John Davenport

History of the forged

John Davenport

History of the forged

ISBN/EAN: 9783337133153

Printed in Europe, USA, Canada, Australia, Japan

Cover: Foto ©ninafisch / pixelio.de

More available books at **www.hansebooks.com**

HISTORY

OF THE

FORGED

"MOREY LETTER:"

A NARRATIVE OF THE

DISCOVERED FACTS RESPECTING THIS GREAT POLITICAL FORGERY, ITS INCEPTION, GROWTH, AUTHORSHIP, PUBLICATION, ENDORSEMENT AND SUPPORT, WITH COPIES AND FAC-SIMILES OF ORIGINAL TELEGRAMS, LETTERS, ORDERS AND RECEIPTS CONNECTED THEREWITH. ITS FRAUDULENT CHARACTER EXPOSED, AND THE FALSE SWEARING, PERJURIES, AND ADDITIONAL FORGERIES, PERPETRATED IN THE EFFORT TO SUSTAIN THE ORIGINAL FORGERY, MADE CLEAR.

BY

JOHN I. DAVENPORT,

UNITED STATES COMMISSIONER AND CHIEF SUPERVISOR OF ELECTIONS, SOUTHERN DISTRICT OF NEW YORK.

PUBLISHED BY THE AUTHOR.

NEW YORK.

1884.

PREFACE.

On the eighth day of November, 1880, and shortly after the Presidential election of that year, General James A. Garfield—President elect—wrote me: "I want you to press the prosecution of the Chinese forgery case until every rascal concerned in it is punished. * * * The subject must not be dropped, but pushed until the forger is discovered."

One week later—under date of November 15th, 1880—General Garfield again wrote me: "I hope you will persevere until the whole thing is discovered."

Until within a week past I have not been able to say my work was completed, and yet I was in position, shortly before President Garfield was assassinated, to exhibit to him some of the original documents of which copies and *fac-similes* are given herein, and to satisfy him that there was little doubt the entire history of the forgery would be obtained, and the fraud exposed.

The "hunt" has never ceased, and this volume has been written, not as a campaign document but as a *history* of the Morey letter and of the ascertained facts respecting its authorship, publication, endorsement and support.

The wishes of General Garfield, as expressed to me in his letters, have, so far as possible, been carried out. The subject has not been "dropped," and I have "persevered" in the work to the best of my ability.

I THEREFORE DEDICATE THIS BOOK TO THE MEMORY OF THE LATE PRESIDENT,

JAMES A. GARFIELD,

AS A TRIBUTE OF RESPECT AND ESTEEM.

J. I. D.

New York, May 31st, 1884.

INTRODUCTORY.

This work has a three-fold purpose:

First. To recall to public attention the forgery during the Presidential campaign of 1880 of the name of the late James A. Garfield to the so-called Morey letter.

Second. To present to the country a plain historical recital of all the facts—those heretofore known as well as those until recently undiscovered—connected with the origin of the forgery, its appearance, and the false swearing, perjuries, alterations of documents and additional forgeries resorted to in the effort to sustain the letter after its publication.

Third. To awaken sufficient interest in the public mind to the great danger incident to the commission of such offenses in connection with our elections, and thereby to secure such legislation as will tend to prevent in the future the introduction of forgery as an element of party success at such times.

Having devoted the greater portion of two years of time to the investigation and study of this matter, and having ascertained the facts in relation to the document in question, its authors, aiders and abettors, I desire to say that I have neither the wish nor the intention to do injustice to any person, or to misrepresent the action of any political organization.

If, therefore, in the recital here made, the facts presented reflect severely upon any individuals, or any committee, organization, or party, it is solely because of their or its own action.

I seek only to narrate "the truth of history," and where there are different versions of any transaction I have presented the statement of each individual connected therewith, so far as I have been able to obtain it. Those who participated in the events of which I treat must stand or fall by their own conduct. My task is to present the record of their acts.

Before passing to the story, it seems not inappropriate that a few words should be written as to my object in devoting to the investigation of this matter the time and labor I have given it.

Holding decided and radical views as to the absolute necessity, under our form of government, of unqualified freedom and purity in our elections, I believe that the surest preventive of fraud at elections is publicity at each and every step taken, from the announcement of the fact that an election is to be held, to the declaration of the result thereof by the last and highest tribunal called upon to take action in regard thereto. Forgery and fraud thrive only in secret. Publicity not only tends to the prevention of crime, but leads to its detection, and subsequent exposure and punishment.

No fraud connected with, or incident to an election, should ever be considered as condoned, either by reason of its failure to accomplish the results sought, or by the fact that the day of election has passed. As a people, we have been, and we are to-day, far too remiss in this matter. The moment an election is over, the tendency is to treat whatever transpired during the canvass in the way of political offenses, as matters which were at the time of their commission both annoying and dangerous, but which are to be overlooked and forgotten in the general result. To this view is to be largely attributed the frequency of such offenses as libel and forgery during exciting and hotly contested elections.

Failure to reap the results intended by the commission of a political offense, perpetrated prior to or at an election, should never be regarded as a plea in bar to its investigation and exposure, nor should the close of an election be considered as a statute of limitations against its punishment. Investigation and exposure should follow the perpetration of any act committed with intent to improperly affect the result of an election. If it be possible, the offender should be punished; but, if the law has attached no penalty to the act, it should, none the less, be investigated and exposed. In this way only will the needed legislation be speedily obtained and future protection secured.

It took ten long years of patient and arduous labor to secure the evidence respecting the fraudulent naturalization certificates issued by the New York Courts in the year 1868, in such completeness as that the certificates might be "impounded" and no longer voted upon. It was finally demonstrated that the long period of time which had elapsed since their issuance, neither prevented the discovery of their fraudulent character nor sanctified their possession; and this fact will, it is believed, be of great service in preventing the repetiton upon any extended scale of similar frauds in the near future.

Entertaining these views, and looking back at most of the Presidential elections of the past twenty years, I observed that each such election seemed to have developed a new species, or form, of fraud whereby the result was sought to be affected. It appeared that at least once in every four years, partisan zeal had devised some new scheme to attain party success in other than the only proper and legitimate channel—the will of the people, freely expressed, honestly returned and lawfully declared.

I. In 1864, to defeat Lincoln and Johnson, frauds were attempted in the receiving and returning of the votes of the soldiers, and riots were threatened in New York.

The early exposure of the first mentioned plot led to its failure, while the clear head and rare executive ability of Major-General Butler, exercising the powers of a Department Commander, alone caused an abandonment of the latter project and maintained the public peace.

II. In 1868, to defeat Grant and Colfax, the most gigantic and systematic efforts were made to over-ride the popular will by means of organized repeating and wholesale frauds in naturalization.

These efforts led to the enactment of the National Election Laws, and to similar legislation by many of the States, by which the future perpetration of such offenses was guarded against, and their punishment provided for.

III. In 1876, to defeat Hayes and Wheeler, organized violence and terrorism were resorted to in several States, tissue ballots were used without number, returns were altered, the attempt made to bribe electors, and, as a novelty, the famous "cipher dispatches" were used to accomplish results not reached by the votes cast.

IV. In 1880, to defeat Garfield and Arthur, a new device was resorted to, in the publication and dissemination, shortly before the day of election, and at a date so late as almost to preclude their efficient exposure, of forged letters in the names of Presidential candidates.

Each of these several efforts had its own specific purpose.

That of 1864 was intended to deter peaceful and law-abiding citizens from giving expression to their choice of candidates through fear of violence and disorder.

That of 1868 was meant to carry the election by the casting and counting of thousands of false and fraudulent votes.

That of 1876 combined the two preceding schemes, and added the attempt to purchase members of an Electoral College.

The effort of 1880 differed from the others in that it was intended to deceive the voters into casting their ballots for candidates other than those of their choice, by means of forged letters which gave expression to sentiments not entertained by their alleged authors, and views which were repugnant to a large class of voters.

Of all the devices referred to, that of 1880, was, in many respects, the most dangerous, because the least readily to be met and controverted before its purpose was consummated, and the least likely to be thereafter reached, if successful.

If an election be carried by either violence, fraudulent voting, false naturalization, bribery, false canvassing, or forged or altered returns, investigation is certain to follow, exposure to ensue, and legal measures to be taken, not only to punish the offenders but to oust the incumbents, and thereby, to give to the people "their own again."

If, however, an election should be carried by reason of forged expressions of views on the part of candidates, whereby the voters either withheld their votes from their party nominees or cast them for those of the opposite party, not only would there be no method of punishing the guilty parties, if discovered—and the chances of discovery would be infinitesimal—but there would be no means by which the wrong could be remedied. The votes cast, although in fact falsely and fraudulently obtained, would stand, and the beneficiaries of the forgeries would alone profit thereby.

In view of the facts recited and of the opinions entertained by me upon these subjects, coupled with the earnest requests both of General Garfield and General Arthur, I determined that the forgery of the Morey letter should not lie buried in an unknown grave with the passing of the election, notwithstanding the fact that the candidates whom it was designed to defeat—and whom it came near to defeating—were successful.

THE PRESIDENTIAL ELECTION OF 1880.

THE PARTY ORGANIZATIONS.

The nominees of the Republican party for President and Vice-President of the United States were General James A. Garfield, of Ohio, and General Chester A. Arthur, of New York. Those of the Democratic party were General Winfield S. Hancock, of Pennsylvania, and William H. English, of Indiana, while the Greenback-Labor party nominated General James B. Weaver, of Iowa, and Benjamin J. Chambers, of Texas.

Each of these political organizations was represented by a National Committee charged with the duty of organizing and conducting the canvass on behalf of the party and its nominees.

The officers of the Republican National Committee were the Hon. Marshall Jewell, of Connecticut, Chairman; the Hon. Stephen W. Dorsey, of Arkansas, Secretary, and Colonel George W. Hooker, of Vermont, Assistant Secretary.

The Greenback-Labor Committee chose George O. Jones, of New York, Chairman; Lee Crandall, of Washington, D.C., Secretary, and Dyer D. Lum, of New York, Assistant Secretary.

The National Committee of the Democratic party organized on the 13th of July, 1880. The Hon. William H. Barnum, of Connecticut, was elected Chairman, and the Hon. Frederick O. Prince, of Massachusetts, Secretary, and Edward B. Dickinson, of Massachusetts, Washington, D. C., and New York, Official Stenographer. From the whole committee an Executive Committee of eighteen members was appointed, prominent among whom were the following named gentlemen, most, if not all, of whom were also appointed from the Executive Committee as an Advisory Committee: William H. Barnum, of Connecticut; Frederick O. Prince, of Massachusetts; Outerbridge Horsey, of Maryland; Orestes Cleveland, of New Jersey; Abram S. Hewitt, of New York; William L. Scott, of Pennsylvania, and Bradley B. Smalley, of Vermont.

On the 23d of July, the Democratic National Committee formally opened its headquarters at No. 138 Fifth Avenue, in the city of New York.

Mr. William H. Barnum, the Chairman of the Democratic National Committee, and ex-officio Chairman of the Executive Committee, had been a member of Congress, and a Senator of the United States from the State of Connecticut, and was a prominent member of the Democratic National Committee of 1876. He is known in the councils of his party as an ardent Tilden man, but his public career has not been such as to inspire the country with any decided respect for himself or his political practices or methods.

Mr. William L. Scott, of Erie, Pennsylvania, was also a member of the Democratic National Committee of 1876 and a strong adherent of Mr. Tilden. He is an aggressive man, well known as a leader in the art of bolstering up party confidence by heavy and widely published wagers upon the success of his party. His ability to make large contributions and to aid in the raising of considerable sums of money toward the campaign fund of the Committee has never been lost sight of in its make up.

Mr. Abram S. Hewitt, of New York, was the Chairman of the Democratic National Committee in 1876. He is a gentleman of large wealth, marked ability, and great nervous energy. Most unfortunately, however, his judgment, speeches and action are constantly warped and controlled by his impetuosity, vanity, and other infirmities. This naturally results in his frequently assuming positions upon public questions which are not only untenable, but which are surrounded by much which is irritating and embarrassing to one possessed of his culture, experience, and sensitiveness.

Mr. Frederick O. Prince, of Massachusetts, may well be considered a life member of the National Committee, having been named thereon as early as the year 1860, in which year he was first chosen its Secretary, a position which he has ever since held. He was also, in 1880, the Mayor of the City of Boston, and did not give that attention to Committee matters during that year which it had previously been his habit to do. He is a gentleman possessed of some popularity in his State; is ambitious for still higher political honors, and desirous of a reputation for so conducting himself as to receive the suffrages and command the respect of those not recognized as strict party adherents.

Mr. Edward B. Dickinson, the Official Stenographer of the Democratic National Committee in 1880, had been, I believe, an attaché of the Committee previously. He was originally from Boston, has great capacity for work, and is pos....d of an extended acquaintance among the public men of his party. While h... osition with the Committee, in 1880, was, upon its face, a subordinate one ... was, *in fact*, the Acting Secretary of that body, and the duties discharged by him were laborious, confidential, and important.

Subsequent to the election of 1880, Mr. Dickinson occupied, for a time, offices with the Hon. Smith M. Weed, of New York, whose connection with the attempts to control the Canvassing Board of South Carolina at the Presidential election of 1876, by means which have become historical, will not soon be forgotten. He has also been carried upon the pay-rolls of the Department of Public Works of the City of New York as an "axeman"—but the $75 a month allowed him under that title, as well as the other sums which he has received from the appropriations granted that Department, have been given him for other work than that which an "axeman" is generally called upon to perform.

THE CHARACTER OF THE CAMPAIGN.

The Republican canvass was conducted with unusual energy, and while it cannot be asserted that errors of judgment were not committed, it is true that they were infrequent and of no special importance. The fairness and decency of the campaign waged on behalf of its candidates was a marked feature, of which Governor Jewell, as Chairman of the National Committee, had reason to be proud.

In this respect the canvass on the part of the Democratic party was in striking contrast, being mainly distinguished for its abusive and scandalous character.

It seems proper that some reference should be made to a few instances illustrative of the justness of the criticism here indulged in:

1. By the terms of a contract entered into between the telegraph companies and the Democratic National Committee, it was agreed, at the opening of the campaign, that all telegrams sent or received by the Committee were to be returned to it at the end of each week, as vouchers for the bills rendered. By the blunder of an employé of the Western Union Telegraph Company, two telegrams of the Republican National Committee, addressed to parties in Florida, found a place in the package of messages forwarded the Democratic Committee on the 20th of October. Those two dispatches were sent by Governor Jewell. The first was to a gentleman in Florida, whose services, and those of a friend, were desired upon the stump, informing him of the compensation which would be allowed them.

This telegram read as follows:

"Rush."   NEW YORK, October 12th, 1880.

To Hon. CHARLES J. NOYES,
    Care of H. Jenkins, Jr.,
        Jacksonville, Fla.

I telegraphed yesterday. I will provide, as requested, two hundred each for Callender and yourself as compensation.

17 pd.   MARSHALL JEWELL.

The second telegram read:

"Rush."   NEW YORK, October 12th, 1880.

To F. W. WICKER,
    Collector, Key West, Fla.

"City of Dallas" took 150; "City of Texas," 100; "Colorado," 100, for Key West. Men on dock instructed to say nothing about it.

26 pd.   MARSHALL JEWELL.

This dispatch was sent under the following circumstances: On the 8th of October, Governor Jewell received information of the sailing of a number of men, during the preceding week, for Florida. He immediately sent the following message:

To F. W. WICKER,   NEW YORK, October 8th, 1880.
    Collector, Key West, Fla.

Mallory steamer of last week had 200 or 300 workmen for some railroad. Looks to me as though they were sent to Key West to vote.

MARSHALL JEWELL.

Pursuing his inquiries as to the shipment of these men, Governor Jewell, on the 11th of October, received the following letter:

CUSTOM HOUSE, NEW YORK.
Collector's Office.
DEAR SIR.   NEW YORK, October 11th, 1880.

I have just received the enclosed memorandum from a perfectly trustworthy person. You remember my telling you the other night I would try to get at the facts.

Yours in haste,
TREICHEL.

To the Hon. MARSHALL JEWELL,
    Chairman, etc.

The memorandum enclosed read :

"City of Dallas," 150; "State of Texas," 100; "Colorado," 100; men on dock instructed to say nothing about it. Denied in office at dock that any had gone.

Upon this information and memorandum, Governor Jewell, very properly, sent his telegram of October 12th, 1880, apprising the Collector at Key West of the reported facts.

Instead of acting as a gentleman would naturally do, and immediately returning the telegrams to the company and observing silence as to their contents, Mr. Barnum exhibited them to Mr. Abram S. Hewitt, who proceeded to the steps of the Sub-Treasury in Wall Street, where, to an admiring audience, he spoke as follows: *vide New York World*, October 22d, 1880.

" We are surrounded by fraud. I have myself seen to-day a telegram sent by Marshall Jewell, the Chairman of the Republican National Committee, to his agent in Florida : " *We ship you* 200 men on such a vessel, 200 by another steamer, 100 on another."

This extraordinary statement of Mr. Hewitt was followed, late in the evening of the day on which it was made, by a long address from Mr. Chairman Barnum, " to the public," in which was printed the telegrams with the declaration that they were "then being lithographed" for general distribution. Their publication led at once to a statement of the facts by Governor Jewell, and the sensation " died a bornin'," the telegraph company demanding the immediate return to it of the dispatches and following its demand by proceedings in the courts to compel prompt compliance therewith.

II. The calumnious address of Mr. William H. Barnum issued on September 17th, relative to the Maine election, in which, among other charges, he declared that the Republicans " had stopped the returns coming in, and delayed them until they could be altered."

The fact was, that in the year 1878, on the Monday of the week following the Tuesday of the election, the returns from but 476 towns had been received ; that in the year 1879, on the Monday of the week following the Tuesday of the election, but 479 towns had been heard from. In 1880, of which Mr. Barnum spoke, there had, on the night of Friday, September 17th, the date of the issuance of his address—only three nights after the Tuesday of the election—been received *and published* the returns from 490 towns.

III. The scurrilous and simultaneous placarding and defacing, upon a fixed day, in all the large cities and villages of the country, of dwellings, public buildings, lamp posts, fences, trees, pavements and gutters, with the figures " 329."

This action was intended to cast a slur upon General Garfield, and if not done at the instigation of the Democratic National Committee, received the warm approval of members of that body and excited the admiration of the Democratic press.

IV. The conduct of the Democratic National Committee in the matter of the so-called Morey letter.

PART FIRST.

THE MOREY LETTER.

THE POLITICAL SITUATION PRIOR TO AND AT THE TIME OF ITS PUBLICATION.

To the end that the political situation at the time of the publication of the Morey letter may be clearly understood, a brief reference to the then, and shortly preceding, condition of the canvass appears necessary.

The State election in Maine, in September, had resulted in the choice of General Plaisted as Governor, upon a fusion ticket of Democrats and Greenbackers. This gave the Democracy strong hopes of success in the National canvass, then but six weeks off, while it warned the Republicans that they must put forth their best efforts if they expected to win in November. Ohio and Indiana were to hold State elections on the 13th of October, and it was practically conceded that the result in those States would forecast the issue in November.

Fortunately, the lessons of the Maine election brought wisdom to the minds of the Republican leaders. The result was the laying aside of many old and threadbare topics of discussion, which were quite as well understood by the great mass of the people as by most of the stump orators of the day. In place thereof there was precipitated into the canvass a living issue—the tariff question. The platform of each party had proclaimed the party position upon this issue. That of the Republicans demanded " a tariff that will discriminate in favor of American labor," while that of the Democrats favored " a tariff for revenue only."

Instantly, the character of the campaign changed, and all along the Republican lines was felt the pressure of the recruits who came crowding in upon its ranks. New interest was everywhere awakened. The young men, who were about to cast their first votes for a President, were found flocking to the Republican cause. The business men of the country were seen taking the most lively interest in the success of the Republican candidates. The employés of the great manufactories, mills, foundries and shops became aroused and clamorous for "tariff cards" and "tracts," while on every side there was manifested the greatest activity and the warmest enthusiasm in the Republican canvass.

At this time, and under these circumstances, was conceived a scheme to cheat and defraud the voters of the Nation, by obtaining their ballots for the Democratic candidates. The means adopted was a forged letter, which purported to have been written by the Republican nominee for President, at a date months prior to his nomination, wherein he was made to give expression to views the reverse of those declared to be held by him in his letter of acceptance, and the wording of which was so framed as to be obnoxious to a large class of voters.

The Democratic party of the country, fearing defeat, through its National Committee and other prominent leaders caused this letter to be published, in *fac-simile*, endorsed and circulated it, and to the last hour of the active life of the Committee, in the year 1880, supported, sustained and defended it, though a palpable and pronounced forgery, for the sake of party success.

Its Publication.

On the morning of Tuesday, October 19th, 1880, *Truth*, a comparatively unknown penny paper published in the city of New York, announced that on the following day it would "produce positive evidence that James A. Garfield is [was] a pronounced advocate of Chinese cheap labor." On the morning of Wednesday, October 20th, *Truth* published, in type, the following letter:

"GARFIELD'S DEATH WARRANT."

"Personal and Confidential."

"House of Representatives,
Washington, D. C., Jan. 23d, 1880."

"Dear Sir:
Yours in relation to the Chinese problem came duly to hand. I take it that the question of employes is only a question of private and corporate economy, and individuals or companys have the right to buy labor where they can get it cheapest.

We have a treaty with the Chinese Government which should be religiously kept until its provisions are abrogated by the action of the general Government, and I am not prepared to say that it should be abrogated until our great manufacturing and corporate interests are conserved in the matter of labor.

Very truly yours,

"H. L. Morey,   J. A. GARFIELD."
Employers' Union,
Lynn, Mass."

The publication was accompanied by a statement that "the foregoing is a true copy," which was not in exact accord with the facts, as was disclosed two days thereafter upon the appearance of a *fac-simile* of the letter. It was added that the letter "was mailed at Washington by the Republican candidate for President to *Henry* L. Morey, a prominent member of the Employers' Union, Lynn, Massachusetts. At his death, which recently occurred, it was found among his effects."

Summary of the subsequent course of "Truth" and of the Daily Press of New York, respecting the Morey Letter, prior to the arrest of Kenward Philp.

From the day of the first publication of the Morey letter by *Truth*, down to a date long subsequent to the day of election, its treatment of General Garfield, of the letter itself, and of every one who questioned its authenticity, was coarse and brutal in the extreme. The tone and character of its editorials may be judged by the following extracts:

On Thursday, October 21st, it declared that General Garfield, in causing to be sent the press denial of the genuineness of the letter, was "a liar."

On Friday, October 22d, it published, in *fac-simile*, both the letter and the envelope in which it was claimed to have been mailed to Morey, declared General Garfield's name to be "synonymous with treachery and falsehood," pronounced him a "stupid liar," as "guilty of a sneaking lie," and as a "desperate" and "stupid liar."

On Monday, October 25th, it styled him a "doubly branded liar," and charged him with resorting to "black lies and foul slanders to save his failing cause."

On the morning of Thursday, October 21st, a press denial from Mentor, Ohio, made on behalf of General Garfield, was published in most, if not all, the New York dailies.

The *fac-simile* of the Morey letter, as published in *Truth* on October 22d, was found to be quite different in essential particulars from the letter as printed by it in type. The *fac-simile* disclosed the fact that at least three words, and apparently a fourth, were incorrectly spelled. They were "companies," which was written "companys," the word "economy," which was written "ecomomy," and the word 'religiously," which was written "religeously." Of these the word "companys" alone was printed as it appeared in the letter and the *fac-simile*, while the printed copy, from its first appearance to its last, contained the word "employes," which, in both the letter and the *fac-simile*, was spelled "employees."

It also appeared, from the *fac-simile*, that the signature to the letter, as written, was not J. A. Garfield, as printed, but "J. A. Garfield"—the "r" in Garfield being dotted and not the "i."

The presentation of the letter, for two days, in so grossly inaccurate a form was, at least, a very grave error. The blunders in orthography, in the original letter, were of great gravity in their character, and the printed copy should have shown them.

Another noticeable fact disclosed by the *fac-simile* of the face of the envelope—which alone was published—was the absence from the Washington postmark of the month, day of month and hour of mailing.

In its issue of Saturday, October 23d, *Truth* declared that Samuel J. Randall, the Speaker of the National House of Representatives, when shown the original of the Morey letter, "compared it carefully with letters in his possession, scrutinized each word, mark and letter, and declared that it was truly in James A. Garfield's handwriting."

It also claimed the credit of having "slain" General Garfield "and the [Republican] party," and asserted that if General Garfield would "say, over his own signature, or by affidavit, that he did not write this letter, *Truth* will [would] instantly prove *the existence of the man to whom he wrote it*, and that man's business and character and General Garfield's perjury once again." Three days previously it had stated that Morey had no existence, having been dead for some months.

An attempt was also made to account for the want of a date and hour in the Washington postmark, as shown in the *fac-simile* of the envelope published on the previous day, and which, with the letter, it re-published. It said: "The date of the postmark on the envelope is not very legible, and in the original it is blurred;" but added that a microscopic examination showed the date to be "January 23d."

All the morning journals of the same day—October 23d—published an address from the Republican National Committee, issued on the previous evening, denouncing the letter by General Garfield's authority.

On Sunday, October 24th, the morning papers printed a despatch from Governor Jewell, dated eight P. M. of the previous evening, embodying a telegram, received by him from General Garfield, denying the genuineness of the letter, and declaring it "the work of some clumsy villain."

The *New York Star* of the same day contained a letter addressed to the Hon. E. H. Gillette, a Greenback member of Congress from Iowa, which purported to be signed by "J. B. Weaver," the Greenback candidate for President. This letter was received by the *Star* about the same time that *Truth* received the "Morey" letter. Instead of at once printing it, the *Star* held it until it could publish it in *fac-simile* form. This, practically, threw the letter open to the inspection of all, and it was at once observed that the handwriting of the Weaver letter bore a marked resemblance to that of the "Morey" letter. General Weaver promptly denounced the letter to Gillette as a forgery, and the latter gentleman declared that no such letter had ever been received by him from Weaver. These statements were practically accepted by the *Star*, and there the Weaver forgery ended.

The *New York Times* of October 25th contained a special dispatch from Columbus, Ohio, stating that on the previous day the forged letter was "being scattered throughout every county and school district in the State."

The *New York Tribune* of the same date published a telegram from Captain John G. B. Adams, Postmaster at Lynn, Mass., to the effect that Henry L. Morey was unknown to the clerks and carriers of his office, and that no such name appeared either in the "City Directory or on the Post Office or carriers' books."

The *New York Herald* of Tuesday, October 26th, published a *fac-simile* of General Garfield's letter of October 23d to Governor Jewell, denying the authorship of the Morey letter, and declared, editorially, that "this [Garfield's letter] settles the question of the character of the Morey letter, and the public at large * * * will, with the *Herald*, accept General Garfield's denial as final and conclusive upon the matter."

Truth of the same day—the 26th—declared that it would "satisfy the people that James A. Garfield is [was] the enemy of the workingman and the liar it has [had] charged him with being."

On Wednesday, October 27th, it published a reprint of the *fac-similes* of the letter and envelope. It was at once observed that the date in the postmark upon the envelope had been *inserted* with great distinctness as "Jan. 23." The fact was that its date was that of a day subsequent to February 15th. *Truth* also declared that Mr. William H. Barnum had "examined the original letter, *and pronounced it wholly in the handwriting of James A. Garfield;*" that Mr. Abram S. Hewitt, after an examination of the document, "*letter by letter*, had stated that *there could be no doubt of its genuineness*," and that Mr. Samuel J. Randall had declared that it was written by James A. Garfield, "*body and letter.*"

SUMMARY OF THE PUBLISHED ACTION OF THE DEMOCRATIC NATIONAL COMMITTEE AND OF INDIVIDUAL MEMBERS THEREOF PRIOR TO THE ARREST OF KENWARD PHILP.

Immediately upon the publication in *Truth*, on Wednesday, October 20th, of the Morey letter, and before even the wires could be used to convey a word upon the subject from the alleged author of the letter, Mr. Chairman Barnum telegraphed the *Cincinnati Enquirer:* "*The letter is authentic. It is in General Garfield's handwriting.* DENIAL IS WORSE THAN USELESS."

At the same time, Mr. Abram S. Hewitt—with the rashness which is both customary and characteristic with him in his political career, and as if striving to outdo Barnum in zeal and pertinacity—hastened to Chickering Hall, where on the evening of the same day—*vide New York World*—he asserted in a public speech, that "some people may [might] incline to pronounce it [the Morey letter] a forgery. I have seen it. I am familiar with General Garfield's signature, and I have compared it with his letters in my possession, and I have no doubt it is genuine."

On the afternoon of the same day—October 20th—the publisher of *Truth* presented himself at the headquarters of the Democratic National Committee, and exhibited the original of the Morey letter and envelope to the members and others who were present. Of this interview, which lasted some time, *Truth*, on the following day, declared that, after an examination of the letter, Messrs. Barnum, Randall, Hewitt, Smalley, "and the other principal members of the National Democratic Committee who are familiar with James A. Garfield's handwriting, signature, and modes of expression, *all pronounced the letter absolutely genuine beyond a doubt.*"

Messrs. Barnum and Hewitt, and *Truth*, having each publicly declared the letter "genuine," or "in Garfield's handwriting," and "the other principal members of the National Democratic Committee" having passed upon General Garfield's "modes of expression" and "pronounced the letter absolutely genuine," it seems to have been assumed that General Garfield could not fail to concur in their views, public notice having been given by Mr. Barnum that "denial" would be "worse than useless." Orders were therefore speedily given for the making of a large number of *fac-simile* plates of the letter and for the printing of thousands of copies therefrom. The plates were very generally distributed throughout the country, and the columns of the Democratic press—from the larger and more influential journals down to the most insignificant and vicious of the party sheets—were alike adorned with the *fac-simile*.

The situation is worthy of being recalled, even though the spectacle presented is far from being either elevating or edifying.

Here was the Democratic National Committee, the highest representative body of the party, circulating a letter purporting to be from a candidate for the high office of President of the United States, and declaring it to be "genuine," when it had no knowledge of its ever having been seen by its alleged author, had taken no steps to ascertain whether there ever was such a person as the individual to whom it was declared it had been sent, and had never inquired whether the "Employers' Union," to whose representative it was addressed, had ever existed.

On the other hand, the story of the manner in which *Truth* came by the letter should, of itself, have aroused the greatest suspicions of its authenticity. Moreover, the letter itself not only gave expression to views at variance with the sentiments entertained by its alleged writer as avowed in his letter of acceptance of the nomination for President but three short months before, but, in fact, presented no marked similarity, either in the body of the letter or the signature, to the handwriting or signature of General Garfield, while upon its face it bore the best evidences of its false character in the spelling, in the very marked and unusual peculiarities of the penmanship, and in its general ensemble. To these facts was to be added the press dispatch denying, for General Garfield, the authorship of the letter. It is difficult, therefore, to understand how any individual acquainted with General Garfield or his handwriting, unless he desired to believe the Morey letter genuine, could ever have claimed it to be from General Garfield, even without a denial of its authenticity.

Some of the morning journals of Sunday, October 24th, contained a report from the *Newark* (N. J.) *Daily Journal*, of an interview had by an attaché of that paper with the Hon. Orestes Cleveland, a member of the Democratic National Committee, which threw some light upon the action of that body and its expectations. It read as follows:

REPORTER. What is being done with it? [the Morey letter.]

MR. CLEVELAND. In the first place, we telegraphed the text of it to every State Committee, and have had it published broadcast all over the country. And in the next place, we had it photographed, and have procured several thousand electro-plates of it. These are now being forwarded to every leading Democratic and Independent paper in the country. In four or five days, the letter, in *fac-simile*, will be scattered all over the Pacific slope.

REPORTER. What will be the effect?

MR. CLEVELAND. Why, that it will give us New York, New Jersey, Connecticut, California, Nevada, and probably Pennsylvania and Indiana.

On the evening of Monday, October 25th, Mr. Abram S. Hewitt, in a speech delivered in the city of Rochester, New York, said that he did not think the body of the alleged Garfield-Morey letter—which *Truth* had declared he had asserted to be in General Garfield's handwriting—was written by him (Garfield), but he considered the signature to be genuine and that "Garfield *did not deny* the genuineness of the *signature*."

On the evening of Tuesday, October 26th, Mr. Abram S. Hewitt addressed an audience at Stuyvesant Hall in the city of New York. He again asserted that when he first saw the original letter, he "compared the handwriting with three letters of Mr. Garfield's which he had in his possession, and he then said that he believed the signature to the Morey letter to be genuine."

THE ARREST OF KENWARD PHILP OF TRUTH UPON A CHARGE OF CRIMINAL LIBEL.—HIS EXAMINATION.—SUMMARY OF THE TESTIMONY.—OPINIONS AND CONDUCT OF THE PRESS.—THE ACTION OF TRUTH AND OF THE DEMOCRATIC NATIONAL COMMITTEE DOWN TO THE CLOSE OF THE PHILP CASE BEFORE JUSTICE NOAH DAVIS.

Late in the afternoon of Sunday, October 24th, I was called upon at my office by a gentleman who introduced himself as Mr. Thomas E. Lonergan, formerly an attaché of the United States Secret Service. Mr. Lonergan stated that he was then the publisher, or connected with the publication, of the *Hotel Mail*, and was also the head of a private detective agency. He claimed to be possessed of important information relative to the Morey letter, referred to the Hon. Emory Storrs, of Chicago, then temporarily in the city, as a gentleman who would vouch for him as a faithful and reliable person, and stated that he had been advised to call upon me. Upon my expressing a willingness to hear him, Mr. Lonergan declared that he had reason to believe that Kenward Philp, then an editorial writer upon *Truth*, and who had long been known as a most able and dangerous imitator of handwriting, was the author of the "Morey letter." Mr. Lonergan further stated that he was possessed of all the editorial and reportorial manuscript, or "copy," for the issue of *Truth* of October 22d, and that much of said editorial "copy," particularly that relating to the "Morey letter," was in Philp's handwriting, and that those to whom he had shown it and who had compared it with the *fac-simile* of the Morey letter believed the writing in that letter to be that of Philp. He added that Philp had stated to a friend, who was also an acquaintance of his—Lonergan's—that he—Philp—had written the Morey letter, and apparently regarded the matter as nothing more serious than a newspaper hoax.

Mr. Lonergan then offered me the manuscript "copy" in his possession, for such examination as should be deemed advisable to make of it, adding that if those to whom it should be submitted were of the opinion that the "Morey letter" was written by Philp, and the services of any detectives became necessary in an investigation of the matter, he should expect to be employed, but under no circumstances would he receive any compensation beyond the usual pay for the time actually devoted to the work, and such disbursements as might necessarily be incurred. Believing the matter worthy of being inquired into, the manuscript "copy" was accepted, and Mr. Lonergan's conditions agreed to. Immediately thereafter, the "copy" and Lonergan's statements were laid before General Arthur, who, as the candidate for Vice-President upon the ticket with General Garfield, was more directly and personally concerned in the matter than any one individual save General Garfield.

General Arthur, after listening to an account of my interview with Mr. Lonergan, requested me to consult with Colonel George Bliss, the Hon. E. W. Stoughton, Colonel Robert G. Ingersoll—who was then in the city—Governor Marshall Jewell and others. Such consultation was had, and resulted in an unanimous decision that the question of the identity of the handwriting of the "Morey letter" with that of General Garfield and of Mr. Philp, should be submitted to the best living experts in handwriting. In accordance with this conclusion, Mr. Joseph E. Payne, of New York, Mr. Albert S. Southworth, of Boston, and, subsequently, Mr. William E. Hagan, of Troy, New York, who were universally conceded to be at the head of their profession as experts in handwriting and photographic and microscopic examinations thereof, were summoned to New York. Mr. Daniel T. Ames, of New York, was also called upon, as an expert, for an opinion in the matter.

On October 26th Mr. Payne and Mr. Southworth arrived in the city, and, with Mr. Ames, were speedily furnished with genuine letters of General Garfield, the *fac-simile* of the "Morey letter" as published in *Truth*, photographs of the letter, the manuscript "copy" of *Truth* of October 22d, furnished by Lonergan, and some letters and other writings of Philp, which had been obtained.

The only questions submitted to them were these :

First.—Is the "Morey letter," in your opinion—either body or signature—in the handwriting of General Garfield?

Second.—Is the "Morey letter," in your opinion—either body or signature—in the same handwriting as the manuscript "copy" and other papers furnished you?

Late that night each of them submitted, in writing, his conclusions and the grounds of his belief. An examination of the several reports disclosed the fact that the three gentlemen were a unit in the expression of their views, although each had reached his own conclusion by a different process, and without consultation, or conference, with either of his associates.

The decision of the experts, stripped of technical expressions, was that they were prepared to say, affirmatively and positively, that the "Morey letter" was not—either body or signature—in the handwriting of General Garfield, while they were of the belief that the writer of the editorial in *Truth* of October 22d, entitled "Lying and Sticking to it," was the writer of the "Morey letter." After consultation, it was decided that Colonel George Bliss should act as complainant in a proceeding charging Kenward Philp with criminal libel in writing the editorial mentioned. The formal complaint was at once prepared, and to it were attached affidavits of the experts and the manuscript "copy" of the editorial libel written by Philp. These papers were submitted to the Chief Justice of the Supreme Court in the First Judicial District—Judge Noah Davis—who, after a careful examination of the same, entertained the charge and granted his warrant for the arrest of Kenward Philp.

One of the most competent and trustworthy officers of the Police Department, Sergeant David F. Crowley, was assigned to the duty of executing the warrant and was given the assistance of such officers as he requested.

At about noon on October 27th, Kenward Philp was arrested in Brooklyn, and at once brought before Judge Davis at the Supreme Court room in New York. There appeared for the prosecution, Assistant District Attorney Joseph Bell, Colonel George Bliss, the Hon. E. W. Stoughton, Henry E. Knox, Esq., and Mr. John I. Davenport. For the accused, Charles W. Brooke, Esq., and General Roger A. Pryor. An examination was immediately entered upon against the strenuous protest of Mr. Brooke, who sought to waive it. The complaint and accompanying affidavits of the experts were read, and a motion was then made on behalf of the accused for his discharge, upon the ground that the allegations of the complaint were insufficient to justify the issuance of the warrant. The motion was denied, an adjournment taken to the following day, and $5,000 bail furnished for the appearance of the accused during the examination.

On the evening of the day of Philp's arrest Mr. William H. Barnum telegraphed over the country that the arrest was simply " a device to break the effect of the publication of *Garfield's* letter in favor of Chinese labor."

It is worthy of special mention that the New York *Sun*, while bitterly hostile to General Garfield, had the manliness, in its issue of October 28th, to refer to the forged letter in the following terse English :

"If there are not enough facts and sound arguments against General Garfield—and we have supposed there were more than enough—to defeat his election, then let him be chosen. Nothing could argue a poorer cause than an attempt to support it by forgery."

The examination in the Philp case was resumed on the morning of October 28th. Colonel A. F. Rockwell, the classmate and life-long friend of General

Garfield, was sworn as a witness. He produced several letters from the General to himself, from which it was apparent that the Morey letter was not in General Garfield's handwriting, either body or signature. A demand was then made for the original Morey letter received by *Truth*, and a recess was taken to afford Mr. Hart, the publisher of that journal, an opportunity to produce it, which he did, but without the envelope. He was directed to bring the envelope in the morning and agreed so to do.

Colonel Rockwell then resumed the stand, and being shown the original Morey letter sent *Truth*, pronounced it a forgery. He was followed by witnesses who were acquainted with Kenward Philp and his handwriting, and also by Mr. Ames, the expert, and each expressed the opinion that Philp had penned the Morey letter. An adjournment was then taken to the following day.

On the evening of Thursday, October 28th, Mr. Abram S. Hewitt spoke at a meeting held at Irving Hall, in the City of New York. He again reiterated his belief that the Morey letter was a genuine letter of General Garfield's, and said: "The original letter was shown me and I said the *signature*, I believe, to be his—Garfield's—the body of the letter, I think, is not written by him."

The witnesses examined at the hearing in the Philp case on October 29th were the experts in handwriting, the microscopic expert and the officials of the New York Post Office. Mr. Hart also produced the envelope of the Morey letter.

The *New York World*, of October 30th, published an extract from a speech prepared by Mr. Abram S. Hewitt for delivery on the previous evening at a meeting held at Terrace Garden, in the City of New York. Mr. Hewitt's voice having failed him he had been unable to speak, but, as appeared from the published extract, he had somewhat toned down his public utterances. In his intended remarks Mr. Hewitt sought to change the issue. Instead of claiming either the letter or the signature to be genuine, he declared that the "sentiments and declarations" of the letter were in full accord "with the votes of General Garfield and the course of the Republican party on the Chinese question." Party demands and exigencies had so entirely warped Mr. Hewitt's judgment, as to force him to take every position but the right one. If Mr. Hewitt failed to see that such was the case, the great mass of the reputable, reading, thinking public did not.

The *New York Sun* of the same day well stated the popular sentiment when it remarked editorially:

"He—Hewitt—certainly must know that to stick to a libel and a forgery, throwing aside all question of principle, as a mere matter of policy, must be exceedingly unwise. Then how is he going to account for a scholar like Garfield—to whom Mr. Hewitt himself pays most extravagant compliments—spelling companies, "companys"?

In another editorial the *Sun* said:

"If a party requires such infamous aids [as forgers and libellers], that party, by whatsoever name it may be called, deserves to perish."

In the Philp examination on October 30th, the prosecution rested its case after putting in the evidence of the Washington Post Office officials as to the post-mark upon the Morey envelope. The defense opened by calling to the witness box each of the counsel for the prosecution; then offered the evidence of, persons who claimed to be familiar with Philp's handwriting to show that the Morey letter was not written by him, and attempted, by one or two unknown persons, to establish the existence of an Employers' Union at Lynn.

From Tarrytown, N. Y., Pittsburgh, Penn., Lowell and Lawrence, Mass., Cumberland, Md., and San Francisco, Cal., there were telegraphed —within the twenty-four hours immediately preceding the election— dispatches from persons who claimed to have known Henry L. Morey. It may be added that not one of the statements published as from these individuals was true, and most of them were promptly denied by their alleged authors.

In the Philp examination on Monday, November 1st, the prosecution examined Captain J. G. B. Adams, Postmaster of Lynn, Mass., who testified that the Morey envelope had never passed into the Lynn Post Office through the mails. The Hon. Samuel P. Bubier, an ex-Mayor of Lynn, a resident of that city for sixty-four years and a manufacturer of shoes there for forty years, was also sworn as a witness. He testified that there never was an Employers' Union in Lynn, and that he never knew or heard of such a person there as Henry L. Morey.

The defense examined one Samuel S. Morey, of Lawrence, Mass., who has been previously alluded to. He testified that Henry L. Morey was his uncle, formerly of Fisherville, New Hampshire, but that in the fall of 1877, and the winter of 1877-78, he saw Henry in Lynn, and again in the spring of 1879. He was then shown the hotel register of the Kirtland House, Lynn, and identified an entry therein, under date of Tuesday, February 25th, 1879, which read: "H. L. Morey, Lowell, D.," as being in the handwriting of his uncle. Also an entry in the same book under date of October 17th, 1879, which read: "H. L. Morey, Lynn."

On cross-examination the witness testified that he last saw Henry L. Morey in June, 1879, at the house of a brother in Lawrence, Mass.; that he came to New York to testify by reason of a telegraphic summons from the Democratic National Committee, sent to A. G. Clark, of Lawrence, the proprietor of a pool room in that city; that Clark informed him that he was to go to New York with him—Clark—and that his expenses would be paid. He further testified that Clark and himself arrived in New York on the night of Saturday, October 30th, and went directly to the headquarters of the National Committee, and that he had first seen the Lynn hotel register on the morning of the day he testified, when it was shown him in *Truth* office.

Mr. Abram S. Hewitt was then called as a witness on behalf of the defense. He testified that he was "reasonably" familiar with General Garfield's handwriting; that he had three letters from the General, which were signed by him, Garfield; that he had once seen the original Morey letter, and as to the signature thereto, he said : "*I think* it is General Garfield's." Being questioned as to his qualifications to pass upon the question of a similarity of handwriting, the witness testified that he considered himself an "expert" in handwriting "enough to satisfy *myself*" [himself].

On cross-examination Mr. Hewitt swore that he saw the original of the Morey letter at about two o'clock in the afternoon of Wednesday, October 20th—the day it first appeared in type in the columns of *Truth ;* that at that time he also saw the envelope, and *looked* "*at the post-mark*," but "only cursorily," and did not observe that the month had been erased therefrom; that after he had made a very careful examination of the original letter, at the time it was shown him, he came to the conclusion that the *body* thereof was *not* in General Garfield's handwriting, and "*said so*."

Mr. Kenward Philp, the accused, then took the stand, and admitted writing the article entitled "Lying and Sticking to it," but denied all knowledge of the Morey letter, as well as any connection therewith, whereupon an adjournment was taken.

The returns of the election, received on Wednesday, November 3d, showed that while the forged letter had not accomplished all that was hoped for by its authors and sponsors, it had beyond doubt cost the Republican candidates the electoral votes of California, Nevada and New Jersey. It was also quite clear to all careful observers of the political situation, that but for the evidence of the fraudulent character of the Morey letter, produced upon the examination of Kenward Philp, the forgery would have succeeded in electing the Democratic nominees.

On Thursday, November 4th, *Truth*—while practically conceding General Garfield's election—declared that he deserved "no respect from any one. * * * He has recently written himself down a cowardly liar, and stamped himself a foul and reckless slanderer."

The examination in the Philp case was resumed on November 4th. The first witness called was Mr. Joseph Hart, the publisher of *Truth* He testified that he found the original of the Morey letter upon his desk on the evening of October 18th; that it was accompanied by the envelope which he had produced in court, the letter from J. W. Goodall, and a "tariff card," hereinafter referred to; that the envelope in which these several documents were enclosed he had thrown away upon tearing it open, and that subsequently, upon ascertaining its contents, he had been unable to distinguish it from other envelopes which he had similarly torn open and cast aside while going through his mail; that upon discovering the Morey letter, he, and two of his subordinates, examined it, and then prepared the announcement for the next morning's paper, to the effect that, on the following day, *Truth* would print a letter from General Garfield upon the subject of Chinese cheap labor; that later in the evening the same party compared it with the *fac-simile* of a letter from General Garfield to one H. H. Hadley, which his (Hart's) paper had published on October 6th; that on the following morning—October 19th—he and his friends resumed their comparisons, and came to the opinion that the letter was genuine, whereupon he printed it on the morning of October 20th.

It will not fail to be noted that no claim was made that either of the three individuals, who thus undertook to pass upon the genuineness of the Morey letter, had ever known General Garfield, had ever seen him write, had any acquaintance with either his handwriting or his signature, or at that time had ever seen anything which they supposed was written by the General save the letter to Hadley. The fact was, that at the time these parties were comparing the Morey letter with the letter to Hadley, they believed the Hadley letter to be in General Garfield's writing, while the signature alone was his. The value of such comparison, and of any opinion based thereon, may be readily determined.

Mr. Hart further testified to his visit to the headquarters of the Democratic National Committee, where the letter *and the envelope* were submitted to Messrs. Barnum, Hewitt, Randall, Cooper, Scott and some eight others, and to the subsequent publication of the *fac-simile* of the letter.

On cross-examination, he swore that Mr. Hewitt—who, as we have seen, had repeatedly declared in the most unequivocal manner, that his declaration respecting the letter, when he first saw it, was that the *signature only* was General Garfield's—had, "at the end of a half hour's" examination, "pronounced *the body and signature* the same," and that the signature was that "of General Garfield himself;" that the Democratic National Committee had been furnished by *Truth* with from 150,000 to 200,000 copies of the *fac-simile* of the letter, and that he had given the Committee full authority to have made all the *fac-simile* plates it desired and to forward them wheresoever it pleased. He explained the *substitution* in the post-mark upon the envelope, as shown in the *fac-simile* published on October 27th, of the letters and figures "Jan. 23," by saying that the maker of the plates informed him that the reason why it appeared in that issue, when it had not appeared in the *fac-simile* published on October 22d, was because the plate used on the 27th had more labor bestowed upon it—it had taken more time to make.

The absurdity of this statement may be best judged by recalling to mind the fact that the word "Jan." had *never been stamped upon the post-mark*. What the word was which had been there stamped, was neither visible to the naked eye nor discernible by the aid of a microscope, and the individual who would accept such an explanation as Mr. Hart testified was given him, must have been, at the time—as Mr. Hart undoubtedly was—so far carried away by his prejudices and his surroundings, as to have been willing to receive any statement made him without properly weighing the probabilities of its truthfulness.

There was also examined for the defense Mr. David A. Carvalho, a photographer. This gentleman declared that Philp did not write the Morey letter, and expressed the opinion that both the body and signature thereof were written by General Garfield.

The Philp examination was resumed on Saturday, November 6th, but the proceedings on that day were mainly confined to the further questioning of the expert witnesses. An adjournment was then taken, at the request of the defense, to November 9th, for the purpose of enabling them to re-produce Samuel S. Morey, of Lawrence, and to present a new and unnamed witness.

On Monday, November 8th, *Truth* again charged General Garfield with writing the letter and sending it to H. L. Morey, and declared that "James A. Garfield's experience proves that perjury is a sure stepping-stone to the White House."

The Philp examination was resumed on November 9th.

The witness Samuel S. Morey, of Lawrence, Mass., was produced, in accordance with the stipulation of counsel for the defense, for cross-examination. During the time which had elapsed since the last hearing, Mrs. Clara T. Morey, of Lynn, whose step-son Samuel S. Morey was, had been found, the false character of Samuel's previous testimony ascertained, and the appearance in New York of Mrs. Morey, her son George E. C. Morey, and officer John W. Morey of the Boston police force, Sam's uncle, arranged for the 9th instant. District Attorney Sherman, of Lawrence, and Mr. R. T. Kimball, of his office, had also found Mr. Frank P. Moore, a son of a married sister of Samuel S. Morey, and Mr. Kimball had brought him to New York.

Upon cross-examination by Colonel Bliss, the witness, Samuel S. Morey, testified to the names of his brother, step-mother, brothers and sisters, both full and half, and also of his father's brothers, but wholly failed to mention Henry L. Morey as being a brother of his father, as he had testified was the case upon his examination in chief.

The next witness was placed upon the stand by Mr. William F. Howe, the attorney of Mr. Hart ot *Truth*. He was introduced as "Robert Lindsay," and was the witness whose attendance was promised at the last hearing but whose name was then withheld.

The testimony of "Robert Lindsay" was that he was a detective in the employ of a secret organization of workingmen; that he first knew Henry L. Morey, in Lynn, Mass., as connected with the Employers' Union, and carried to Morey a letter of introduction from the Consolidated Coal Company of Alleghany County, Maryland; that he had last seen Morey between the 4th and 10th of February, 1880, and that Morey at that time read and exhibited to him a letter from General Garfield. Being shown the original of the Morey letter, he identified it as being similar to the letter shown him by Morey.

This was all the direct testimony. The great caution displayed by Mr. Howe in the questioning of this, his own witness, was apparent to all present. The reader may judge thereof from the statement that the above summary covers every point testified to, and that the official report of the entire direct examination, questions and answers included, contains only 309 words.

The cross-examination of "Lindsay" was looked forward to by counsel for the people as likely to prove exceedingly fruitful of interesting, and generally unexpected, results. Owing to the vigilance and good judgment of Colonel Henry J. Johnson and Captain William E. Griffith, two well and favorably known citizens of Cumberland, Md., the prosecution had been kept posted as to matters at Cumberland connected with a "Robert Lindsay" letter written from that city to the *Washington* (D. C.) *Post*. The prosecution believed that an attempt would be made to support a certain affidavit which had been sent to the press on the eve of election day by the Democratic National Committee, and which purported to have been made by one "Robert Lindsay," and therefore had communicated with Colonel Johnson and requested him to be present at the hearing on the 9th inst., together with such other parties from his city as he deemed it necessary to bring with him.

Promptly at the hour for the hearing to proceed, on the 9th of November, Colonel Johnson, Captain Griffith, Mr. James Reed, steward of the almshouse at Cumberland and formerly a deputy sheriff and police officer in that city, and Ransom T. Powell, a "dock boss" at Eckhart Mines, Maryland, filed into court with counsel for the people. No one connected with the defense knew them or was acquainted with the fact of their presence.

When the short, timid and hesitating direct examination of the so-called "Robert Lindsay" was completed, the witness was taken in hand by Colonel Bliss for cross-examination. He swore that he resided on the road running from Frostburg to Cumberland, in the County of Alleghany, Maryland, and had been "around there for the last nineteen years," sleeping where it was most "convenient;" that since he was eight years of age he had been in the employ of the man with whom he now was—the president of a secret organization of workingmen—and was a detective of that organization, but being bound, as he said, by an oath, not to reveal any of the secrets of the organization, he declined to mention the name of its president. The name being insisted upon, Mr. Howe came to his assistance and argued that he should not be compelled to state it. Judge Davis held otherwise, and, after a consultation with Mr. Howe, the witness replied, "William H. Thompson," who was, he stated, a lawyer residing on West Baltimore Street, in West Cumberland, just opposite the jail, about a block or two blocks from the Court House; that he, the witness, had resided for twelve years in Mr. Thompson's family, but did not know the name of any street which crossed West Baltimore Street, on which he had so long lived; that he rarely ever saw Mr. Thompson, receiving all his instructions from him by letter, which documents, together with his pay, he always found "in a niche in the wall in the Eckhart mine;" that his principal occupation at home was "walking around the mines," and yet he "knew none of the mine superintendents or foremen, and none of them knew him." He could neither name any man he ever saw working in the Eckhart mines, nor any man who ever knew of his being there; the mines which he "walked around in" were the "Eckhart," the "Consolidation," the "Borden" and the "Cumberland," all of which he entered "on a level;" when he traveled from Frostburg to Cumberland, by railroad, he always went by "the Baltimore and Ohio road."

As to the "Lindsay" letter, the witness testified that he had written the letter to the *Washington Post* signed "Robert Lindsay," and had made an affidavit in Cumberland respecting Morey. His reason for making the affidavit he stated to be due to the fact of his having seen an advertisement in a Cumberland paper, signed by one Price, and calling for information respecting "Robert Lindsay," and "as a gentleman and a Democrat, I [he] thought it would be valuable." He was unable to give the name of the paper in which he saw the advertisement, and could not fix the time of his seeing it, save that it was "*after*" he had made the affidavit. He also testified to an acquaintance with Henry L. Morey, which began in the fall of 1874, when he saw him once, and that he met him twice thereafter, early in the year 1880. As to his presence as a witness, "Lindsay" stated that he came to New York at the request of one Walton, whom he met in Cumberland.

In response to a question he stated that his right name was James L. Barry, but he considered himself entitled to the name of "Robert Lindsay," because his father's name was Robert, and his "mother's maiden name was

Lindsay." He denied ever having been in Georgetown, D. C.; but had been in Washington at one time, for a few hours only.

At the close of the cross-examination, which was most skillfully conducted by Colonel Bliss, who was greatly aided by the information which Colonel Johnson, Captain Griffith and the other Cumberland witnesses were able to furnish him, it was evident to every person in the court room that the witness was a stupid, yet cool, deliberate and determined perjurer.

The Cumberland witnesses were then called and examined. Their testimony established the fact that no single essential statement of "Robert Lindsay," in so far as it related to anything in Alleghany County, Maryland, was true, save that he left there on November 5th.

As illustrative of the complete and unqualified manner in which these gentlemen broke down "Lindsay's" story, it may be stated that it was shown that no "William H. Thompson" resided in Cumberland, where he had located his employer; that the Eckhart mine, into which he daily walked and where he received all his letters and his compensation, had been closed some twelve years, being full of water; that some of the mines mentioned by him had no existence in that section of country; that no one of them was located where he placed it, and that the Baltimore and Ohio Railroad did not run to Frostburg.

The next witness examined was Mrs. Clara T. Morey, of Lynn—the stepmother of the witness Samuel S. Morey, previously examined on behalf of the publisher of *Truth*. Mrs. Morey was questioned by Assistant District Attorney Joseph Bell. She testified that she resided in Lynn, which city had been her home for some twelve or fourteen years; that previously, she had lived in Lowell for over twenty-five years; that she was a widow, her only husband having been Samuel C. Morey, who was dead. She then gave the names of her children and step-children—living and dead—and of her husband's brothers and half-brothers, and testified that she had never known or heard of a person by the name of Henry L. Morey, while it was beyond question that Samuel S. Morey never had an uncle by that name. The cross-examination of the witness disclosed nothing new save that among the cousins of her husband there was no Henry or H. L. Morey. Mrs. Morey was followed by her son, George E. C. Morey, of Medford, Mass.; John W. Morey, of Boston—for over thirty years a police officer in that city—and Frank P. Moore, of Lawrence, Mass.—a nephew of the witness Samuel S. Morey. Each of these witnesses corroborated the testimony of Mrs. Clara T. Morey, as to the names of their male relatives, the places of abode of such of them as were living, and the fact that Samuel S. Morey had no uncle by the name of Henry L. Morey, while each also testified that he had never known nor heard of any person by that name.

Dr. Jonathan W. Goodell, of Lynn, Mass., was the last witness called by the prosecution. He testified that he was a physician of large practice and extended acquaintance in Lynn, but he had never known a man by the name either of Henry L., or H. L. Morey; that he had never heard of any one in Lynn, other than himself, by the name either of J. W. Goodell, or J. W. Goodall; that *he* did not write, cause to be written, or have any knowledge respecting the "Goodall letter," nor did he ever see it until it was shown him in court; that he had never been the administrator of Henry L. Morey, and knew nothing either as to the life or the death of such individual, if he ever had an existence.

The case was then submitted without argument, and an adjournment ordered until Saturday, November 13th, 1880. Immediately, Sergeant Crowley and Detective-officer Richard Fields, acting under instructions from Assistant District Attorney Bell, took the witnesses "Robert Lindsay" and Samuel S. Morey into custody upon the charge of perjury. They were removed to the District Attorney's office, and subsequently were taken before Police

Justice Bankson T. Morgan, when Colonel Bliss presented, in each case, a formal complaint, and the prisoners were remanded to the Tombs to await examination on the following day.

On the morning of Wednesday, November 10th, the prisoners Morey and "Lindsay" were before Justice Morgan for examination. Each of them at once pleaded guilty to the crime of perjury, as charged, and expressed a desire to confess the part and lot taken by him in the proceedings of the Philp examination. Opportunity was afforded them, and their statements, when completed, were filed with the District Attorney, the prisoners being remanded to await the action of the Grand Jury.

The confession of each of these individuals will be found in full in the Appendix, and the investigation which has been carried on since they were made has shown that the statements they contain are in the main correct and truthful accounts, so far as they go, of the occurrences of which they treat.

The man who had testified under the name of "Robert Lindsay" acknowledged that his right name was James O'Brien, and that his home was at Georgetown, D. C. He made one or two statements in his confession which, in justice to political opponents, I am constrained to notice. He said that he passed the day of election in 1880, in Baltimore, Md., having gone there on behalf of the Republicans for the purpose of detecting repeaters from Washington who might visit Baltimore in the interest of the Democrats. I regret to be obliged to say that my investigation of this statement has satisfied me that it is not true, but that O'Brien, with others, went from Washington to Baltimore for the purpose of repeating in the interest of certain local Republican candidates. It was to this fact that his subsequent visit to Cumberland, which resulted so disastrously to himself, was mainly due. He feared remaining in Washington, and when upon the stand as a witness and questioned by Colonel Bliss respecting his residence in Georgetown, his fears led him to deny that he had ever been there.

It goes without the saying that Wilde, *alias* Walton, disclaimed having any conversation with "Lindsay" on the cars as to what he was to swear to, and declared that he believed the man to be the individual he claimed to be, and to have made the "Lindsay" affidavit.

The above completes the statements of all the individuals then in New York whose names have been connected with these disgraceful proceedings, and each statement has been fairly summarized. *Truth* alone remains to be heard from, and, although its statement was not made until the morning of November 12th, a summary thereof is inserted at this place, so that the reader may have before him everything then published respecting the matters being treated of.

The statement of *Truth* began by expressing its then conviction that the Morey letter was "genuine." This was followed by some details of what it claimed had been its course in respect to the two perjurers.

It alleged that it had received "two letters" from or relating to John W. Goodall, one of which stated that he had recently gone to Florida. This letter *Truth* did *not* print, but did print the other letter, which was dated October 29th, 1880, and was signed "John Q. A. Sheakly," who claimed to be about to start for Florida to bring Mr. Goodall back, and promised to have him in New York by November 7th.

As to its connection with the witness Samuel S. Morey, *Truth* said:

First.—That "on the Sunday preceding the election"—October 31st—Mr. Hart and Mr. Post "casually" visited the rooms of the Democratic National Committee, where they were informed by Mr. Dickinson and Mr. B. B. Smalley, who alone were present, "that Henry L. Morey's nephew was there"; that they were thereupon introduced to Samuel S. Morey and Albion G. Clarke.

Second.—That Mr. Post questioned Morey to ascertain what information he possessed; that Morey stated in substance the story which he subsequently testified to, and that upon being shown the "Goodall" letter, with the signature covered, he declared that he had no doubt it was his brother Frank's writing.

Third.—That on the morning of the day when Samuel S. Morey first testified he was brought to *Truth* office "to meet counsel," before going to court, and was there shown the register of the Kirtland House at Lynn—which had some days previously been sent to *Truth* by the Democratic National Committee—and immediately declared the signature, "H. L. Morey," to be "in his uncle's handwriting," although on the preceding evening, upon being asked whether he could recognize Henry L. Morey's handwriting, he replied that he was "not certain."

Let us pause for a moment and examine this statement.

Truth knew the "Goodall letter" was dated *at* and mailed *in* the City of New York. By its own statement the portion of that letter shown Sam Morey set forth the fact of its being written in New York, and contained the first announcement which he had received that his uncle Henry was dead, and that his—Henry's—administrator was then in the city. The fact that the receipt of this sad intelligence neither threw Sam into one of his frequent epileptic fits, nor drew from him any expression of surprise, and that it did not even lead to any inquiry upon his part as to where he could find his brother Frank, whose handwriting he "had no doubt whatever" the letter was in, would have suggested to any one, other than the very intelligent and capable young lawyer who had become an editor of *Truth*, that extreme caution was necessary in dealing with Samuel S. Morey and his statements.

Again, the positive identification of the Goodall letter by Sam Morey, as being in his brother's handwriting *from New York*, when Sam had previously stated in the same interview that he had a letter from Frank only "*six weeks*" before, dated at Venezuela, South America, in which Frank wrote that he and Henry L. were going "to Columbia," should have led even this editor of *Truth* to look with suspicion upon the proffered and willing witness.

Yet further. If the editor believed Sam Morey's statement that the Goodall letter was in Frank Morey's handwriting, he, of necessity, knew that the statements made by Frank in the letter were false. If he believed Sam Morey mistaken in his identification of the handwriting of his brother, and that in fact Frank had not written the "Goodall letter," upon what ground did he assume that a witness who did not know *his brother's* writing, was entitled to belief, when, upon being shown on the following day the hotel register, he "immediately" identified the signature "H. L. Morey" as in *his uncle's* handwriting? The pertinency of this inquiry is the more marked when the fact is remembered, that before seeing the hotel register, Sam. Morey had informed the editor that it was doubtful if he could tell his uncle's writing.

Truth, having explained its action in the Sam Morey matter to the satisfaction of no one who would not have been satisfied without an explanation, proceeded to state its connection with the "Lindsay" incident, which it declared to have been as follows:

First.—The first intimation *Truth* had of the existence of the witness, O'Brien, who testified under the name of "Robert Lindsay," came from Stilson Hutchins, the editor of the *Washington Post*, who sent it the letter signed "Robert Lindsay."

[Note—The "Lindsay" letter was forwarded *Truth* by Mr. Walter S. Hutchins, not Mr. Stilson Hutchins, who was not in Washington at the time.]

Second.—That Mr. Stilson Hutchins had informed *Truth* that he had not been able to find "Robert Lindsay," whereupon *Truth* forwarded the "Lindsay letter" to the Democratic National Committee with a request to that body to look into the matter; that thereafter it received from the Committee the dispatch containing Price's telegraphic copy of what purported to be the "Lindsay affidavit."

[Note—It was Mr. Walter S. Hutchins, and not Mr. Stilson Hutchins, who gave *Truth* the information referred to.]

Third.—That finding the National Committee disposed to do nothing toward bringing "Lindsay" to New York, *Truth* sent an agent to Cumberland under the assumed name of Henry L. Walton; that its representative, upon arriving at Cumberland on the morning of Thursday, November 4th, went directly to see Mr. William M. Price, who expressed a doubt as to his being the authorized agent of *Truth;* that it had removed these doubts of Mr. Price, and Walton, with the assistance of that gentleman, had then found "Lindsay," and brought him to *Truth* office, where he—Walton—stated that "Lindsay" had been identified to him by Mr. Price; that thereupon Mr. Post—the lawyer-editor of *Truth*, whose *brilliant* success in examining Samuel S. Morcy we have already observed —and Mr. Howe, the personal counsel of Mr. Hart, the publisher of *Truth*, examined "Lindsay" and then placed him "in charge of a trusted employee" with instructions to permit no strangers to communicate with him. The *Truth* statement further declared that "Lindsay's" story, as told at that time, was as he "gave it in court;" that "he was subjected to a rigid cross-examination, but upon most collateral points he declined to answer on the ground of his obligation, thus evading the detection which followed in court, when he was compelled to answer;" that "relying upon the integrity of the source from which he came," and deceived by his story of being a detective in a secret society, they believed his statements, and accepted him; that upon his arrest Mr. Hart telegraphed Mr. Price to "come on," and received a reply that he could not leave.

This was *Truth's* story of "Lindsay," and the same is doubtless in the main correct. It contains one statement, however, which should not pass without notice; I refer to the claim of *Truth*, that "Lindsay," when cross-examined by Messrs. Post and Howe, "upon most collateral points" in his story "declined to answer on the ground of his obligation"—his oath as a member of a secret organization—"thus evading the detection which followed in court when he was compelled to answer."

The official report of the examination—direct and cross—of the witness "Lindsay," fills one hundred and seven letter sheet pages, of which nearly *one hundred and five are devoted to the cross-examination;* from the time he was sworn to the moment of his leaving the stand, he declined to answer *but a single question*, and was "compelled to answer" but that one, *viz.:* "What is the name of the man who employs you?" It may be added that before this question was answered, the prosecution had more than half closed their cross-examination. It had therefore no opportunity in this respect, which was not equally open to the editor and attorneys of *Truth*, save that the Court compelled the witness to give the name of the president of a mythical secret organization to which he pretended to belong, which name was wholly immaterial, so far as the breaking down of his testimony was concerned.

If the excuse of *Truth* had been that the "*rigid*" character of the "cross-examination" of "Lindsay" by its representatives, Post and Howe, had so shattered the mind of the witness as not to permit of his recalling the precise facts when produced by them in Court, the statement would have appeared quite as accurate and much more probable than the one which was offered.

The comments of the metropolitan press on Thursday, November 11th, upon such facts as they had obtained respecting the disclosures made by the perjurers in their statements of the previous day—the documents themselves not having yet been made public—were of substantially the same tenor. The *Tribune* said: "The Democratic campaign of 1880 surely reached the utmost limits of mean trickery." The *Times* said: "An excellent opening seems to present itself for introducing some more or less eminent Democratic statesmen to the corrective discipline of State Prison." The *Herald* declared that the facts stated by the perjurers led to the conclusion "that Henry L. Morey, the nominal recipient of the letter, is as mythical a personage as Sairey Gamp's Mrs. Harris. It is mortifying to every honorable Democrat to think that the result of the presidential election came near being determined by such a vile fraud." The *Sun*, with great frankness, said: "It strikes us that the worst fraud practiced in the latter part of the campaign was the forgery and circulation of General Garfield's alleged Chinese letter."

Truth, of the same day, expressed the opinion that the question of the truth or perjury of these witnesses "had no real bearing upon the question of Garfield's guilt;" reiterated the statement that Messrs. "Hewitt, Randall, Cleveland and half a dozen other reputable honorables" stated the letter was in Garfield's handwriting; declared that Garfield's innocence was not proved "without Garfield's testimony," and inquired: "Why did not James A. Garfield deny the letter under oath?"

The Grand Jury being in session, the witnesses in the perjury case against Samuel S. Morey, and James O'Brien, *alias* Lindsay, were examined by that body on November 11th.

On Saturday morning, November 13th, the *New York Tribune* published an interview with Mr. Hewitt in which he said: "*I do not yet know that the Morey letter is a forgery.*" He finally admitted, however, that "in view of the facts disclosed during the examination in the Philp case," he had "*doubts* of its genuineness; I think any man would in view of the most suspicious circumstances."

Mr. William L. Scott was also caught by the same interviewer. His opinion was that the Republicans had better not continue to stir up "this mare's nest." He declared that "the Republicans are [were] trying to throw mud at us [them]. They will [would] find out that the other side [the Democrats] can [could] throw mud before they get [got] through."

On November 13th Justice Davis decided to hold Kenward Philp to await the action of the Grand Jury upon the charge of libel, on which he had been arrested.

The Later Action of "Truth."

About the first of December, 1880, the Grand Jury of the Court of General Sessions of the City and County of New York found an indictment against Kenward Philp for writing, and Joseph Hart, Charles A. Byrne and Louis F. Post, for publishing, in *Truth* "a certain false, scandalous, malicious and defamatory libel of and concerning the said James A. Garfield," to wit: the editorial of October 22d, 1880, entitled "Lying and Sticking to It," in which article General Garfield was charged with having lied when he denied having written the Morey letter.

Shortly after this indictment was presented I became satisfied that Kenward Philp was not the penman of the Morey letter, and I so stated to the District Attorney and those with whom I had been associated in the prosecution of the libel proceedings before Justice Davis. It was then determined that no action should be taken in the matter of the trial of the indictment above referred to, pending the investigation I was prosecuting into the authorship of the letter.

On Wednesday, December 8th, 1880, *Truth* said: "That letter [the Morey letter] is not a forgery. It is genuine."

Two days thereafter, on December 10th, its publisher, Mr. Joseph Hart, sent a letter to General Garfield. The following is a copy thereof, save that the names of certain individuals are omitted. This letter has never before been published.

OFFICE OF "TRUTH,"
142 Nassau Street,
NEW YORK, December 10th, 1880.

The HON.
JAMES A. GARFIELD,
President elect of the United States,
Mentor, Ohio.

SIR:—From the day that it was discovered that the envelope supposed to have enclosed the Morey letter had been tampered with, I have devoted time and expense to ascertain the truth in respect to its origin, and the result of my investigations has conclusively satisfied me *that the letter is a forgery.*

Moreover, I feel assured that before you are inaugurated—probably long before—we shall have positive legal proof, not alone of the fact, but of the guilty parties.

Permit me therefore to express my sincere regret, that I and my journal should have been used to injure you in the late campaign, and my gratification that the outrage against you was not successful to defeat you.

I and my associates have acted in entire good faith in this matter throughout, and in this connection I desire to say that the only parties in this city professing to act in your interest, who have really acted in good faith, with a sincere desire to unravel the mystery and ascertain the truth, are * * * * * * * *. My opportunities for knowing this are such that I make this assertion without hesitation or doubt.

It is proper to explain that the course of *Truth* in respect to this matter at the present time, is suggested and approved by your friends, and is intended to assist in detecting the criminals by allaying their suspicions.

You will please not regard this letter as intended to solicit your favorable consideration in any respect, or for any purpose, but purely as an acknowledgment of the wrong I have unintentionally done you, and an assurance of my determination to right it, so far as it is in my power to do so.

You will appreciate the necessity of regarding this as confidential for the present.

I am, with great respect,
Your obedient servant,
JOSEPH HART.

On Tuesday, January 4th, 1881, *Truth* published an open letter to General Garfield in which it publicly admitted the Morey letter to be a forgery.

Subsequently I succeeded in satisfying those with whom I had acted in the prosecution of Philp for libel, that the trail struck early in December, 1880, was undoubtedly the only one which would ever lead to the disclosure of the author of the Morey letter, and that while the hunt was destined to be a long one, it would, if persistently followed, prove successful. I also laid before them such evidence as established the fact that Philp was not the writer of the letter and thereupon the District Attorney decided to enter a *nolle prosequi* in the matter of the indictment for libel against Philp, Hart, Byrne and Post. This he did on the 19th of May, 1881, filing with the papers in the case the following memoranda:

THE PEOPLE, ETC.,
vs.
KENWARD PHILP,   New York:
CHARLES A. BYRNE,   Oyer and Terminer.
LOUIS F. POST,
JOSEPH HART.

By leave of Court I enter a *nol. pros.* on the indictment herein pending, which charges the above named defendants with libel. That libel is alleged to consist of the writing and publishing in a newspaper called "*Truth*" a certain editorial article entitled, "Lying and Sticking to It." Prior to the publication of the article in question, there had been printed in the said newspaper what purported to be a *fac-simile* of an autograph letter bearing the signature James A. Garfield and addressed to Henry L. Morey at Lynn, Mass.

The pretended *fac-simile* was accompanied by certain editorial comments, declaring that it was a veritable reproduction of a letter theretofore written by Mr. Garfield and received by Henry L. Morey at Lynn.

In the subsequent issue of *Truth* containing the article which was the foundation of the indictment, it was declared that Mr. Garfield denied that he was the author of the letter referred to, and, under the heading of "Lying and Sticking to It," it was stated in various forms that such denial was false, and that its author was guilty of lying.

It was for this publication that the defendants were declared by the indictment to have been guilty of libel.

At the time the prosecution was instituted there was evidence in the possession of the District Attorney strongly tending to prove that the defendant, Philp (who was employed on the staff of the *Truth* newspaper, edited and published by his co-defendants), was himself the writer of the letter above referred to, which purported to be a *fac-simile* of a genuine letter of James A. Garfield.

The prosecution against Philp and his co-defendants was, in a great degree, based upon the theory, supported by evidence which seemed to deserve credence, that the editorial entitled "Lying and Sticking to It"—admittedly written by Philp—was known by him, at the time of its publication, to be false, malicious and libellous, because the so-called "Morey letter" was known by him to have been written by himself, and not by Mr. Garfield.

Upon careful inquiry and examination, I have, since the finding of the indictment, been led to doubt whether Philp was in any wise concerned in the authorship or writing of the "Morey letter," now universally conceded to have been a forgery, and avowed to be such by the *Truth* newspaper itself. Indeed, in the light of the investigation which has been made since the indictment was filed, I am decidedly of the opinion that Philp was *not* the author or the writer of the letter in question. And upon the evidence now within reach of the prosecution, I should not feel justified in asking a conviction for any offense which involved the participation of Philp in the preparation of that letter.

While the defendants may in strictness be chargeable with criminal libel, even though no one of them may have taken part in the forgery of the letter, or have had guilty knowledge at the time when it was editorially declared to be genuine, that it was in fact a forgery, it seems to me that a prosecution under such circumstances would be both undeserving success and unlikely to succeed.

If the defendants, prior to the publication of the alleged *fac-simile*, believed the Morey letter to be genuine (and the prosecution is not prepared to show the contrary), such belief may well have been strengthened by the confident assertions made to certain of the defendants by the prominent members of the Democratic National Committee that the letter was in truth in Mr. Garfield's handwriting.

In the course of the preliminary examination in this cause before the Presiding Justice of the Supreme Court, sitting as a committing magistrate, at least two of the witnesses on behalf of the defendants committed perjury, as they themselves afterwards admitted. Certain of the defendants were engaged in procuring the attendance of these witnesses, but so far as I am informed their action was in good faith. I am thoroughly impressed with the conviction that the forgery of the Morey letter was a public crime of exceptional gravity, and that whoever perpetrated it, or connived at it, or was wilfully and maliciously concerned in its publication, is deserving of severe punishment.

But in the absence of evidence which seems to me sufficient to show, either that the defendants were parties to the forging of the letter, or had a guilty knowledge that it was forged, at the time when they published it as true, I am unwilling to prosecute this indictment.

DANIEL G. ROLLINS,
District Attorney.

The last meeting of the Democratic National Committee was held on Friday, November 12th, 1880. After a secret session of two hours, and the adoption of a resolution thanking Mr. "Barnum, the Advisory Committee, and the officers of the Committee for the efficient and faithful manner in which they have [had] performed their respective duties," the Committee issued the following statement in reference to the "Morey letter."

First.— Neither the Committee nor any sub-committee thereof, have ever taken any action in reference to that letter.

Second.— That it was first called to the attention of the Chairman of the Committee *on the night before its publication in Truth,* on the 20th of October.

Third.— That the Chairman thereupon requested Mr. Smalley, a member of the Committee, to examine the letter, but permission to do so was refused at the office of *Truth.*

Fourth.— That no member of the Committee ever saw the letter, or any copy or portion thereof, until after its publication, or was in any wise concerned therein or gave any advice in respect thereto.

Fifth.— That Mr. Hart, the publisher of *Truth,* brought the original letter to headquarters, No. 138 Fifth Avenue, on the afternoon of the 20th of October, when it was examined for the first time by any member of the Committee, and it was then scrutinized by several members and by others not members. All of those who were familiar with the handwriting of General Garfield came to the conclusion that the letter was genuine.

Sixth.— That the Committee decided to purchase a reasonable number of the electrotype plates of the *fac-simile,* which had already been prepared by *Truth.*

Seventh.— No denial having come from General Garfield of the authenticity of the letter, notwithstanding the telegraphed demand of the *New York Herald,* and a sharp leader in that paper, the Committee decided to give out the electrotype plates, which was accordingly done. The propriety of this action was not doubted by the Committee, as the letter seemed to be in harmony with General Garfield's views upon the subject therein discussed, as gathered from public records of undoubted genuineness.

Eighth.— That the first complete denial was not published until five days after the original publication in *Truth;* and to this denial, unsupported by any other evidence, the Committee, in view of General Garfield's connection with other scandals, attached no weight.

Ninth.— That therefore when evidence was offered to show that Morey was a real person, and not a myth, the Committee called for its production, as they were bound to do in order to arrive at the truth.

Tenth.— That if the letter has been forged, or any fraud committed in reference thereto, or any false evidence been given, it has been done without the knowledge, consent or privity of the Committee, or of any member thereof. Finally, the Committee approve of all honest measures to prosecute any and all persons, who have committed any violation of law, and have no interest in the matter, but to arrive at the truth of the affair. That there should be a doubt as to the authenticity of the letter is largely due to the failure of the prosecution to put General Garfield on the stand.

By order of the Committee,
W. H. BARNUM,
Chairman.

FREDERICK O. PRINCE,
Secretary.

In view of what was known at the date of this manifesto the document was a most extraordinary one. In the light of the facts since ascertained it would not be difficult for the author to properly characterize it, but, as his readers are about to be placed in possession of the facts respecting the Morey letter and the action of the influential officers, members and agents of the Democratic National Committee in respect thereto, he prefers leaving them free to form their own opinion of the above paper and to speak of it in such terms as they shall, thereafter, feel themselves warranted in doing.

PART SECOND.

THE MOREY LETTER.

The History of its Authorship, Publication and Support, with Fac-Similes of Original Papers, and the Documentary and Other Evidence relating to the Forgery.—Matter, which in the main, has never before been published.

In presenting the hitherto unpublished, and generally supposed unascertainable, facts respecting the authorship, publication, endorsement, circulation and support of the Morey letter, I shall omit as far as may be any reference to the manner in which the information, affidavits, telegrams, letters, receipts and other original documents herein submitted have been obtained. It is sufficient for me to state that they were procured in an honorable manner and one which will bear the fullest investigation. The details of the methods adopted would necessarily be too personal to myself in their character to admit of relation here. However interesting might be any account which could be written of the trail followed, the means employed, the agents used and the negotiations had, in ascertaining the facts and securing the documentary evidence herein presented, it would not add anything of value to the history of the matter and therefore has no place in this work. The people of the country are entitled to be informed of what has been ascertained and established. For personal reminiscences and the details of two years of earnest search and travel the public has no care, and I have neither the desire nor the time to recite them.

The Republican National Convention assembled at Chicago, June 3rd, 1880, and on the 8th of the same month made its nominations. There was at that time, ostensibly engaged in the practice of the law, in the City of New York, one Henry H. Hadley, a native of Perry County, Ohio. He had been, for a greater or less time, a resident, within seven years, of Washington, D. C., and of the States of New Jersey, New York and Connecticut. His business during the major portion of that time had been the organizing, managing, manipulating, or acting as the agent or broker of several insurance companies in New Jersey, West Virginia, Missouri and Washington, D. C. Many of these companies were of doubtful character and standing, and some of them came to an untimely and unfortunate end. He was also connected for some time with a real estate loan and trust company, which guaranteed the title of property—chiefly wild cat lands in the West and South—upon which notes were issued upon engraved forms gotten up by the company. Hadley had many other matters, mainly of an equally precarious and doubtful character, in which he dabbled from time to time, as the occasion offered and the fool presented himself. He also interested himself considerably in politics, in a small way, for some years, but apparently had no fixed political principles. He was not known—certainly of late years—as a Republican, and had no standing as such in that party.

In a letter written by himself on February 27th, 1877, to Lambden Dawson, Raleigh, N. C., he referred to his political position as follows: "Now the writer is not much of a Republican."

In June, 1877, he was the Secretary of a National Greenback Club in the City of Washington, D. C.

In a letter written by himself on February 1st, 1878, to Charles B. Colton, Louisville, Ky., he said: "One has to *manœuver*" (the italics are his own) "these times, while there is a fool in the White House and a fanatic in the Treasury Department."

In personal appearance Mr. Hadley is a man of commanding figure, standing over six feet in height, and weighing in the neighborhood of two hundred and forty pounds. Possessed of some capacity, he is more distinguished for a certain versatility of resource and a strong taste for underhand methods than for reliability. His habits and necessities seem always to have made much larger demands upon his purse than either his natural abilities, rightly applied, or his legitimate earnings would supply. Not possessed of a liberal education, and lacking in stability of purpose and moral character, he naturally, and not wholly unwillingly, fell into the way of relying upon his wits, and an innate love of intrigue, to supply him with that which neither his attainments nor his willingness to make progress slowly, would bring him. The inevitable tendency of such a composition was to lead its possessor to do that which would earn for him a reputation for "smartness" and "cunning," rather than for hard, earnest and honest work. While always "waiting for something to turn up," Hadley was never at a loss for a new scheme, from which, for a time at least, he would not only derive pecuniary benefits, but through which he would be enabled to gratify his vanity by figuring as the attorney, manager, agent or other officer of a corporation. I speak of Hadley, not alone as I judge him from a year and a half's acquaintance, but as I read him from his correspondence, having obtained, and being now in possession of nearly, if not quite, one thousand letters written by him during the seven years from 1873 to 1879 inclusive.

I find Mr. Hadley to be possessed of at least two weaknesses, which are both peculiar and marked.

The first, is a mania for clipping and preserving little extracts from newspaper interviews, published letters, editorials, and other articles to be found in the columns of the daily press, relating to public men and public affairs. This enables him, when the opportunity offers and the "craze" seizes him, to hold communication with public men and others with a semblance of possessing some familiarity both with the subject to which, at the time, he may address himself and with their views thereon. It also assists him in his speeches, where his assurance and his readiness to "quote" some charge, some allegation, some document, convey the impression of a somewhat studied acquaintance with the topic he may be discussing. None of his efforts will, however, bear a moment's careful examination without disclosing not only his sources of information, but the fact that his treatment of his subject is lacking both in originality of ideas and of expression.

The second, is a craving for recognition which seems to manifest itself by an unconquerable desire to dip into politics, and, under one pretext or another, to carry on, from time to time, a correspondence with gentlemen in public life. The utter lack of acquaintance with the individual he might desire to communicate with seems never to have been a bar to Hadley's opening a correspondence with such person.

In the evident belief that the campaign was to be closely fought, and would, at some stage of the canvass, present an opening which might be successfully worked to his advantage, if not profit, Mr. Hadley, on the sixteenth of June, 1880, eight days after General Garfield's nomination, addressed the General the following letter, the original of which is now in my possession.

Law Offices,
H. H. HADLEY,
A. W. KNAPP,
21 Park Row, Rooms 44 and 45.

NEW YORK, June 16, 1880.

Hon. J. A. GARFIELD,
  Washington, D. C.:

SIR—Allow a humble farmer's boy from Perry County, Ohio, to congratulate you and the country upon the result of the Chicago Convention.

I have usually stumpped (sic) Athens, Perry, Hocking, Fairfield, and Franklin and Muskingum counties, my old stamping ground during Presidential efforts, and may have the pleasure of doing so this year.

Resp'y your ob't s'v't,
H. H. HADLEY.

This communication was received by General Garfield on the day following its date, and was answered, on the 26th of June, by a letter written by Mr. J. Stanley Brown, but signed by General Garfield. The reply simply acknowledged the receipt of Hadley's letter of the 16th instant and thanked him for his kind expressions. Shortly after sending the letter of June 16th to General Garfield, Mr. Hadley found an opportunity, at the Fifth Avenue Hotel, to secure an introduction to Mr. William H. Barnum, the Chairman of the Democratic National Committee. At subsequent interviews with Mr. Barnum, Mr. Hadley represented to that gentleman, that he and some friends were undecided as yet who to support for President; that some of the gentlemen to whom he referred were inclined to vote for General Hancock, but had not definitely determined upon their course of action. In the mean time Hadley was vainly endeavoring to secure such an introduction and recommendation to General Arthur, the then Chairman of the Republican State Committee of New York, as would lead to his being able to make an arrangement with the Republicans looking towards his employment in the canvass. His efforts in this direction were not successful, but the Democratic hook on his line finally received a nibble which resulted in an arrangement being made between himself and Mr. Barnum, whereby the latter gentleman, in his capacity as Chairman of the Democratic National Committee, agreed, as Mr. Hadley states, to pay him twenty-five hundred dollars for his services in perfecting an organization which should partake of the nature of a bridge over which disappointed, disgruntled and despondent Republicans might travel on their way to the Democratic camp.

As a preliminary step in his scheme, Hadley, on the 10th of August—nearly two months after the date of his first letter to General Garfield—addressed that gentleman a second letter, the original of which is in my possession and reads as follows:

21 PARK ROW,
NEW YORK, August 10, '80.

HON. JAMES A. GARFIELD,
  Mentor, Ohio.

DEAR SIR—Thanking you for your favor of 26th of June, permit me, as a life-long Republican, a soldier who was with you at Murfresboro (sic), a native of the State of Ohio, and one who desires the perpetuity of the Republican party in its original purity, to ask you with great respect, a few plain questions for the satisfaction of myself and a large circle of my Republican friends.

The questions I desire to ask you are as follows:

First—Can you not make a more satisfactory answer to the charge brought against you in the De Golyer matter than has thus far been made public?

Second—Can you not make a more satisfactory refutation of the charges of perjury against you in the Oaks (sic) Ames controversy? Can you refer me to any reliable source where such answer and refutation can be procured?

Third— Please do me the favor to state before which Bar you were admitted as a lawyer, and the date.

These questions entering largely into the present campaign, I claim the right as an American citizen, a voter, a soldier through the late war, a native of your own State, and an earnest and conscientious Republican, to a canded (sic) and early answer.

Awaiting your early reply,

I remain,

Yours respectfully,

P. O. Box, 1585.   H. H. HADLEY,

21 Park Row, New York.

This letter was received at Mentor on August 11th, and on the following day, August 12th, Mr. J. Stanley Brown, General Garfield's private Secretary, replied thereto and enclosed Hadley some documents bearing upon the matters referred to by him.

The letter sent Hadley read as follows:

MENTOR, Ohio,
August 12th, 1880.

Mr. H. H. HADLEY,
21 Park Row, N. Y.

MY DEAR SIR:—In response to your letter of August 10th, I send some documents which I think answer your inquiries. Won't you please read them carefully and let me have your opinion in regard to their merits in answering the charges made against me.

Very truly yours,

J. A. GARFIELD.

In referring to this letter subsequently, General Garfield said to the author: "I was not in the habit at that time of reading answers prepared for me to sign to letters asking for documents, etc.; and therefore I was not aware of the nature of this letter until I afterwards saw it in print. Nor, until that time, did I see the letter to which mine was a reply. I can only say that the letter from me of August 12th was written by Mr. Brown, my Secretary, and signed by me without reading it. It was one of two mistakes which Brown made during the campaign, and I am bound to say, that with the pressure of work upon him and the great care and responsibility necessarily exercised by him, the only wonder to me is that he should have made so few errors of judgment, for I really remember but two. In this instance, if he had replied in any manner to Hadley's insolent letter, he should never have gone beyond the first sentence of his answer. To have requested from a stranger any expression of opinion as to my conduct in the matters of which Hadley wrote, was something which never should have been done. If I had seen Hadley's letter of August 10th, it would most assuredly have remained unanswered."

It will be borne in mind by the reader, that Mr. Hadley, by the 14th of August, had secured two letters bearing General Garfield's signature. Let us now see what use was made of them.

In every year of great political excitement there spring into existence various political associations or clubs, which seek to aid in carrying out the wishes of the regularly appointed and thoroughly organized party committees. The year 1880 was prolific in these mushroom associations, but most of them were so purely local in their character and purposes as to call for no mention here.

There was one, however, which demands notice. It was styled "The Association of Conservative Republicans and Independent Voters of the United States," but was commonly referred to as the "Hancock Republican Association," and was, at the time, believed to be simply "a tender" to the Democratic National Committee.

The first public notice of this Association was contained in the *New York Star* of September 10th, which stated that it had secured headquarters at No. 21 West Twenty-fourth Street, while "every member has pledged his sacred honor not to vote for James A. Garfield for President." To that hour, this long titled body had never been heard of. Some curiosity was therefore manifested among Republicans as to who were its sponsors, who its members and how much "sacred honor," to "pledge," they possessed. It was soon ascertained that Henry H. Hadley was its most active promoter, and that at an adjourned meeting of the Association held on the 15th of September, its organization was completed by the election of Leonard W. Jerome, Esq.—who had determined to support General Hancock—as President, and Henry H. Hadley as Secretary.

So far as the membership of this Association comprised individuals who had at any time acted with the Republican party, neither in numbers nor in character—with a few exceptions—did it take from the Republicans any whom they could not amply afford to spare and whom they were not most willing to dispense with.

On the evening of September 24th, a public meeting was held at Chickering Hall, New York, under the ostensible auspices of this association. Mr. Jerome presided, Mr. Hadley read a long address prepared by himself and issued by the organization to its followers, and speeches were delivered by Colonel John W. Forney, of Philadelphia, T. B. Wakeman, Esq., and Dr. George H. Mitchell—the latter of whom was, at the time, amusing himself by posing as the President of "The Hancock and English Republican Campaign Club." Among the "distinguished" stage performers at this assemblage were General George P. Este, formerly of Ohio, but for years a claim attorney at Washington, D. C., Colonel H. G. Worthington, of Nebraska and South Carolina, Paul S. Forbes, Samuel S. Patterson, John T. Green, Thomas A. Jones and George Sweitzer.

I am possessed of a copy of Mr. Hadley's "address" issued by the association. It covers eleven pages of printed matter, and about one-half thereof consists of editorial extracts, resolutions, news reports, etc., published from time to time in the columns of the daily press. There is, however, one very indicative charge in the paper in question. It is therein alleged that General Garfield held "various positions" as to several matters, among which is enumerated "*the rights of the Chinese.*"

I cannot find that at the time this charge was so made—September 24th, 1880—there had been theretofore uttered any such allegation save in the "Campaign Text Book" of the Democratic party, published by its National Committee. This fact possesses peculiar significance when taken in connection with Mr. Hadley's statements, hereinafter presented, respecting the manner in which a certain paper—subsequently constituting the body of the original draft of the Morey letter—originated, and the *time* of its origin.

The expenses of the meeting at Chickering Hall were met, by money received from the Democratic National Committee. And here it may be well to relate the account Mr. Hadley gives of a performance of Mr. Barnum's in respect to the first payment made by the latter to Hadley. Being called upon for some funds, Mr. Barnum said to Hadley that he desired so to conduct their financial arrangements as that he might be able to deny any charge made that he had paid him—Hadley—any money. He therefore suggested that the better plan of arranging the matter would be for Hadley to make his individual note for thirty days for the amount of $500, payable to the order of some friend; that Hadley should then send his friend, with the note, to him—Barnum—and he would hand to the gentleman presenting the note the amount called for. This was agreed to, Hadley making a note for $500 for thirty days and giving the same to a member of the New York Bar who occupied offices on the same floor with Hadley at 21 Park

Row, and whose relations with him may be designated as close and peculiar. With the note thus prepared, Hadley, accompanied by his friend, proceeded to the Democratic headquarters, and there the note was delivered to Mr. Barnum, who handed over the amount called for.

On the 18th of October the *New York Sun*, the *World*, and the *Star*, each published a long address from the Hadley Association of "Conservative and Independent Voters." It bore date *on the day of its publication*, was addressed, "To the friends of General Hancock and of the Constitution and the Union," and called "upon the people to come forward and unite with us at once in raising by single subscriptions of five dollars a great popular fund for the defense of the polls." Contributions were to be sent to Mr. Charles J. Canda, Treasurer of the Democratic National Committee, Mr. Edward Cooper, Mr. Abram S. Hewitt, and a long list of prominent local Democrats in the City of New York.

Both the *New York World*, and the *Star*, almost daily thereafter, printed specimen letters claimed to have been received in response to this call for a "Voluntary Poll Tax." These letters were reported to have contained sums of money ranging from one dollar to one thousand dollars, and the total amount acknowledged by the Democratic National Committee as received under this call of its "decoy" was something over $18,000.

There have been, from time to time, various inquiries made as to what amount of these subscriptions Hadley himself received, and what became of them. So far as my knowledge extends these inquiries have never been satisfactorily or definitely answered. It has also been remarked that with but a few exceptions all the alleged contributions referred to by the press were from individuals who seemed to be either ashamed of their names or their contributions, and therefore forwarded their money as "Elizabeth Street," "Ten Working Girls," "Seven Bowery Tailors," "For God and the Right," "A Cash Boy at Ridley's," "Ten Cotton Brokers" and "Fifteen Workingmen."

A perusal of these communications afforded amusement if not instruction. As illustrating the absurdity of the performance and the supposed credulity of the public take the letter of the "Ten Cotton Brokers," who were published as forwarding one thousand dollars because they "would rather *die* than see Hancock defeated."

In any criticisms hereinafter made upon the action, either of the "Conservative and Independent Voters' Association," or of its individual members, it should be understood that Mr. Leonard W. Jerome is not included. My information is that he knew but little of what was done by this "Association," and that late in the campaign, upon learning of some of its more recent action, he expressed his disapproval and condemnation thereof, and took immediate steps to prevent the further circulation of certain cards containing upon one side a reprint of the Morey letter.

About the last of September, 1880, the greatly improved condition of the Republican canvass had not only attracted the attention of the Democratic leaders, but had seriously alarmed them as to the future of their cause. To the end that he might personally view the situation in the October States, and, if possible, stem the tide which was so strongly running in favor of the Republicans, Mr. Barnum determined to visit Ohio and Indiana. Leaving New York for that purpose he arrived in Cincinnati on the evening of Monday, October third.

Mr. Hadley has stated to me, that shortly before Mr. Barnum left for this trip, he—Barnum—was strolling through the corridors of the Fifth Avenue Hotel one evening, when he met General George P. Este—the Washington claim agent before mentioned, who was formerly a resident of Dayton, Ohio —of the Hadley Association, and Hadley himself; that Mr. Barnum stopped and spoke to General Este, who stepped aside with Barnum; that Mr. Barnum stated to General Este, in substance, that he was not pleased with the appearance of the Democratic canvass; that the change of policy upon the part of the Republican leaders in forcing the issue upon the tariff question had greatly demoralized the Democratic party, and that numbers of working-men and artisans, who had hitherto voted with the Democracy, were disposed, at this time, to follow their employers in sustaining the tariff plank of the Republican platform. He announced his intention to go personally to the West, look over the field and see what could be done to counteract the defeat he feared was coming.

In response to an inquiry from General Este—who had been taking an active interest in the election of General Hancock, and who had been devoting some time to preparing himself for discussing upon the stump the questions of the tariff and of Chinese labor—as to what was proposed to be done and as to what suggestions he—Barnum—could offer as to the means to be adopted to counteract this unfortunate state of affairs, Mr. Barnum responded that he really did not know what to advise. He was inclined, however, to believe, that if something was prepared, presenting, in an offensive manner, General Garfield's views upon the subject of Chinese Cheap Labor, it might be put to good use—by being printed upon a small card and circulated as "a dodger"—in counteracting the effect of the "tariff cards" of the Republicans. In his—Barnum's—opinion, something of this character might be of practical benefit, but beyond this he could suggest nothing.

Aware of the fact that General Este's home was in Ohio, and that he had been for years well acquainted with General Garfield, Mr. Barnum inquired of Este if he was familiar with General Garfield's views and record upon the Chinese question. To this General Este made answer that he was, to some extent, and could readily inform himself thoroughly; that he was fully alive to the situation and would at once see what could be done in the matter.

The above statements have been given as Mr. Hadley has related them to me upon several occasions, and it is but fair to all parties mentioned that I should say that they rest solely upon Mr. Hadley's word—General Este having died shortly after the election. It is also due to Mr. Hadley that it should be stated that he does not claim to have heard the entire conversation, he and Este having been together when Mr. Barnum called Este one side; that Barnum and Este then conversed earnestly together for a few moments, when Barnum left and Este rejoined him—Hadley—and related the entire conversation to him as he stated it to the author, and as the latter has here presented it.

Assuming that Mr. Barnum will deny the story, and knowing that General Este's mouth is closed, we are compelled to judge of its probability by other facts and subsequent events which are clearly established.

Mr. Hadley further states, that on the evening of the first or second day following the conversation between Barnum and Este, he—Hadley—was shown by General Este, in the rooms of the Independent Voters' Association, a memorandum which Este had prepared in accordance with Mr. Barnum's suggestion; that at Este's request, he—Hadley—wrote, upon a sheet bearing the stamp of the "Independent Voters' Association," from Este's dictation, two sentences, which were intended to be printed upon a small card bearing some such heading as this:

"The following are General Garfield's views upon the subject of Chinese Cheap Labor, as expressed by him in a recent interview."

The two sentences written by Hadley as above mentioned read as follows:

"'I take it that the question of labor is only a question of private economy and individuals have the right to buy labor where they can get it cheapest. We have a treaty with the Chinese government which should be religeously kept until its provisions are abrogated by the action of the government, and I am not prepared to say that it should be abrogated until our great manufacturing interests are conserved in the matter of cheap labor.''

I am possessed of further information, the sources of which I need not here disclose, which tends to confirm Mr. Hadley's statements as to General Este's assistance in the preparation of the draft of the original "dodger." It is but just, however, to say, that it is claimed that, at the time, none of those who aided in the framing of these sentences had any other idea than the preparation of something which could be circulated as a "dodger," be claimed to be General Garfield's expressions, as made by him in a recent interview with a person not named, and thus, by trick and device, be used to create such doubt and uncertainty in the public mind as to General Garfield's real opinions upon the Chinese question, as to result in a revulsion of popular feeling against him and his party.

I have heard the assertion frequently made that he, or they, who framed the Morey letter must, necessarily, have possessed considerable shrewdness and ability, the wording of its two sentences being regarded as establishing the averment. To the ordinary reader, this claim will doubtless appear well founded; but those who are familiar with the literature of the subject of Chinese Immigration, will observe, on the most casual reading of the letter, that neither in ideas nor in mode of expression, did the Morey letter possess aught of originality. Mr. Hadley informs me that, as matter of fact, it was prepared after an examination of the "Campaign Text Book" and of the records and documents of Congress upon the subject of which it treats.

I give below, in one column the Morey letter—the sentences being, for convenience, divided—and in the opposite column, a few extracts from the Congressional Records. This will enable the reader to see from whence each idea, contained in the Morey letter, was obtained, and, also, where the words themselves were culled from.

The Morey Letter.	Congressional Records.
	"I think the Chinese come here for pecuniary benefits. The question to them is a money question. The question to us is both a money question and a question of political economy."
	[Chas. Wolcott Brooks, page 492, testimony before Committee on Chinese Immigration, 44th Cong., 2d Sess.]
"I take it that the question of employees is only a question of private and corporate economy."	"'The question of the employment of labor appears to me to be entirely a question of whether capital can be invested at a profit."
	[John M. Divine, page 418. Statement before Wright's Committee on Depression of Labor.]
	"The question of wages is merely a question of the distribution of the product between the parties engaged in the production."
	[Henry George, page 276. Testimony before Committee on Chinese Immigration.]

"Labor, like gold and silver, naturally seeks the best market, and no laws can prevent capitalists employing it in preference to that which is higher priced."
[Answer of Dr. S. Wells Williams, of U. S. Consulate in China, to inquiry of Committee of California, in 1876.]

"The various interests of capital and labor will be advocated on one side or the other, depending upon whether the speaker has *to buy labor* or to sell it."
[Admiral Chas. Rogers, page 1,021. Testimony before Committee on Chinese Immigration.]

"And individuals or companys have the right to buy labor where they can get it cheapest."

"I believe they (capitalists) will get labor as cheap as they can. It is human nature to get anything as cheap as we can."
[Rev. Wm. W. Brier, page 574. Testimony before Committee on Chinese Immigration.]

"Can an *individual or company* come here (China) and engage Chinese to be employed for a term of days?"
[Inquiry of U. S. Consul at Hong Kong of Secretary of State, Nov. 19th, 1869, quoted by John K. Luttrell, M. C., of California, in his speech on Chinese Immigration in 43d Congress, Second Session.]

"I have no occasion to insist upon the more general considerations of interest and duty which sacredly guard the faith of the nation in whatever form of obligation it may have been given."
[President Hayes' veto message of Chinese bill.]

"If then we cling to the history of the past, follow the beaten tracks of our forefathers, stand fast by treaties, observe contracts and *religiously fulfill* national obligations, our flag will be welcomed on every shore, etc."
[A. W. Cutler, M. C., of New Jersey. Speech on veto message of Chinese bill, March 1st, 1879.]

"We have a treaty with the Chinese Government which should be religeously kept until its provisions are abrogated by the action of the general government."

"Treaties bind nations as contracts bind individuals."
[C. G. Williams, M. C., of Wisconsin, on veto message of Chinese bill, March 1st, 1879.]

"The President * * * rests his veto chiefly on the ground that the bill is a breach of national faith, and is violently subversive of the terms of a treaty entered into with a foreign government at our own solicitation."
[Wm. A. Phillips, M. C., of Kansas, on veto message of Chinese bill, March 1st, 1879.]

See language of Senators Matthews, Davis, Merrimon, Edmunds, Howe, Maxey, and others, in Part Third of this work.

"The real point in this question (as to the effect of Chinese immigration upon California and the United States as regards industry) is probably * * * whether it interferes with the labor already there, so as to entail damage upon the interests connected therewith; and the condition and needs of that industry should decide the answer."

[Dr. S. Wells Williams, of U. S. Consulate in China, in answer to the Committee of State Senate of California, in 1876.]

"If we are to keep up the high prices of labor in this State, we can never compete with the East, and we never can have successful industries in the State. We must have cheap labor, if we are to compete with the East."

[Rev. Otis Gibson, page 338. Testimony before Wright's Committee on Depression of Labor.]

"It seems desirable that Chinese immigration should be discouraged by all honorable means. * * * Still I cannot see how we can well dispense with the Chinese, because cheap labor is a great desideratum."

[John A. Collins, page 335. Testimony before Wright's Committee on Depression of Labor.]

"And I am not prepared to say that it should be abrogated until our great manufacturing and corporate interests are conserved in the matter of labor."

"Is it just to those who have made great investments in farms, manufactories and vineyards, to threaten them with a loss of labor, whereby alone their operations can be prosecuted to the advantage of the whole country?"

[J. C. G. Kennedy. Argument on behalf of the "Chinese Six Companies," before Committee on Chinese Immigration.]

"Let the Chinese be driven away, and all the manufacturing interests would be seriously affected, if not stopped."

[Rev. Augustus W. Loomis, page 458. Testimony of Committee on Chinese Immigration.]

"Your whole course (the Republican party) during the past sixteen years has been *in the interest of corporations, in the interest of cheap labor.*" * * * "This contest between free labor and cooly slavery * * has been maintained by the leaders of the Republican party, *in order that great corporations might have the benefits of cheap labor.*"

[J. K. Luttrel (Dem., of Cal.). Speech on veto message of Chinese bill, page 60. Appendix Cong. Record, 45th Cong., 3d Session.]

"Every act of the Republican party for the last sixteen years, has been *in the interests of corporations and capital.*"

[J. K. Luttrell (Dem., of Cal.). Speech on veto message of Chinese bill, page 84, same volume as above.]

Upon the completion of the Hadley draft it was taken, Mr. Hadley states, by General Este and himself to the Democratic National Committee rooms; Hadley remained—as he claims—below stairs in conversation with a member of the Executive Committee, while Este took the draft to the floor above, on which were the private rooms of Mr. Barnum, the Executive Committee of the National Committee, and Mr. Edward B. Dickinson: that after being gone some time General Este came down stairs and rejoined him—Hadley—and they left the building together; that after reaching the sidewalk General Este said to him that the character of the paper had been changed; that instead of being a pretended interview it was now a letter; that Este then exhibited to him—Hadley—his (Hadley's) draft which he found contained certain changes, interlineations and erasures; that the two then went to their own rooms—the "Hancock Republican Association" headquarters—and there a clean copy of the paper, as altered and amended, was made by Mr. Hadley. It is due to Mr. Barnum to say, that Mr. Hadley avers that he—Barnum—was not at the Democratic Committee headquarters when the draft of the proposed "dodger" was taken there for submission and was changed.

In proof of his statements as to the changes made in the original paper Mr. Hadley has exhibited to me a letter sheet, which bears in the upper left-hand corner the heading of the "Conservative and Independent Voters' Association," and which contains certain writing thereon. This paper he asserts to be the original draft which he wrote, as herein above described, and on which the changes referred to, were made at the Democratic headquarters.

It reads as follows, the words in italics being the words which Hadley claims were interlined, or added, at the Democratic Committee rooms, when the purpose of the paper was changed from "a dodger" to a letter, and the words in brackets being words which were at that time stricken out of the draft of the "dodger."

Dear Sir: Yours in relation to the Chinese problem came duly to hand.

I take it that the question of [labor] *employees* is only a question of private *and corporate* economy, and individuals *or companys* have the right to buy labor where they can get it cheapest.

We have a treaty with the Chinese government which should be religeously kept until its provisions are abrogated by the action of the *general* government, and I am not prepared to say that it should be abrogated untill our great manufacturing *and corporate* interests are conserved in the matter of [cheap] labor.

Very truly yours,

J. A. G.

A clean copy of this paper, as corrected, was made by Hadley—save that "J. A. G." was written out "J. A. Garfield"—after the return of General Este and himself from the Democratic headquarters, and was, Mr. Hadley states, forwarded the Democratic National Committee.

The name of Henry L. Morey, a Republican Member of Congress, from the State of Ohio—the former home of both General Este and Mr. Hadley—was taken to furnish the letter with an address.

Let us analyze Mr. Hadley's story for a moment, and see if we can arrive at the facts, for there are parts thereof as to which there is abundance of evidence to prove that Hadley has concealed a portion of the truth. Hadley's statements, summarized, are as follows:

I. That General Este and himself were at the Fifth Avenue Hotel one evening late in September, 1880, when Mr. Barnum met them, and calling Este aside, spoke with him as to the then poor prospects of the Democratic party.

This statement is probably true. All three of the parties named were frequently seen by the writer and others, in and about the corridors of the Fifth Avenue Hotel during the canvass. Hadley and Este were both members of Barnum's "Auxiliary Committee," while Hadley, as I shall hereafter show, was the most trusted Agent of the Democratic National Committee, and Este was an active and earnest advocate of Hancock's election. That Barnum was, at the time mentioned, exceedingly anxious respecting the political outlook, was an open secret in well-informed political circles.

II. Hadley says that Barnum's conversation with Este related to the damaging effect upon the Democratic canvass of the preparation and circulation by the Republicans of their "tariff cards," and included a suggestion that, as an offset thereto, "a dodger" should be prepared and circulated, containing what purported to be a statement of General Garfield's views upon the Chinese question, so worded and phrased, as to irritate and offend a large class of the community.

This is by no means an improbable or unlikely story. The proposed "dodger" was a comparatively safe and fairly shrewd investment, and General Este was, at the time, a man not unlikely to be spoken with respecting the project. He was from the State of Ohio, a lawyer by profession, a resident of the City of Washington for more than a half-score of years, familiar with the debates in Congress upon all public questions, and an old acquaintance of General Garfield's, whose defection was a surprise to Garfield and his friends. In addition to these facts, General Este had made it a point in the campaign, prior to the date of the alleged interview with Barnum, to devote himself to the study of the labor question and the Chinese problem, and had given much attention to the discussions in the press and in Congress upon these subjects.

III. Hadley admits that he made the draft of the "dodger," and that such draft was taken by General Este and himself to the Democratic headquarters.

This statement may be assumed to be, and I have no doubt is, true, so far, certainly, as it relates to Mr. Hadley.

IV. Mr. Hadley says that when General Este and himself arrived at the Democratic Committee rooms, the General took the draft of the "dodger" up-stairs, where were the private rooms of the principal officers, and of the Executive Committee of the National Committee, and that when he returned, he exhibited the paper to him, Hadley, with the changes therein as I have described them, by which the document was made to assume the form of a letter, instead of a mere statement of a pretended interview with a person not named.

This statement—General Este being dead—rests solely upon Mr. Hadley's word. To substantiate it, that gentleman has exhibited to me the paper heretofore set forth, which he claims to be the original draft made by him, and which contains the changes referred to. My examination of that paper has satisfied me that the alterations made therein, while they may have been suggested by another, were actually made by Mr. Hadley; and while this is doubtless the fact, yet it does not necessarily affect the main point of his statements, to wit: that some of the members or officers of the Democratic National Committee were cognizant of the Morey letter, prior to its publication. There appears to be considerable evidence tending to establish this alleged fact. Let us see how the news traveled.

First.—I am in possession of correspondence showing that on or about the twenty-third day of October, 1880, Frank W. Torrey, Esq., the then Chairman of the Maine Democratic State Committee, made to a personal friend of his, a resident of and merchant in the City of Richmond, Maine, and a gentleman of standing and integrity, the following statement : "Mr. Barnum sent me that letter (the Morey letter), whether the original or a copy was not stated—about two weeks before its publication in *Truth* (*Note.—That would make it about October 6th*), with the request that I cause it to be published with such sharp comments as I saw fit. I did not see fit to publish it at all and I refused it."

Second.—On Thursday, October 14th, it was whispered on the Stock Exchange that a letter of some such character as the Morey letter was known to the leaders of the Democracy and would be produced. This information was supposed to have filtered through Mr. William L. Scott.

Third.—On the afternoon of Friday, October 15th, Captain Blake and Major MacFeely, both well known and reputable citizens of Washington, D. C., were at the St. James Hotel in New York. They there met General W. W. Averill, an ardent Democrat and an acquaintance of theirs. General Averill said to them that he had just come from Governor's Island—the official residence of General Hancock—and was feeling very good; that he had heard some glorious news, and that in a few days there would "a letter of such a startling nature appear that General Garfield would be wiped out." In response to their request for some information as to its character, Averill replied that as yet "it was a secret," but that Garfield would "not carry a Pacific Coast State."

Fourth.—The editor of a small Democratic paper published at Cleveland, Ohio, on the evening of November 12th, informed Dr. E. H. Peck, a practicing physician in that city, that about ten days before the publication of the Morey letter (*Note.*—This would make it about October 10th), he received a slip, purporting to come from the Democratic National Committee in New York, notifying him of the fact of the coming publication of an important letter of which in due time a *fac-simile* plate would be sent him. The gentleman who made this statement to Dr. Peck, subsequently repeated it to the author in the Doctor's presence. He also stated in that interview that subsequent to the receipt of the aforementioned slip he received a *fac-simile* plate of the Morey letter and that a day or two thereafter Mr. W. W. Armstrong, the member of the Democratic National Committee from the State of Ohio, and the editor of the *Cleveland Plaindealer*, returned from New York and sent to him for the plate which he had received, stating his—Armstrong's—desire to use it in the *Plaindealer*. It was sent to Mr. Armstrong and a *fac-simile* of the letter appeared in his journal.

Fifth.—The *Lincoln* (Nebraska) *Journal* of a late day in November, 1880, published a statement of Mr. N. S. Harwood, of that city, to the effect that he was in California several weeks before the election and that the Morey letter was quietly circulated in the remote districts of that State *prior to its publication in Truth.*

While I know nothing respecting Mr. Harwood, beyond what appeared in the *Journal*, I believe there is foundation for the statement in view of what is contained in the following paragraph which came to me from a gentleman, who is vouched for by those whom I well know, as being a man of high character, undoubted veracity, and good social standing.

Sixth.—Mr. R. A. Parker, an attorney at law in the City of Detroit, Michigan, has made to me, in writing, a statement of this character. Prior to the election in November, 1880, he was in the State of California. On the evening of Friday, October 15th, he arrived at Oroville, Butte County. On Monday, October 18th, he "started for Granite Basin, and reached that evening a mountain house called 'Buckeye,' about thirty-five miles north-east of Oroville. Staid there that night. The next day—October 19th—we drove into the basin and back to 'Buckeye,' and *that evening*, at that hotel, if I am not very much mistaken, I saw a circular containing the text of the Morey letter." Mr. Parker adds that he went to "Buckeye" the succeeding week, but, he says: "*I am certain, however, that it was on the first occasion* [the evening of October 19th,] *I saw this circular*, from these reasons."

A. "It was the first I saw or heard of the Morey letter, while two or three days later I heard it discussed on the Oroville train for Sacramento, by people going to attend a grand Republican barbecue there."

B. "On the second occasion of going to Buckeye I stopped on my way *up*, but the succeeding evening we drove to a point ten miles nearer Oroville on our return. Our horses ran away and we were forced to spend the night there"—Oroville.

Mr. Parker adds: "As for the dates and other events I have referred to, they are beyond question—the only doubt which could arise is that of my being mistaken as to the *occasion* and of *that I have no doubt but the first one is correct.*

Seventh.—A week or ten days before the publication in *Truth* of the Morey letter, Mr. Charles A. Dana, of the *New York Sun*, was, I am informed, told that such a letter was in existence, and upon his expressing a doubt thereof, his informant assured him that such was the case and that he believed he could obtain it and show it to him—Dana. To this Mr. Dana replied, that he did not care to see it for the reason that he believed, if any such letter was in existence it was a forgery and he wished to have nothing to do with it.

From this incident grew the story related by Mr. Abram S. Hewitt, that Mr. Dana had possession of the Morey letter before its publication in *Truth*. Mr. Dana, I am assured, never had the letter, and his treatment of it, both before and after its publication, was honest and manly.

Eighth.—I am reliably informed that on Monday, October 18th, 1880, two days before the appearance of the Morey letter in *Truth*, General Dwight Morris, formerly the Democratic Secretary of State of Connecticut, said to more than one of his friends in the city of Bridgeport, Connecticut: "You wait a few days and you will hear of something that will startle the country from one end to the other and elect General Hancock."

Ninth.—In Norwalk, Conn., and at other places in that State, notably in the locality of Mr. William H. Barnum's business interests, it was spoken of by Democrats before its publication, and their Republican friends were warned of the dire disaster which was to follow the publication of some document in the possession of the Democratic National Committee.

V. Mr. Hadley admits that after the changes were made in his original draft of the "dodger," he wrote the original draft of the Morey letter, but, *at times*, he claims that he never knew what became of it thereafter, save that it was forwarded to the Democratic Committee and subsequently appeared in *Truth*, re-written, upon a sheet of paper bearing the letter head of the House of Representatives. Mr. Hadley's admission is doubtless true, but it is unquestionably untrue that he did not write the letter in the shape in which it finally appeared. I have the statement of a friend of Hadley's to whom he admitted the fact that his hand had penned the letter. I can produce a gentleman—a member of the bar of this city—who was asked by the most intimate friend Hadley has in New York—also a member of the bar—to allow himself to be introduced to Hadley, who was described to him as being a very remarkable man and the writer of the Morey letter. The gentleman referred to was finally taken by Hadley's confidant to Hadley's office, where Hadley was pointed out to him as the writer of the letter.

Other facts within my own knowledge make it clear, beyond a shadow of a doubt, that Hadley's friend was not only in a position to know whereof he spoke, but did in fact know that what he said of Hadley was true.

But there is still other testimony, and that from one who, by Mr. Hadley's statement, was a party to the original scheme and fully cognizant of the entire matter. I refer to General Este, whom I had known for some fifteen years, and with whom shortly before his death I had an interview. I had just previously entered upon the investigation of Hadley's connection with the Morey letter and expressed to General Este my belief that Hadley wrote it. Este said to me that I was correct in my view, adding that when my investigation of Hadley's relationship to the letter was completed, if I felt that

I desired any additional information or needed any corroboration of facts found, he—General Este—would supply me with what might be necessary to place the matter beyond all dispute.

Later on I shall lay before my readers other and very substantial evidence that H. H. Hadley penned the letter sent to *Truth*.

But to resume the narrative where I left it for the purpose of considering and testing Hadley's statements by the discovered and well authenticated facts.

At about the time of the completion of the original of the Morey letter, there was furnished by Mr. Hadley to *Truth* what purported to be a copy of his letter to General Garfield, of date August 10th, 1880, and General Garfield's reply of August 12th. These documents were subsequently published in *Truth* in its issue of October 6th, the former letter appearing in type and the latter being published in *fac-simile* form. Both of these letters were also published by Hadley's "Independent Voters' Association," in what purported to be *fac-similes*, for general distribution. The Hadley letter of August 10th, as printed in *Truth* and as published by the "Independent Voters," in what purported to be *fac-simile* form, was not the letter sent General Garfield, which letter has been set forth on a preceding page exactly as written. The bad spelling of that letter was corrected both in *Truth* and in the Hadley publication, and aside from those corrections, both of those publications contained the following changes from the original, viz.: ten words were added, forty words were left out, two words were transposed and three words were substituted for three others. The published letter was certainly neither a copy nor a *fac-simile* of the communication sent by Hadley to General Garfield.

There was also printed in *Truth* at the same time, and as an addendum to the correspondence in August, an open response from Hadley to General Garfield's letter of August 12th. The publication of the "Independent Voters' Association," previously referred to, also contained this communication in *fac-simile*. It is worthy of mention that this reply—although dated September 18th, 1880, five weeks after the date of the letter to which it purported to be an answer, and nearly three weeks prior to its appearance in *Truth*, the *New York World* and the *Star*—was never sent General Garfield, while it was not furnished the public until the journals named, printed it on October 6th. From this it would seem that it was not prepared until about the date of its publication, and was then ante-dated. The letter itself was low in tone and insulting in character, while it was apparent that its conception was an afterthought, following the organization of the "Conservative and Independent Voters' Association," of which Hadley was the Secretary and practically the body itself, and preliminary to something yet to be sprung upon the public, but for the time concealed.

Simultaneously with the reports current from Maine to California that the Democratic leaders were about to resort to some desperate expedient, in the hope of thereby attaining success for their party at the polls, the editorial columns of *Truth*, on October 16th, contained an article, which, in view of subsequent events, cannot but be regarded as significant.

This editorial—entitled "The Real Danger"—was remarkable in its character, while the time and place of its appearance, followed as it was by the publication of the Morey letter, gave it special significance.

I have devoted much time to the task of ascertaining the history of this "tell-tale" editorial, and I find the fact to be that it was not written by any one employed upon or connected with *Truth*. I have also ascertained the fact, that it was the practice of the Democratic National Committee to send to various of the city journals, editorials prepared by or under the auspices of the Committee, and that many such editorials were in fact received by *Truth* and published in its columns. I am in possession of one such editorial so sent *Truth* for its issue of October 27th, 1880. It is headed "Is it [the Morey letter] Forgery? Let Us See." This article is a hektograph copy, and is upon law size sheets, bearing at their top the printed heading of the Democratic National Committee.

It is susceptible of perfect proof that the editorial in question, "The Real Danger," was an article sent to *Truth*, and while it is now impossible, by reason of the destruction of the "copy," to absolutely prove the fact that it came from the Democratic Committee, it is the belief of Mr. Hart, the publisher of *Truth*, that it was one of the many furnished the paper at about that time by that Committee. It certainly bears upon its face the strongest evidences of having been prepared with great care, and my own investigation of the matter has satisfied me that Mr. Hart is correct in his conviction, and that it was sent to *Truth* as a forerunner of the Morey letter. Let us examine it, keeping in view the fact that it reached *Truth* from *outside of its own office*, and that many such editorials came from the Democratic National Committee.

The editorial as it appeared in *Truth* read as follows:

"THE REAL DANGER."

"It is full time that Democratic voters came to a clear understanding of the slip-knot they are tying about their necks in voting the Republican ticket. They have been frightened into this by the specious pleas of Republican speakers, by the pamphlets issued by the Republican National Committee on the tariff question, and by the threats of employers that they must cut down their force if the Democrats get into power.

Like sheep, Democratic workingmen have been led to the slaughter thoughtlessly, heedlessly, cowardly.

It is not only not in the disposition of the Democratic party to abolish protection, but it would in any case be an absolute impossibility. There is no Democratic leader in the whole country who is against protection, and in favor of unqualified free trade.

The very notion is a bugbear, and nothing else. Nevertheless, it has been an effective campaign weapon in the hands of Republicans.

But there is one pet Republican scheme infinitely more dangerous to the American workingman than even free trade. We speak of Chinese labor.

In 1866 Mr. Burlingame, the American Minister in China, signed, with the sanction of Mr. William H. Seward, a treaty of commerce with China, by which the American Government pledged itself to put no bar on the importation of Chinese into this country. This treaty was, at that time, issued in ignorance of the dire effects that would follow. Since then the fatal error in the Burlingame treaty has become apparent. In the past thirteen years 250,000 Chinamen have come to this country. Thus far they have domiciled in dangerous numbers on the western side of the Rocky Mountains; but within six months a fleet of Chinese steamers has been put in motion, capable of bringing here 100,000 Chinese laborers every year. They come in swarms, and settle down in our fair land and devastate it. Wherever a Chinaman appears there must a white man give way. In the far Western States white labor is ruined, for the Chinese, who can live on next to nothing, underbids the white man, and drives him out.

For years the workingmen of San Francisco have been agitating this question, and crying that the Chinese must go. Eastern people cannot realize the desperation that exists among them. One by one all the various employments are slipping out of the hands of the whites, because they cannot live on the wages with which Chinamen are happy and prosperous. The Chinese build the railroads, act as house servants, laundrymen, day laborers, tobacco workers, hotel help, mechanics, indeed all the avocations hitherto belonging to the poorer classes of white men and women, who are driven to misery and starvation by this impossible rivalry. The Chinese will work at fifty cents a day, and the white man who asks for one dollar, or one dollar and a half, is jeered and laughed at. Mining is almost the solitary calling left to the white man in the Pacific States.

Again and again the people of these States have appealed to the National Government for help. They have been ignored. They beg only that no more Chinese be allowed, but the

Republicans have turned a deaf ear to their solicitations. Month by month the state of affairs grows worse, and the white man of the West is gradually driven out of the land which he settled and civilized, by this horde of barbarians, who, like locusts, leave nothing behind them in their onward march.

It is probable that the Eastern workingman believes that the day is still far distant when he will be affected by the Mongolian invasion. But is this true? Already the Chinese are appearing in our manufacturing centres—a few at a time, but in slowly increasing numbers. Now, however, that the flood of Chinese immigration has become larger than ever before, the time is near at hand when the Eastern laborer must suffer like his Western brother.

Who is responsible for all this—the Republican party? They it is who have encouraged Chinese labor from the first. Sharon and Jones, Republican Senators, are primarily responsible. They have made enormous fortunes by encouraging Chinese labor, and when the time comes, the Vanderbilts and the Goulds and other Republican millionaires will push aside the white man in the East to obtain Chinese cheap labor.

President Hayes had it in his power to put a stop to this invasion, but he decided in favor of the Chinese. At Chicago it was attempted to fit a plank in the Republican platform against Chinese immigration, but it was frowned down. At Cincinnati, on the contrary, the Democratic platform affirmed the danger of Chinese cheap labor and pledged the party to take action against it.

From the first the Republicans have proved the friend of the Chinaman and the enemy of free white labor.

With this momentous, this all-important danger staring Eastern workingmen in the face, they are led astray by the question of the tariff, which the Democrats no more intend to alter than the Republicans themselves.

There is no graver question involved in the present canvass than that of Chinese immigration. To put the Republican party in power once more is to assure the continuance of a policy which must sooner or later beggar every workingman in the land.

Where is the remedy now, we will be asked—a simple and a direct one? A Democratic administration will tear up the Republican Burlingame Treaty and put head money on every Chinese arrival in the United States, say of $100. This would crush out the Chinese immigration in an instant.

Let American workingmen pause to consider this all-important subject. Let them no longer be deceived by Republican false representations, while the Republican party stand the sponsor and the patron of Chinese Cheap Labor. This will be the battle cry for Democratic orators from now until the 2d of November.

The political situation at the time was this. The tariff issue had driven the Democratic party to the very verge of despair and desperation. The more intelligent among the file of its following were deserting it. The Morey letter had, as we have seen, been prepared and one or more unsuccessful efforts made to float it. Only about two weeks of the canvass remained. Unless the letter could be got before the public within a day or two the purpose sought to be attained by its preparation and publication would be beyond the possibility of accomplishment. It was clearly apparent, in view of the previous failures to secure its publication, that both the public mind and the columns of the organ through which the public were to be reached must be prepared to receive the letter. What, then, was more natural, and what indeed better calculated to divert suspicion from the real authors of the letter and cast it upon others, than to first secure the publication of such an editorial as the above?

The careful reader will not have failed to note the several steps taken in this remarkable article, but I deem them worthy of being recalled.

I. The *concession is made* that "Democratic voters" are about to vote "the Republican ticket."

II. "Democratic workingmen" are addressed and the *assurance given* them that it is "*not in the disposition of the Democratic party* to abolish protection."

III. They are informed that *"there is no Democratic leader* * * * who is against protection and in favor of unqualified free trade."

IV. They are told that "the very notion is a bugbear and nothing else," but are warned of the existence of *"one pet Republican scheme"* which they have to fear as being "infinitely more dangerous to the workingmen than even free trade. *We speak of Chinese labor."*

V. Their attention is then called to the dire results to their fellows on the Pacific coast, which, as alleged, have followed the immigration of the Chinese to California, and they are told that already the Chinese are appearing at the East "in our manufacturing centres."

VI. "Eastern workingmen" are sympathized with for the reason that in the face of the fact, as asserted, that the Republican party, as "the enemy of free white labor," had brought all this about they were now being "led astray by the question of the tariff, which Democrats no more intend to alter than the Republicans themselves."

VII. A *remedy is suggested* in the election of a Democratic administration.

VIII. A *pledge is given* that *"a Democratic administration will tear up"* the *Burlingame treaty,* "and put head money on every Chinese arrival in the United States, say of $100."

IX. A final appeal is made to the workingmen "to pause," and be "no longer deceived * * * while the Republican party stand the sponsor and the patron of Chinese Cheap Labor."

X. In closing, *an affirmative announcement* is made of the future action of the Democratic party. Protection and free trade are no longer to be even discussed. Democratic speakers are instructed to ignore the tariff question, and are notified that a new issue has, from that hour, entered the canvass, to wit: that "the Republican party stand the sponsor and the patron of Chinese Cheap Labor," and that *"this will be the battle cry for Democratic orators from now until the 2d of November."*

But aside from the tone of authority which pervades this article, in its demands, warnings and pledges, as well as in the announcement of the future policy of the Democratic party, there are certain facts of marked significance which claim attention.

First.—There is the fact that this was the first article—certainly at the East—which formally thrust the question of Chinese labor into the canvass.

Second.—There is the fact that on December 7th, 1877, Mr. Shelley (Democrat), of Alabama, introduced in the House of Representatives a bill to restrict Chinese immigration by levying a *per capita* tax upon every subject of China entering the United States, except officers or duly accredited agents of the Chinese government and their families; that on January 14th, 1878, joint resolutions of the Legislature of California were presented in Congress asking for the passage of Mr. Shelley's bill; and that M. J. Donovan, an ex-member of the Senate of the State of California, averred before the Wright Committee on Depression of Business and Labor (page 358) that the only way to stop the immigration of the Chinese was for Congress to allow the State of California to tax all foreigners, or any particular class of foreigners, * * * " and the Chinaman "is the only foreigner you have got to distinguish against * * * $100 a head per year."

This, it will be noted, the editorial in question declares would be "the remedy" which "a Democratic administration" would apply.

Third.—There is the fact of a most remarkable coincidence in form and manner of expression between a portion of the editorial and certain matter contained in "The Campaign Text Book" of the Democratic party for the year 1880.

The editorial contains the following expression, in speaking of Chinese labor: "There is *one pet Republican scheme."*

I have before me, as I write, a copy of "The Campaign Text Book." It was prepared for, and adopted by, the Democratic National Committee, and bears upon its outer and its inner covers the words: "Issued by the National Democratic Committee. New York, 1880." On pages 261, 262 and 263 of this document are to be found extracts from the "Views of the late Oliver P. Morton," United States Senator from Indiana, who as Chairman of a Joint Committee of Congress, went to California in 1876, and investigated the question of Chinese immigration. These extracts are occasionally broken by comments of the compiler, or editor, of the "Text Book." On page 262 one of these comments appears. After charging that Mr. Morton was solicitous of making the Chinese citizens of the United States, the editor asserts that in an extract, which he is about to give from the Senator's views, his adherence to "*another pet Republican dogma*," to wit: that of "undeviating hostility to American commerce," is betrayed.

Fourth.—The fact that on the second day following the publication of "The Real Danger," to wit, on Monday, October 18th, the publisher of *Truth* found upon his table, among other letters addressed to himself, an envelope, which, upon being opened, disclosed the following documents, viz.:

I. A blue "tariff card," so called—a campaign card gotten up by the Republicans showing the difference in the rate of wages of skilled employés in the United States and Great Britain.

II. A letter purporting to be from one "John W. Goodall, of Lynn, Mass."

III. An envelope addressed to "H. L. Morey, Lynn, Mass.;" and

IV. A letter purporting to be from "J. A. Garfield," to "H. L. Morey, Employers' Union, Lynn, Mass.," relating to the subject of *Chinese cheap labor.*

In view of the facts recited, and of the history of the Morey letter—its origin and support—as detailed in this work, the inference is irresistible, and the intrinsic evidence overwhelming, that the editorial, "The Real Danger," was prepared under the auspices of, and furnished to *Truth* by, the Democratic National Committee.

On Tuesday, the 19th of October, *Truth* printed at the head of its columns the following double-leaded announcement:

"TO THE WORKINGMEN OF AMERICA."

"To-morrow morning *Truth* will produce positive evidence, over his own signature, that James A. Garfield is a pronounced advocate of Chinese cheap labor."

This notice fell flat, no morning paper in the city referring thereto on the following day.

During the day of Tuesday, October 19th, Mr. Edwin R. Meade, a former Democratic member of Congress from the city of New York, called at *Truth* office for the purpose of seeing Mr. E. C. Hancock, the managing editor of that journal and a personal friend of Meade's. While there, Mr. Hart, the publisher of *Truth*, expressed a desire to have the members of the Democratic National Committee see the letter, and requested Mr. Meade to see some one connected with the Committee, and arrange an hour when he (Hart) could show them the letter. Mr. Meade agreed to endeavor to bring about the interview desired, and, leaving *Truth* office, went to the office of Mayor Edward Cooper, in the City Hall, where he induced the Mayor's secretary, Colonel John Tracy, to go with him to see Mr. Barnum. Their visit resulted in a request from Mr. Barnum to Mr. Bradley B. Smalley, the Vermont member of the Committee, to see Mr. Hart. This Mr. Smalley did, and Mr. Hart informed him of the character of the letter in his possession, but declined exhibiting it, until after its publication on the following morning, when, he said, he would be pleased to have an interview with the Committee and show its members the original letter.

On the morning of Wednesday, October 20th, the Morey letter appeared in type, in *Truth,* as previously printed herein.

The letter which accompanied the Morey letter read as follows:

NEW YORK, October 18th, 1880.

DEAR SIR: In administering on the effects of the late Henry L. Morey, I found the enclosed letter, which I send to you, with the accompanying card, which was sent me in Lynn by somebody in this city as an answer thereto.

I am of the opinion that as there never has been in this country for a hundred years such a thing as "free trade," there is not much danger of it now. We have a greater danger.

I am truly yours,
JOHN W. GOODALL,
of Lynn,
Mass.

The reader who has borne in mind the editorial sent to *Truth,* and published by it on the 16th instant, entitled "The Real Danger," cannot fail to see that the last two sentences of the above letter clearly refer to the matters discussed in that editorial.

The letter was the sequel to the editorial and its "earmarks" are those of the latter.

The *editorial,* said that free trade "would be an absolute impossibility," and declared "the very notion is a bugbear and nothing else."

The *Goodall letter,* asserted that free trade had not existed "in this country for a hundred years," and "there is not much danger of it now."

The *editorial,* declared "the real danger," "the momentous, * * * all-important danger" was not free trade, but "Chinese labor" and "Chinese immigration."

The *Goodall letter,* said "we have a greater danger" than free trade, and, as an answer to the tariff card published by the Republicans, enclosed a letter purporting to be from General Garfield, in which both "Chinese labor" and "Chinese immigration" were favored.

In the *editorial,* the words "free trade" were twice used, and each time were given marked prominence by the use of capitals, thus: "Free Trade."

In the *Goodall letter,* the words "free trade" occur, and the very unusual course was adopted of *quoting* them.

Taken in connection with the striking similarity of thought and expression apparent in the two documents, not only is the inference justifiable that the words in quotation marks in the Goodall letter were quoted from the editorial, but the confirmation is strong of the correctness of the views heretofore expressed, that the purposes of that editorial were to prepare the minds of the managers of *Truth* for the Goodall letter and its enclosure—the Morey letter—and to divert suspicion from the really guilty parties and cast it upon the paper, and those connected therewith, when the Morey letter should appear. At the same time, the soundness of Mr. Hart's opinion, that the editorial in question was the work of the Democratic National Committee, and was furnished *Truth* by, or on behalf of, that body, is made the more apparent.

It is worthy of special note, that the publication of the Morey letter on the morning of October 20th met with the same fate, at the hands of the press, which had befallen the announcement by *Truth,* on the 18th instant, of its future printing. No metropolitan journal of the 21st, save the *Star,* either copied the letter or made any editorial comment thereon.

On the afternoon of the 20th instant, Mr. Bradley B. Smalley called again upon Mr. Hart. At that interview, he was permitted to see the original letter, whereupon he urged that it be at once published in *fac-simile* for wide distribution. Mr. Hart responded to this suggestion, by saying that he would not allow it to be so printed or circulated, until it had first been examined by members of the Committee and others familiar with General Garfield's handwriting, when, if they pronounced the letter genuine, he would *fac-simile* it as desired. Mr. Smalley then stated, that he had called for the purpose of saying that the Committee was prepared to receive Mr. Hart and to examine the letter, whereupon it was taken by Hart to the rooms of the Committee.

There were present at the time of the letter being shown at the Democratic headquarters—about two o'clock in the afternoon of the 20th of October—Mr. William H. Barnum, Mr. Abram S. Hewitt, Mr. Samuel J. Randall, Mr. Orestes Cleveland, Mr. Edward Cooper, and others; most, if not all, of those to whom it was then shown, declared, with much promptness, that the letter was "absolutely genuine."

In view of the facts, as they are now known, the scene at the Democratic Committee rooms, on this "exhibition day," must have been most interesting, and the inquiry can but naturally arise in the mind of the reader, whether the members of the Committee, and such others as were present, did not, like the Roman augurs of old, "look in each other's faces and laugh."

The exhibition having finally closed, Mr. Hart was taken by Mr. Smalley to Sarony's, where the letter was photographed. Preparations were then made for its appearance in *Truth* in *fac-simile*. Leaving Sarony's, Mr. Smalley accompanied Hart to *Truth* office, and while there Mr. Hart remarked to Smalley, that already the air was full of reports that the letter was a forgery, and that measures should be at once taken to substantiate its authenticity. Among other matters which Mr. Hart mentioned as seeming to him worthy of attention, was the obtaining of evidence to establish the fact of the existence of the "Employers' Union" at Lynn, and he inquired of Mr. Smalley if the Democratic Committee could not aid in making that fact clear. Mr. Smalley replied that he believed there would be no difficulty in that regard, whereupon he left *Truth* office, saying he would give it immediate attention.

Within a very short time—Mr. Hart's recollection is that it was not to exceed one hour—two men entered *Truth* office, and made themselves known to Mr. Hart as John Pope Hodnett and William H. Grace. The former claimed to be "President of the United Labor League of America," and the latter "Chief Central Organizer." These illustrious demagogues proceeded to state that they had been sent by Mr. Smalley, to furnish evidence respecting the existence of the "Employers' Union," when they were stopped by Mr. Hart, who requested them to put in writing whatever they knew respecting that organization. Hodnett thereupon sat down at a desk, and on a sheet of brown paper, now in my possession, wrote the following, which Grace and himself then signed.

Headquarters United Labor
League of America,
359 Fulton Street,
BROOKLYN, October 20th, 1880.

EDITOR TRUTH: In reply to your inquiry as to what kind of an organization is the Employers' Union, of Lynn, Mass., we beg leave to state that it is an organization of boot and shoe manufacturers, established after the Burlingame Chinese Treaty of 1868, to import Chinese coolie labor into Massachusetts, and employ it in the manufacture of boots and shoes to replace the thousands of American workingmen at this business.

The first importation of these Chinese were taken to South Adams, Mass., and there employed at shoe making, and hundreds of American workingmen discharged by this same Employers' Union, of which the late H. L. Morey was the President, and subscribed largely to replace American workmen by Chinese laborers.

JOHN POPE HODNETT,
President United Labor League of America.

WILLIAM H. GRACE,
Chief Central Organizer, United States.

Messrs. Hodnett and Grace are in no true sense laboring men, nor the representatives of that useful and deserving portion of the community. They are simply noisy and persistent demagogues, who seem to pursue candidates for office, and endeavor to persuade such gentlemen into the belief that they are the representatives of the laboring classes, and that, to some extent, they can influence or control the votes of the workingmen. In 1880, Mr. Hodnett sought interviews with representatives of the Republican party, and subsequently, as early as July 26th, accompanied by a delegation, he called upon General Hancock, at Governor's Island, and informed the General that a convention of the National Labor League would be held in New York, in September, when they would decide whom they would support.

General Hancock referred the party to Mr. Wm. H. Barnum, whom he advised them to see, and to whom he gave them a letter of introduction, *vide New York Sun*, of date July 27th, 1880. The interview with Mr. Barnum must have been of a satisfactory character, for Hodnett, appears to have thereafter been at the service of the Democratic Committee.

I am in possession of memoranda of a conversation which subsequently took place between Hodnett and a friend of his, when Hodnett stated that he did not know H. L. Morey, and upon his friend suggesting that he had averred in his communication to *Truth* that he knew Morey, Hodnett replied "I did not." It will be observed that he *did not* so state, although his letter was of course intended to convey the impression that he knew, or had known, Morey. During the same conversation, Hodnett stated that the way in which he came to go to *Truth* office was as follows: he received a telegram from Mr. Smalley requesting him—Hodnett—to call upon him—Smalley; in response thereto he went to the Democratic National Committee rooms and saw Mr. Smalley, who requested him to go to *Truth* office, which he did.

It would seem almost superfluous to add, that every statement contained in the letter of Hodnett and Grace was absolutely manufactured, without the shadow of anything to rest upon, save the single fact that some years ago, a Mr. Sampson, of North Adams, Massachusetts, employed a few Chinamen in his shop at that place.

On the morning of October 21st, the telegraphic columns of the New York dailies contained the following press dispatch:

MENTOR, Ohio, October 20th.—General Garfield's attention being called to the full text of a letter on the Chinese question purporting to have been addressed by him in January last, to Henry L. Morey, of Lynn, Mass., and published in a New York paper of to-day, promptly and emphatically characterized it as a stupid forgery.

It will be remembered that at the interview with Mr. Hadley at which he told me of the manner in which the original "dodger"—afterwards, as he claimed, changed to the letter—was prepared, he admitted that the first completed draft of the Morey letter was in his handwriting. At the time of his making such statements he spoke to me of his family, and expressed the hope that in any account of the origin of the letter which I might prepare, I would let the matter rest there; that for the sake of his family and his future he did not desire to make any further admissions. I replied to him, that I had never asked him, as he well knew, whether he did or did not write the Morey letter, as I had fully satisfied myself upon that point and was well fortified with evidence to establish the conclusions at which I had arrived.

I have previously herein, enumerated certain facts tending to show Mr. Hadley's connection with the letter. It may now be stated, that by reason of the facts so recited; by reason of the personal examination I have made of the paper claimed to be the original "dodger;" by reason of my personal knowledge of Hadley's handwriting and habits; by reason of his conduct, both before and since the publication of the Morey letter; by reason of Hadley's admissions of the fact that he wrote the letter, which statements were made by him to those whom he supposed to be *his* friends and wholly unknown to me; by reason of the statements made me by General Este before his death; by reason of the many facts yet to be related herein, respecting Hadley and his connection with the letter, and by reason of a mass of other statements and facts in my possession, which are withheld at this time, but which—under circumstances which may possibly occur—will be, hereafter, made public, I am justified in saying that the penman of the Morey letter was Henry H. Hadley, who had previously obtained, as has been shown, two letters signed by General Garfield.

The habits of spelling and penmanship of Hadley, are so marked and peculiar, as, of themselves, to leave little doubt, if no other facts were known, that his was the hand that wrote the Morey letter.

The errors in spelling found in the Morey letter are those of Hadley, and some of them are of frequent occurrence in his correspondence, while his *habits* of penmanship are so very marked and peculiar as to be wholly distinctive and individual in their character.

Among other papers of his now in my possession are several letter-press books. In many of his letters I find the word "companies" used, but never once does it appear spelled by him in any other way than "companys," while the words "copies," "factories," "enemies," are never spelled otherwise than "copys," "factorys," "enemys," as is shown in Plate No. 1, on pages 50 and 51.

The dotting of the "r" and not the "i" in the word "Garfield" in the signature of the Morey letter, which by some was looked upon as accidental, while others regarded it as intentional, was neither. It was simply *a habit*, so strong as to be done naturally, and without observation or thought.

I find that it was his practice to dot his "r," in some words, always, in others, frequently. To illustrate: In the word "diagrams" the "i" was never dotted and the "r" always; in the words "services," "subscribed," "officers," "description," "circumstances," "interview" and "invariable," the same habit prevailed to a great degree, as is shown in Plate No. 2, on page 52.

Indeed, so marked and unconscious was this habit of dotting the letter "r" that he frequently did it in words containing no "i." To illustrate: In the words "perfect," "fraternally," "purpose" and "observe" I find the "r" dotted, while the word "convertible" he spelled without an "i," thus, "convertable," and then dotted the "r," and the word "observing" he would, while dotting the "i," also dot the "r." See Plate No. 3, on pages 52 and 53.

The letter "i" seems to have been his aversion, for wherever it followed an upright letter—save in words ending in "tion"—his frequent habit was to throw the dot to the left of the upright letter, whether an "r" preceded the latter or not. To illustrate: In the words "Chesterfield," "certified," "certificate," "enterprise," "benefit," "opinion," "detectives" and "uncontradicted," and occasionally in the word "confidential," he would not dot the "i" following the upright letter, but would, as in the word "Garfield" in the signature to the Morey letter, throw the dot to the left of the upright letter, thus dotting the letter which preceded the upright one.

On the other hand, if the "i" preceded an upright letter he would frequently throw the dot in exactly the reverse position; that is to say, it would be thrown to the right of the upright letter, and if there was an "r" to be found there, would be placed over that letter. To illustrate: In the words "considerable," "Richardson," and others, I find the "i" not dotted, but the dot carried to the right of the upright letter following the "i," and placed over the "r." See plate No. 4, page 53.

Two other habits, equally as peculiar, are noticeable. In the Morey letter are four words ending in "tion," *viz.*: "relation," "question," "question" again, and "action." In the first three words the dot which should be over the "i" is placed with great apparent deliberation and precision directly over the "n," and in the last word over the "o." I have examined hundreds of Hadley's letters, and I find that it is a habit, *rarely deviated from*, for him to dot the "n" in all words ending in "tion." Wherever this does not occur, and I find the ratio of change therefrom to be as one is to one hundred, the dot is always placed over the "o"—never in an instance elsewhere. See Plate No. 5, pages 54 and 55.

An examination of the Morey letter further discloses the fact that in all words containing a "t," save the words "the" and "that," the "t" is crossed directly through the letter, while every time the words "the" or "that" are found it will be seen that the initial "t" is never crossed through the letter, but directly above it. This is another of Hadley's peculiarities. In more than three thousand instances in the letters of Hadley which I have examined I find hardly an instance in which the habit of *never crossing the initial "t" through the letter*, in the words "the" and "that," is deviated from, while the instances are equally rare where, in words in which the letter "t" occurs, other than "the" and "that," *the line is not run through the initial "t."*

Still another remarkable fact. In the paper shown me by Hadley as being the completed draft of the "dodger" written by himself, the word "religiously" was written "religeously." The reader will find the word so spelled in the Morey letter.

A mere reference to the plates which follow will most forcibly present the very peculiar and marked characteristics of the penman of the Morey letter, while an examination thereof will disclose the fact that each of such characteristics existed in that letter. If no other evidence were presented, the facts shown in the plates referred to, would, alone carry conviction to the minds of all fair-minded persons who examine them.

PLATE NO. 1.

Specimen No. 1—"Companys"—in Morey Letter.
" 2 " in letter of H. H. Hadley to C. B. Rodes, of date Aug. 12th, 1874.
" 3 " " " Lee Clark, " Aug. 6th, 1874.
" 4 " " " John R. Hamble, " Dec. 22d, 1874.
" 5 " " " N. Grabill, " July 20th, 1874.
" 6 " " " O. A. Atwood, " Aug. 11th, 1874.
" 7 " " " Thos. Pryce, " July 14th, 1874.
" 8 " " " " " " "
" 9 " " " Julius H. Stoll, " July 27th, 1874.
" 10 " " " Lyman, Moen & Campbell, " July 21st, 1874.
" 11 " " " Studebaker Bros. M'f'g Co., " Nov. 24th, 1874.
" 12 " " " Wm. De Mott, " Aug. 12th, 1874.
" 13 " " " Denel & Co., " Oct. 29th, 1874.
" 14 " " " Charles Handy, " July 6th, 1874.
" 15 " " " James G. Harrison, " Oct. 31st, 1874.
" 16 " " " Harvey Reid, " July 22d, 1874.
" 17 " " " Michel and Gardner, " May 2d, 1879.
" 18 —"copys of"— " " Richardson & Teal, " Mar. 24th, 1877.
" 19 —"of the copys"— " " F. B. Agens, " April 16th, 1877.
" 20 —"enemys" — " " Lambden Dawson, " Feb. 27th, 1877.
" 21 " " " " " " "
" 22 "two factorys" " " Cole and Thomas, " Jan. 14th, 1875.

51

PLATE No. 1.

Showing the spelling of the words Companies, Copies, Enemies and Factories by H. H. Hadley.

No. 1.
(From the Morey Letter.)

PLATE No. 2.

Showing the habit of H. H. Hadley to dot the letter "r" instead of "i" in certain words.

Specimen No. 1—"Diagrams"—in letter of H. H. Hadley to L. M. Tucker,			of date Nov. 17th, 1884.
" 2 " "	"	"	"	" " "
" 3 " "	"	" A. Larrabee,	"	June 18th, 1874.
" 4 " "	"	" Columbia Ins. Co.,	"	June 17th, 1874.
" 5 " "	"	" J. F. McSnecan,	"	July 31st, 1874.
" 6—"Services"—	"	" Wm. H. Barnum and others,	"	Feb. 5th, 1881.
" 7—"Subscribed"	"	" A. Larrabee,	"	June 18th, 1874.
" 8—"Officers"	"	" Wesley Lyon,	"	Sept. 14th, 1877.
" 9—"Description"	"	" Robert H. Morrison.	"	July 20th, 1874.
" 10—"Circumstances"	"	" Wesley Lyon,	"	Sept. 14th, 1877.
" 11—"Interview"	"	" Wm. H. Barnum and others,	"	Feb. 5th, 1881.
" 12—"Invariable"	"	" Wesley Lyon,	"	Sept. 14th, 1877.

PLATE No. 2.

[Handwriting specimens No. 1 through No. 12]

PLATE No. 3.

Showing Hadley's habit of dotting the letter "r," in words containing no "i," &c.

Specimen No. 1—"Title perfect"—in letter of H. H. Hadley to H. Green,			of date September 27th, 1877.
do. 2—"Fraternally"—	do.	do.	Reuben Michel,	do.	November 2d, 1877.
do. 3—"Purpose"—	do.	do.	E. S. Hubbard,	do.	April 18th, 1877.
do. 4—"Observe"—	do.	do.	Michel & Gardner,	do.	May 2d, 1877.
do. 5—"Observing"—	do.	do.	F. H. Rollins,	do.	April 23d, 1877.
do. 6—"Convertable"—	do.	do.	Hon. T. L. Tullock,	do.	May 10th, 1877.
do. 7—"Liberally"—	do.	do.	Wilson Ager,	do.	February 19th, 1881.
do. 8—"Certain"— From a draft of a law paper of H. H. Hadley's in the year 1877.					

PLATE No. 3.

[Handwritten signature specimens No. 1–No. 9]

PLATE No. 4.

Showing Hadley's habit of dotting the letter to the left or right of the letter "i," as that letter followed or preceded an upright letter.

The forged signature of Gen. J. A. Garfield.

Specimen No.							
"	No. 1—"Chesterfield"	in letter of H. H. Hadley to Seible and Ezell, of date				July 21st, 1874.
"	" 2—"Certified"	"	"	"	Wesley Lyon,	"	Sept. 14th, 1877.
"	" 3—"Enterprise"	"	"	"	Hon. H. C. Kelsey,	"	Dec. 8th, 1874.
"	" 4—"Opinion"	"	"	"	Hon. A. S. Hewitt,	"	May 6th, 1882.
"	" 5—"Detectives"	"	"	"	Wilson Ager,	"	Feb. 19th, 1881.
"	" 6—"Uncontradicted"	"	"	"	Hon. A. S. Hewitt,	"	May 6th, 1882.
"	" 7—"Confidential"	on outside of envelope addressed by Hadley to			Wilson Ager,	"	Jan., 1881.
"	" 8—"Considerable"	in letter of H. H. Hadley to			H. C. Swain,	"	May 10th, 1877.
"	" 9—"Richardson"	"	"	"	Richardson & Teal,	"	Feb. 10th, 1877.

PLATE No. 4.

The forged Signature to the Morey Letter.

[Handwritten signature specimens No. 1–No. 9]

PLATE NO. 5.

Specimens showing the dotting of the letter " n " by Hadley in all words ending in " tion."

No. 1—" relation "—" question " in the Morey letter.
do 2 " questions" (3 times) in letter of H. H. Hadley to Gen. Garfield of date Aug. 10th, 1880.
do 3 " introduction " do do Wilson Ager do Feb. 19th, 1881.
do 4 " actions " do do do do do
do 5 " transactions " do do do do do
do 6 " connection " do do A. Larrabee do June 18th, 1874.
do 7 " representation " do do Reuben Michel do Nov. 2d, 1877.
do 8 " explanation " do do do do do
do 9 " option " do do Hon. T. L. Tullock May 10th, 1877.
do 10 " portion " do do Hon. A. S. Hewitt May 9th, 1881.
do 11 " questions " do do H. C. Swain do May 10th, 1877.
do 12 " resolution " do do do do do
do 13 " precaution " do do do do do
do 14 " questions " do do Michel & Gardner May 2d, 1877.
do 15 " connection " do do Hon. E. S. Hubbard March 30th, 1877.
do 16 " objection " do do Hon. T. L. Tullock April 25th, 1874.
do 17 " portion " do do Hon. A. S. Hewitt March 3d, 1881.
do 18 " conversation " do do Mo. Val. Life Ins. Co. Dec. 29th, 1874.
do 19 " remuneration " do do George E. Morse Feb. 26th, 1877.
do 20 " calculation " do do George H. Bacon July 21st, 1877.
do 21 " production " do do Hon. A. S. Hewitt March 3d, 1881.
do 22 " inception " do do do do
do 23 " convention " do do Gen. J. A. Garfield June 16th, 1880.

PLATE No. 5.

Showing the dotting of the letter "n," by Hadley, in all words ending in "tion."

From the Garfield-Morey-forged Letter.

No. 1 *relation* No. 1 *question* No. 1 *question*

From Letter of H. H. Hadley to Gen. James A. Garfield, August 10th, 1880.

No. 2 *questions* No. 2 *questions* No. 2 *questions*

No. 3 *introduction* No. 10 *portion* No. 17 *portion*

No. 4 *actions* No. 11 *questions* No. 18 *Conversation*

No. 5 *transactions* No. 12 *resolutions* No. 19 *Remuneration*

No. 6 *connections* No. 13 *precaution* No. 20 *Calculation*

No. 7 *representations* No. 14 *Questions* No. 21 *inception*

No. 8 *Explanation* No. 15 *Connection* No. 22 *production*

No. 9 *option* No. 16 *objection* No. 23 *Connection*

It has not, however, been my desire, throughout the long investigation I have conducted as to the history of the Morey letter, nor is it my present purpose, to advertise, or make much of, the mere instrument used to give that document its first circulation. If the hand which penned it had not done it, another would have been found and used. My mission has been to ascertain and present the facts so that the *really* guilty offender or offenders—who caused to be prepared, who published, circulated, endorsed and supported the forgery—should be made to appear in his and their true light. He and they, were, morally, the forgers—not the mere creature who held the pen.

Immediately upon the appearance of the letter the Democratic National Committee, through its Chairman, sent the following dispatch to the country, and the same was printed in many of the leading Democratic journals on the morning of Thursday, October 21st.

NEW YORK, October 20th, 1880.

The following is published in *Truth* this morning. *The letter is authentic. It is in General Garfield's handwriting.* Denial is worse than useless. It should have the widest circulation among all classes, as it unmasks the Republican hollowness and hypocrisy on the labor question through their chief. He declares himself adverse to the laboring man's interest, and in favor of the Employers' Union, advising them to employ the cheapest labor.

WM. H. BARNUM.

[Here followed a printed copy of the Morey letter.]

It has now been conclusively established:

First.—That before the Morey letter was received by *Truth*, prominent Democrats and their allies and confederates had knowledge of the existence of the letter.

Second.—That following its receipt by *Truth*, prominent Democrats—members of their National Committee and others—hastened to pronounce it "absolutely genuine" and to declare it "to be in General Garfield's handwriting."

Almost simultaneously with its appearance, and with these declarations, rumors became current that the Democratic National Committee was in possession of, or able to produce, a *second* letter from General Garfield upon the same subject and of a similar character; that this second letter it was deemed wise to keep from the public until General Garfield should be heard from respecting the Morey letter; that if General Garfield denied writing that letter, the other one would be promptly published.

I have recently come into possession of such facts and evidence as enable me to fix the parentage of this early attempt to sustain the forgery of the Morey letter.

On the morning of October 21st—the day *following* the exhibition of the Morey letter at Democratic headquarters and the day *preceding* the publication in *fac-simile* of that letter—the Hon. Edwin R. Meade called upon his friend Mr. E. C. Hancock, then managing editor of *Truth*, and in conversation with said Hancock and Mr. Hart, the publisher of *Truth*, stated that he had been informed of the existence of *another* letter from General Garfield of a character similar to that of the letter to Morey. Mr. Hart, seeing at once the great value to him of such a letter, and fearing that it might fall into the hands of some other journal than his own, urged Meade to ascertain, definitely, if there was such a second letter, and, if so, to see to it that when it was made public it should be through the columns of *Truth*. Mr. Meade undertook the mission, and leaving *Truth* office went at once to the rooms of the Democratic National Committee, where, in response to his inquiries as to whether there was a second letter from General Garfield similar to that to Morey, he was assured that the fact was so, and that at the proper time it would be published. Leaving the National headquarters, Meade went up to the Democratic State Committee rooms and there wrote and sent to *Truth* office the following letter. It has never before been published, and the original is in my possession. A *fac-simile* of the same, reduced in size, is here presented.

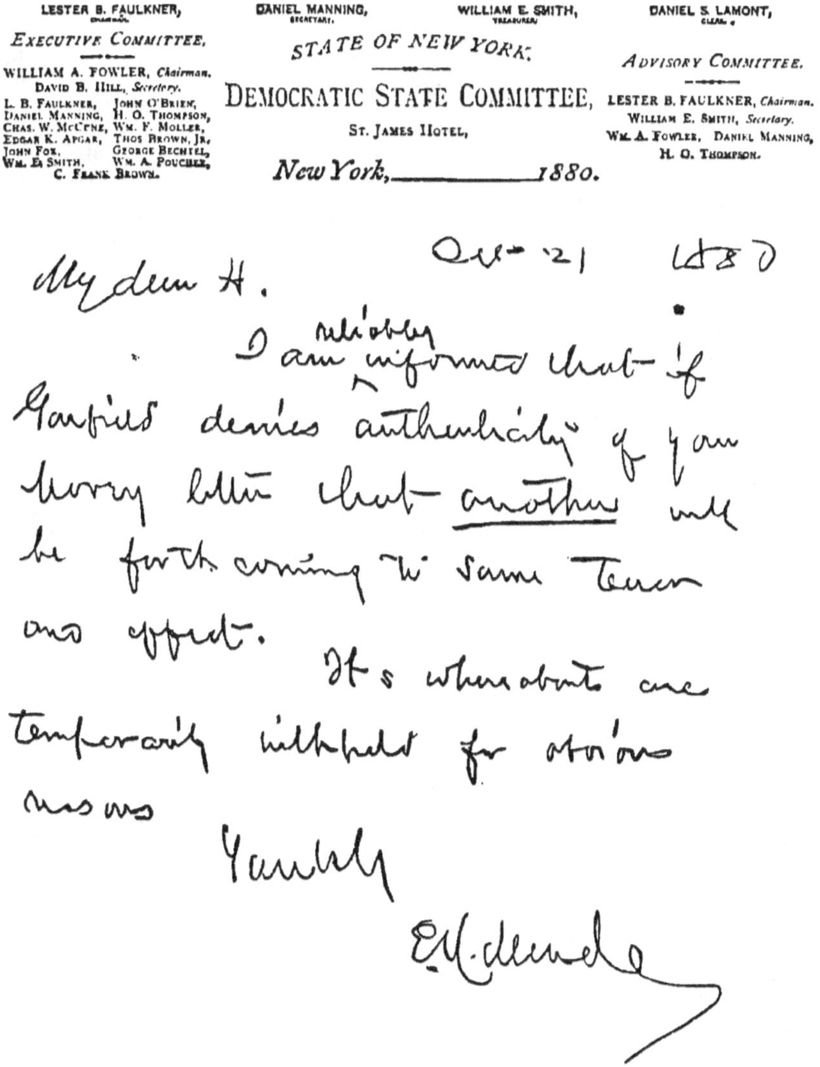

LESTER B. FAULKNER, Chairman.	DANIEL MANNING, Secretary.	WILLIAM E. SMITH, Treasurer.	DANIEL S. LAMONT, Clerk.
EXECUTIVE COMMITTEE.	STATE OF NEW YORK.		ADVISORY COMMITTEE.
WILLIAM A. FOWLER, Chairman. DAVID B. HILL, Secretary. L. B. FAULKNER, JOHN O'BRIEN, DANIEL MANNING, H. O. THOMPSON, CHAS. W. McCUNE, WM. F. MOLLER, EDGAR K. APGAR, THOS BROWN, JR. JOHN FOX, GEORGE BECHTEL, WM. E. SMITH, WM. A. POUCHER, C. FRANK BROWN.	DEMOCRATIC STATE COMMITTEE, ST. JAMES HOTEL, New York, _____ 1880.		LESTER B. FAULKNER, Chairman. WILLIAM E. SMITH, Secretary. WM. A. FOWLER, DANIEL MANNING, H. O. THOMPSON.

[Handwritten letter:]

My dear H.   Oct 21 1880

I am reliably informed that if Garfield denies authenticity of your Morey letter that another will be forthcoming to same tenor and effect. Its whereabouts are temporarily withheld for obvious reasons

Yours &c

E M Meade

I have afforded Mr. Meade, an opportunity to make any statement respecting this letter, and his connection with this matter, which he might be desirous and willing to have published. In response to my offer, that gentleman has said to me that he heard the story which he related to Hancock and Hart, substantially as I have stated it herein; that in compliance with Mr. Hart's request that he should ascertain if there was a second letter in existence from General Garfield, similar in character to the Morey letter, he went to the Democratic National headquarters and inquired specifically as to the existence and whereabouts of such a letter; that at the time of my call—January, 1884—he could not say, positively, of whom he made his inquiries, but his impression was that it was Mr. Bradley B. Smalley, the Vermont member of the Democratic National Committee; that while he might be mistaken as to the individual, he was, however, able to state, as a fact, that his conversation respecting the second letter, was with a person attached to the Democratic headquarters, and at the rooms of the National Committee; that such person was in a position to know, and he—Meade—believed that he did know, as to whether there was or was not such a second letter; and that the note which he sent to *Truth* office contained a fair and accurate statement of what was said to him, at the rooms of the Committee, by the gentleman of whom he inquired touching the matter.

I am able to supplement this statement by a "special dispatch" sent the *Boston Globe*—a Democratic paper—from New York on October 22d, 1880. It read:

"It may be added, *on the authority of ex-Congressman Hewitt*, that in case it [the Morey letter] is disputed, another letter is ready for publication, of the same tenor, written to another party."

If the reader will compare the wording of this "special" with that of Mr. Meade's letter, no doubt will remain in his mind that the authors, aiders and abettors of this foul conspiracy to elect a President of the United States by forgery, false swearing and perjury, occupied such relations of close intimacy and fellowship, with some, at least, of the members and officers of the Democratic National Committee as not to be distinguishable from those gentlemen themselves. This is the more clear when the statement is made that the special to the *Boston Globe* was sent from the Democratic headquarters, and was from one of two of its prominent officials, to wit: Mr. Bradley B. Smalley, or Mr. Edward B. Dickinson. There yet remains to be presented, another fact showing the action of the Committee with respect to the Morey letter. On the day of its first appearance, in type, in *Truth*—October 20th—the Morey letter was telegraphed throughout the country. Among the Democratic journals which received it was the *Boston Globe*. Immediately upon its receipt, and before printing it in that paper, the *Globe* took the exceedingly fair and unusual course, of sending a telegram to the National Committee, asking if the letter could be relied upon as being genuine. To this the Secretary, or Acting Secretary, replied that there could be "no doubt of its authenticity." Thereupon, the *Globe* printed the telegraphed copy of the Morey letter in its late evening editions. In the meantime, however, it had dispatched a representative to Lynn, by the first train, with directions to ascertain the facts respecting the existence of the "Employers' Union." The result of the inquiries made, established the fact that no such organization existed; that during the labor troubles in the winter of 1877–78, there had been an attempt by the boot and shoe manufacturers of Lynn to establish a labor bureau, through which they might obtain, from other cities and towns in New England, workmen to take the place of the strikers; that it was merely a temporary affair, and that none of those engaged in the effort had ever known, or heard of, any Henry L. Morey, nor had several other prominent Lynn people of whom inquiries were made. These facts were at once telegraphed, late in the evening of the same day—the 20th—to Mr. Wm. H. Barnum, who replied the same night in the following remarkable dispatch:

NEW YORK, October 20th, 1880.

The Committee hold that it is of no consequence whether the man to whom it [the Morey letter] is addressed is alive or dead, the important question being as to the genuineness of the signature only. On this point Speaker Randall recognizes the signature, and *Mr. Abram S. Hewitt*, in a public meeting, at Chickering Hall, to-night, *declared* that by comparison with letters in his possession, the signature *is in the handwriting of Mr. Garfield*.

WM. H. BARNUM.

On Friday, October 22d, appeared the fac-simile of both letter and envelope, and the consequent exposure of the errors in orthography. All who were really familiar with General Garfield's handwriting, were at once satisfied of the fact that both in body and signature the letter was a forgery.

A *fac-simile*, of the Morey letter, reduced in size, will be found on the following page.

On the same day that the *fac-simile* appeared in *Truth*—October the 22d—General Garfield sent the Republican National Committee the following dispatch :

MENTOR, OHIO, Oct. 22d, 1880.

To the HON. MARSHALL JEWELL:

I will not break the rule I have adopted, by making public reply to campaign lies ; but I authorize you to denounce the so-called Morey letter as a bold forgery, both in its *language and sentiment*. Until its publication, I never heard of the existence of "the Employers' Union," of Lynn, Mass., nor of such a person as H. L. Morey. If you think best, publish your denunciation officially to-night, by Associated Press, east and west, and make Barnum feel the weight of public indignation for his reckless and dishonorable conduct.

J. A. GARFIELD.

There is no denying the fact that this telegram was a disappointment, both to the personal and political friends of General Garfield. The only denial of the authorship of the letter, to that time, had been that contained in the press dispatch, published on the morning of the 21st instant, and while all who knew the General's writing and signature knew the letter was not his, the cautious wording of this message was a source of great annoyance, the reason therefor not being understood. What was needed was a short, crisp, burning, denial—over General Garfield's own signature—of the letter being his. *The Herald* of the 22d instant, in an editorial upon the subject well represented the popular feeling. It said : "On Wednesday evening," the 20th, we telegraphed General Garfield, " offering if he had not seen the letter to telegraph it to him at once, and opening *The Herald's* columns to him for a denial. To this dispatch we have up to this present writing received no reply." It added : " His denial over his own name would, in our opinion, settle the question."

That denial was soon to appear, and when it came it was in no uncertain words, while it made apparent a cause for the delay.

At eight o'clock in the evening of Friday, October 23d, a second telegram was received by Governor Jewell from General Garfield, who also mailed the Governor, the original draft of the telegram as written by himself. I now have that draft; a *fac-simile* thereof, reduced in size, will be found on page 61. It is placed opposite the *fac-simile* of the Morey letter, so that it may be readily compared therewith. Each reader will thus be enabled to readily distinguish the marked dissimilarities of penmanship and habit.

THE FORGED MOREY LETTER

UPON

GENERAL JAMES A. GARFIELD.

Personal and Confidential.

House of Representatives,

Washington, D. C., Jany 23, 1880.

Dear Sir:

Yours in relation to the Chinese problem came duly to hand. I take it that the question of employees is only a question of private and corporate economy, and individuals or companys have the right to buy labor where they can get it cheapest.

We have a treaty with the Chinese government, which should be religiously kept until its provisions are abrogated by the action of the general Government, and I am not prepared to say that it should be abrogated, until our great manufacturing and corporate interests are conserved in the matter of labor.

Very truly yours

J. A. Garfield

H. L. Morey
Employers Union
Lynn Mass.

A GENUINE LETTER

FROM

GENERAL JAMES A. GARFIELD.

Telegram

MENTOR, OHIO. Oct 23, 1880.

Hon. Marshall Jewell
241 Fifth Avenue N.Y.

Your telegram of this afternoon is received. Publish my dispatch of last evening if you think best. Within the last hour, the mail has brought me the lithographic copy of the forged letter. It is the work of some clumsy villain, who cannot spell, — nor write English, nor imitate my hand-writing. Every honest and manly democrat in America who is familiar with my hand-writing, will denounce the forgery at sight — Put the case in the hands of able detectives at once, and hunt the rascals down

J. A. Garfield

At the same time that the foregoing was telegraphed to Governor Jewell, General Garfield wrote with his own hand, and forwarded to the Governor by mail, the following letter :

MENTOR, OHIO,
Oct. 23, 1880.

Hon. MARSHALL JEWELL,
   Chairman Rep. Nat. Committee,
     241 Fifth Avenue, N. Y.

DEAR SIR: In my dispatch of yesterday and this evening (which are also sent you by mail) I have denounced the Morey letter as a base forgery. Its stupid and brutal sentiments I never expressed *nor entertained*. The lithographic copy shows a very clumsy attempt to imitate my penmanship and signature. Any one who is familiar with my handwriting will instantly see that the letter is spurious.

Very truly yours,
J. A. GARFIELD.

This letter, was received by Governor Jewell on Sunday, October 25th, and was given the *New York Herald*, which published it, in *fac-simile* form, the following morning.

A few words respecting the delay in denouncing the letter as a forgery, as broadly and emphatically as were done in the above telegram and letter, are due General Garfield. They cannot fail to prove of interest, when the statement is made that they were received by me from General Garfield's own lips, while on a visit to him at Mentor, shortly after his election.

Said the President elect :

"The instant I heard of the letter, I declared my belief that it was a forgery. I had no recollection of ever having written such a letter or of ever having heard of H. L. Morey, of Lynn. The date of the letter was, however, for the moment, an embarrassment. It bore date a few days only after my election to the United States Senate, and upon my return, at that time, to Washington, from Ohio, I found the accumulation of several days' mails awaiting me. Many of the letters were congratulatory, and somewhat personal in their character, but all required answers. My friends, Brown [J. Stanley], Nichol [Thomas M.], and others, undertook the task of drafting replies to this mass of correspondence; but all letters so prepared it was understood were to be brought to me to sign, and I believed were so presented to, and signed by me. While, therefore, I was positive that, personally, I had neither at any time written, nor knowingly signed, such a letter as was printed, and had never heard either of Morey or the Employers' Union, I determined, before doing more than expressing my belief, to cause a thorough examination of my letters to be made, and also to personally confer with the gentlemen who so kindly aided me at that time. This would make absolutely certain—what I had no reason to question — that no one of them had written or signed such a letter for me.

"Inquiry of the gentlemen referred to, save Mr. Nichol, whom I could not, at the moment, reach, satisfied me that they were totally ignorant both of the letter and of Morey, while a careful search of my letters, letter-books and stenographer's notes, demonstrated the fact that I had never had such a correspondent as H. L. Morey, of Lynn, Mass. As soon as Nichol could be got to Mentor, I satisfied myself of his entire lack of knowledge of either the man or the letter. Meanwhile, the issue of *Truth* containing the *fac-simile* had reached me, and I was then enabled to brand the letter as a forgery in most emphatic terms. Had it been originally published in that form on the 20th of the month, it would have reached Mentor on the following day, when I could at once have spoken of it as decidedly and definitely as I did in my telegram and letter of the 23d instant, two days later.

"You will see, therefore, what pains I took, and under what difficulties I labored, in my endeavors to make it beyond all question, that neither myself nor any one connected with me had ever written or signed, or had in any manner been connected with the Morey letter."

This was General Garfield's statement. During his life-time, it was a satisfactory explanation to his friends, both personal and political, for his delay in making his full personal denial until the 23d of October. It is a perfect answer after his death, to the suggestions which have since been indulged in by certain journals, to the effect that "possibly" General Garfield signed the Morey letter, not knowing at the time what he was signing; that "perhaps" Nichol wrote it, and signed Garfield's name to it; that "perchance" Stanley Brown penned it, and affixed General Garfield's signature.

It should be borne in mind in this connection, that no such suggestions have ever come from any one who was really familiar with the penmanship, either of General Garfield, Mr. Nichol, or Mr. Brown. They have proceeded, solely, from those whose wish was father to the thought, and whose factional or personal animosities toward General Garfield, could only be relieved, by the circulation of such calumnious innuendoes, long after he had been buried in an honored grave.

Upon the publication of the Morey letter, on Wednesday, October 20th, and for a day or two thereafter, the policy of the Democratic National Committee in respect thereto, was in accord with the declaration contained in Mr. Barnum's dispatch, of the 20th instant, to the *Boston Globe*, to wit: to ignore all questions of fact connected with, and inseparable from, the letter, and to rest all claim of its genuineness upon the bare assertion of its own members and of Mr. Samuel J. Randall.

This policy, did not commend itself to Mr. Hart, of *Truth*, to whom their asseverations of the authenticity of the letter had been made, and who had accepted their statements and vigorously acted thereon. He, therefore, communicated to General Winfield S. Hancock, the nominee of the party for President, his distrust of the loyalty of a portion at least of the Committee toward him—General Hancock—and the interests of the party. I have endeavored to obtain a copy of that letter, but Mr. Hart has been unable to find one. General Hancock, however, must have acted in some manner upon its suggestions or warnings, but such action was not satisfactory to Mr. Hart, and, thereupon, a second letter, of which the following is a copy, was addressed the Democratic nominee for President. It bears date the day following the publication of the *fac-simile* of the Morey letter, and it has never before been published.

OFFICE OF "TRUTH,"
142 Nassau Street,
New York, October 23d, 1880.

General WINFIELD S. HANCOCK.

MY DEAR GENERAL:—If the Garfield letter and the proofs of its genuineness which we shall produce, and have produced, do not elect you, it will be the fault of those who are managing your campaign.

Enclosed is one each of a large quantity of telegrams and letters we have received. Neither mails nor express can be trusted to deliver these papers [copies of *Truth* containing the *fac-simile*, etc., of the Morey letter].

And I say it without hesitation, that there is a lukewarmness about the Democratic papers and managers that will yet defeat you, if you do not see to it that *personal friends* give personal attention to your interests.

To some extent you have done this, *in response to my last letter;* but your real friends in the Committee are so hampered by others, having more authority, that it is necessary for you to do more.

If your friends can furnish the money, I will supply you with men who will faithfully deliver these *fac-similes* and proof to all the centres that can be reached.

Be assured that Wednesday's *Truth* will thoroughly establish our position in respect to the letter.

Resp'y yours,
JOSEPH HART.

What *further* action General Hancock took, after receiving this letter, is not known, but the fact is significant, that, *at that time*, General William F. Smith—more widely known as "Baldy" Smith—who was a Democratic Police Commissioner of the city of New York, and a warm personal and political friend of General Hancock—began to manifest great interest in the dissemination of *Truth*. He ordered, upon his personal credit, several hundred copies of that journal and took upon himself the task of their distribution. It will, hereafter, be necessary to refer to General Smith and to certain conduct of his, somewhat in detail. He has been alluded to here, only for the purpose of showing *when* his interest in the Morey letter first publicly manifested itself, and under what circumstances.

I shall now establish the fact, that, *from the day of the date of this second letter from Mr. Hart to General Hancock*, no charge of inactivity upon the part of the Democratic National Committee, was made, or could have been for a moment sustained, if alleged.

On Saturday, October 23d, 1880, Mr. Bradley B. Smalley, of the Executive Committee of the National Committee, gave Mr. David N. Carvalho, a photographer, a letter to Mr. Hart, of *Truth*. The original is written upon a letter sheet bearing the heading of the Democratic National Committee and is now in my possession. It reads as follows:

JOSEPH HARTT, ESQ.,   NEW YORK, October 23d, 1880.
   TRUTH OFFICE.
MY DEAR SIR: Permit me to introduce to you Mr. Carvalho, of this city.
He will talk to you about photographing the "Garfield" letter on linen. Please give him an interview and see how it strikes you. IT IS A BIG THING AND WILL BEAT "GARFIELD."
                                        Yours sincerely,
                                             B. B. SMALLEY.

I am sorry for my friend Smalley, who, personally and socially, is a most agreeable gentleman, but it is clearly dangerous to allow him absolute freedom with his pen. There are matters which call for skillful treatment and delicate handling, when written of. There are others as to which silence is the best course to be pursued. Mr. Smalley's temperament is, evidently, such as to unfit him for dealing with either of these classes of subjects, but it passes all understanding, how, with his experience and at his time of life, Mr. Smalley has managed to retain all the simplicity and ardor, of his early youth. If it be not due, to a life-long residence in the invigorating and rejuvenating atmosphere of the beautiful city of Burlington, Vermont—situated on the shore of Lake Champlain, where the air from the Adirondacks, on the one hand, intermingles with that from the Green Mountains of his native State on the other—it will never be accounted for, save as a freak of Nature most rare and touching.

The delight of Mr. Smalley over the *fac-simile* of the Morey letter was that of a child over a new toy. His feelings were too much for him. He must give expression to his rapture, and he did. Subsequent events proved his prophetic powers to be somewhat at fault, but for that he was not responsible; yet it is evident, that, in his exuberance, he simply echoed the views and sentiments of the Committee, when he disposed of the serious charge of forgery and the other grave offenses which attached to the Morey letter, by the statement : "*It is a big thing and will beat Garfield.*"

I am confident the Committee will agree with me, that the suggestion to friend Smalley, that when, in the future, he has *finished* the business which he is called upon to transact in writing, it would be wiser for him to stop *right there*, is not open to the objection ordinarily attaching to gratuitous advice. It must be too painfully evident to the members of that body, as it cannot fail to be to all who read Mr. Smalley's letter, that a little curbing of that gentleman, when he ventures to give expression to his views, would be, at least, judicious. *He discloses too much.*

On Monday, October 25th, the forged letter had been for six days before the public, and not a scintilla of evidence had been anywhere produced to establish its genuineness, the former existence of Henry L. Morey, his death, the existence of the administrator of his estate, or of the "Employers' Union." In short, the letter was simply and solely "a big thing," forged "to beat

Garfield," and was without any support other than the bare assertions of Barnum, Hewitt, Randall, Scott, Cleveland, Cooper and other prominent Democrats, that it was "in Garfield's handwriting," or that "the signature was his."

As against these assertions, there was the appearance of the letter itself, with its gross errors in orthography, the then conceded fact that the body of the letter was not General Garfield's, the denial of General Garfield of all knowledge of the letter or the person to whom it was addressed, the evidence that the Washington post-mark had been tampered with, the fact that Henry L. Morey was unknown to any one in Lynn and that there never had been an "Employers' Union" in that city.

The time had arrived, when something had to be done in the way of actively supporting the claims made by the Democratic National Committee, or the effect, which followed their avowals of the genuineness of the letter, would be lost, and a reaction produced in the public mind which would be ruinous to the party and its hoped-for success. It would no longer do to stand upon the platform laid down in Mr. Barnum's telegram of the 20th instant to the *Boston Globe*.

The public required something more tangible from the sponsors of the letter than mere expressions of opinion as to handwriting, or mere allegations of the genuineness of letter or signature, from men who knew nothing as to the facts, and who, when informed that certain intrinsic statements in the letter did not appear upon examination to be borne out by the facts, coolly replied: "It is of no consequence."

It was therefore opportune, that, on the 25th instant, two telegrams should be received by the Chairman of the Democratic National Committee relating to the letter. The original dispatches received by Mr. Barnum are both in my possession. They are written upon delivery blanks of the Western Union Telegraph Company, and are stamped as having been received at the office of the company No. 12 West Twenty-third Street. They are given below in the order of their receipt by Mr. Barnum, and have never before been published.

MANCHESTER, N. H., Oct. 25th, 1880.

To HON. W. H. BARNUM:

Have a reliable man who knows Morey and the Employers' Union, and has seen him and Garfield together in Washington.

23 collect.

J. C. MOORE,
Daily Union.

To this message the answer was returned:

"Obtain his affidavit and send him along."

Then followed the second telegram from Manchester, which was as follows:

MANCHESTER, N. H., Oct. 25th, 1880.

To W. H. BARNUM:

Edgar E. Mann, two hundred eight Broadway, Lawrence, Mass., has stated to our reporter that he knew H. L. Morey, in Lynn, Lawrence, Haverhill and Washington. Has seen him in Garfield's company in Washington. He would not make sworn statement, but said he was going to Lynn to examine certain records to fortify his position. He says he knows of other letters from Garfield that Morey received at different times. He will go to Lynn and we fear he will sell out to Republicans if approached. If you have an agent in Lynn look out for him. Mann is about fifty-five years old and a cripple. Has leg crooked up and walks with a crutch.

116, collect.

DAILY UNION.

Both of these telegrams, were from the office of the *Manchester* (N. H.) *Daily Union*, of which Dr. J. C. Moore, who signed the first message, was the editor. He was also a Democratic State Senator in New Hampshire. It is but fair to add, that the information telegraphed by Dr. Moore was received by him from one John B. Mills, then a reporter in the employ of the *Daily*

Union, who claimed to have obtained the statement, which he imparted to Dr. Moore, from one Edgar E. Mann, of Lawrence, Mass., who possessed neither reliability nor principle.

Immediately upon the receipt of these telegrams from Dr. Moore, it was determined by Mr. Chairman Barnum to take definite action in the way of supporting the story of the forged letter. Mr. H. H. Hadley, to whom the reader has been previously introduced, was, at the time these telegrams were received by Mr. Barnum, on the second floor of the Democratic headquarters; he was called by Mr. Edward B. Dickinson, who informed him that Mr. Barnum desired to see him, whereupon he started for Mr. Barnum's private room by the way of the hall, where he was met by Barnum, who there informed him that it was his—Barnum's—wish, that he—Hadley—should go at once to Boston, Lynn, and such other places as might be found necessary, to obtain, as Mr. Hadley states, what he could, to "bolster up the weak points in the [Morey] letter." After some hesitation upon the part of Hadley, whose wife was about to be confined, he at last yielded to Barnum's importunities and accepted the mission. He was then furnished by Mr. Barnum with a letter of introduction to the Hon. Frederick O. Prince, the then Mayor of Boston, and the Secretary of the Democratic National Committee. That letter introduced Mr. Hadley under the assumed name of O. M. Wilson, Mr. Barnum stating to Hadley, that he so acted for the reason that the proximity of Boston to New York rendered it unwise for him—Hadley—to travel or pass under his own name, and that by adopting an assumed name he would render detection of his movements less probable.

Christened anew by Barnum, and equipped with his letter of introduction, Mr. Hadley left for Boston that evening, and arrived there on the morning of Tuesday, October 26th, when he registered at the Parker House as follows:

O M Wilson   Brooklyn n y   56

Upon presenting Mayor Prince his letter from Barnum, Mr. Hadley, *alias* Wilson, was welcomed, and furnished with four letters of introduction. Each of those letters was written upon the official note paper of the Democratic National Committee, and the originals are all in my possession. One of them is addressed to a gentleman, of national prominence, in Massachusetts, and is written and signed by Mayor Prince. That letter, was not used by Mr. Hadley, and the gentleman to whom it was addressed never heard of it until informed thereof by myself. I deem it but fair to him, therefore, to make no further reference to the paper.

Each of the other three letters, was, by the Mayor's direction, written and signed by Mr. Charles Albert Prince, his son and Secretary. They are respectively addressed to Ben. Palmer, Esq., editor of the *Boston Globe*; Charles Saunders, Esq., a lawyer of Lawrence, Mass.; and W. C. Thompson, of Lynn. Mr. Hadley called two or three times at the office of the *Boston Globe*, but failed to meet Mr. Palmer, and I am not aware that he saw Mr. Saunders. Mr. W. C. Thompson was the Chairman of the Essex County (Mass.) Democratic Committee, and a candidate, that year, before the D─── ─tic Congressional Convention in his district for the nomination to C ─── death,

The three letters to Palmer, Saunders and Thompson a ──rs' Union." alike, but the one to Thompson is the more important of th─ged "to beat of what followed. It is therefore selected for presentation in *fac-simile* form. It has never before been published, an─ ─eads:

HANCOCK AND ENGLISH.

Headquarters National Democratic Committee,
138 FIFTH AVENUE.

DUNCAN S. WALKER, 1st Assistant Secretary.
JOSEPH L. HANCE, 2d Assistant Secretary.
EDWARD D. DICKINSON, Official Stenographer.

Hon. WM. H. BARNUM, Chairman.
Hon. F. O. PRINCE, Secretary.
CHARLES J. CANDA, Treasurer,
52 William Street, New York.

Boston ~~New York~~, Oct. 26th 1880.

My dear Thompson.

This note will introduce to you Mr. O. M. Wilson, of New York. He desires to consult with you please give him your entire confidence

Yours truly
Charles Albert Prince

Upon the receipt of these letters Mr. Hadley proceeded to Lynn, where he registered at the Sagamore House as follows:

O. M. Wilson   B. Ten ny. D. 54

Both o~~f~~
Daily Union,
editor. He wa~~s~~ hompson upon the street, and explaining to him his mission,
but fair to add, endorsed upon the back of the letter addressed to him by

young Prince, and over his own signature, the following words, which are given in *fac-simile* form:

Ref. to O. S. Roberts at Hotel
Chas. H. Clark, Munroe St.
W. C. Thompson

He then returned the letter to Hadley, *viséd* as above. Mr. Hadley thereupon called upon Mr. Roberts, at the Sagamore House, and exhibited to him the letter of Prince, endorsed by Thompson. Upon stating the purpose of his call and requesting Roberts' assistance, that gentleman suggested that Mr. Clark would be more likely to be of service to him in the matter and advised him to see that gentleman. This advice Mr. Hadley followed, and through Clark, he made the acquaintance of one Alfred A. Mower, of Mower Brothers, prominent Democrats and shoe manufacturers of Lynn. These gentlemen—F. B. Mower, Alfred A. Mower and Martin F. B. Mower—with one James Phelan, then caused to be prepared, signed, and before Joseph F. Hannan, a Justice of the Peace in Lynn, swore to a statement to the effect that "in 1877 and 1878 an Employers' Union was formed" in their city "for the purpose of resisting the demands of the Crispin organization, and procuring cheap labor in our factories. The association had a place for meetings, several of which were held. We discussed the situation fully, and formed plans as to what had best be done to protect its interests. The undersigned were members of said organization, and know that it existed and was in active operation, and embraced nearly every other large manufacturer in Lynn." Then followed the names of eight individuals or firms, who, it was declared, were members of this Employers' Union, and the statement that "John Shaw, second, was President thereof, and Alfred A. Mower was Secretary."

As soon as the contents of the Mower Brothers' paper were made public, its statements were promptly met and shown to be without foundation, as will appear by the following:

LYNN, Oct. 28, 1880.

The morning papers contain a sworn affidavit by three of the brothers Mower and James Phelan, all Democrats, to the effect that an "Employers' Union," of which they were members, was formed during the strike of 1877-78, and that John Shaw, second, was President of the organization. Concerning the above statement, I, John Shaw, second, do on oath depose and say that there never was, to my knowledge, any such organization formed in Lynn, before, during or since the strike of 1877-8. On one occasion only I presided at an informal meeting of a few manufacturers, when the question of forming some permanent organization was discussed and it was unanimously decided to be inexpedient.

JOHN SHAW, SECOND.

COMMONWEALTH OF MASSACHUSETTS, } ss.
Essex County, Lynn, Oct. 28, 1880.

Subscribed and sworn to before me, N. N. HAWKES, *Justice of the Peace.*

This affidavit was accompanied by a statement, signed by each of the eight individuals or firms, mentioned by the Mower Brothers and Phelan as being members of the **Employers' Union**, and by eleven others of the largest shoe manufacturers in Lynn, denying the statements made by the Mowers and Phelan, and asserting the facts to be : that during January and February, 1878, there were a few informal meetings of Lynn manufacturers held at various places in the city at which different gentlemen acted as chairmen; there was never any formal organization, nor any president or treasurer, and at no meeting was the term "Employers' Union" ever used or suggested. The object of the coming together of these gentlemen was not to obtain "cheap labor," but by all fair means "to secure experienced workmen." An office was opened for the purpose of conferring with applicants, and advertisements were issued, signed by J. L. Robinson "per order MANUFACTURERS' COMMITTEE." Two other agents, named Alley and Foster, were employed, and sent to the shoe manufacturing districts of Maine and New Hampshire to secure workmen, but there was never any man by the name of H. L. Morey employed, nor was such a man ever heard of by said manufacturers or either of them.

Thus effectually, was the attempt to sustain the forged letter, in the matter of establishing the existence of an "Employers' Union," stamped out and disposed of.

The next effort of the Democratic National Committee was to prove that Henry L. Morey had at one time lived, breathed and had an existence. It came about in this manner. Mr. Hannan, the Justice before whom the Mower Brothers and Phelan affidavit was made, informed Hadley *alias* Wilson, that he had heard of a physician in Lynn who knew a Morey in that city, and he promised to obtain and furnish Hadley with the doctor's address. Later in the day, Mr. Hadley received from Hannan the following letter, the original of which I have :

LYNN, Oct. 26th, 1880.

Mr. WILSON.

DEAR SIR: As I am obliged of [to] go out of town to-night to address a Dem. meeting, I leave the certificate with you. [Certificate of Clerk of Court that Hannan was empowered to administer oaths and take acknowledgments.] If you are in town to-morrow have the Clerk of Police Court attach it.

The name of that man who knew a Morey in Lynn is Dr. Ahearne, who resides on Church Street, Lynn.

In haste,

J. F. HANNAN.

Mr. Hadley, *alias* Wilson, at once called upon Dr. Ahearne and obtained from him the address of Mrs. Clara T. Morey, a lady of some sixty years of age, whom he at once sought and found.

In a written statement made by Hadley, which is in my possession, he thus relates his subsequent action :

I drove to Mrs. Morey's house, taking a sheet of note paper with me. I found no one but an old lady, apparently very poor. I asked her where her son Henry was, as I wanted to see him. She was greatly confused and said he was away. I told her that a statement had been made that no family of Moreys had lived in Lynn for ten years (referring to the Lynn Postmaster's statement), and asked if she was willing to state in writing that she and her son had lived there for ten years or more. She said, "Yes, if George O. Tarbox says so." She said her son had not been in Lynn for "three months," and I afterwards understood her to correct it to "eleven months" or "ten." I then drew up the statement, and read it to her, pronouncing the name Henry L. Morey with emphisis (sic). She then interrupted me, and pointed to the photograph of a dead man on the wall, and said, "I will tell you how that was. My husband's name was George S. Morey. I had a boy named after him—George S. My husband died, and that photograph was taken of him while he lay a corpse. Shortly afterwards George died and I then changed the name of this boy—then the baby--to George S. Morey." This was said in a confused way which I attributed to embarrassment and age, and I then and there made up my mind that her affidavit would be of no value further than to establish the fact that there was a family of Moreys in Lynn, notwithstanding the certificate of the Republicans in Lynn to the contrary. I had written the statement in haste on my knee, with my stylographic pen, and before reading it to her, had, I then thought, returned my pen to its usual place in my pocket—the left side upper vest pocket. I felt there for it that I might correct the statement; not finding the pen readily, I felt in some of my other pockets, and looked on the floor. Still not finding it, I took my pencil and with it crossed out the name of "Henry L. Morey" on the statement and wrote above it the name "Geo. S. Morey"—I thought then and still think plainly, with the pencil. I then returned to George O. Tarbox's store, read it to him, and asked him to accompany me to Mrs. Morey's and take her affidavit or acknowledgment, which he did. He commenced reading the statement to her, but before concluding a line handed it to me to read, which I did, to her aloud as corrected. She then signed it, and Mr. Tarbox and I returned to his store. I wrote the jurat on the second page of the statement which Mrs. Morey had made, and Mr. George O. Tarbox signed said jurat as Justice of the Peace. I paid him one dollar, and had previously paid Mrs. Morey, voluntarily, five dollars for her trouble, which she accepted, saying "that is enough." I considered the affidavit of so little importance that I did not hand it to the Democratic National Committee until the evening of Saturday (?) the 29th of October. I had carried it in my pocket meantime, and it had not been altered or tampered with in the least, and I handed it to them just as I received it from Mrs. Morey and Mr. Tarbox—with the name "Henry L. Morey" crossed out with a pencil and the name "Geo. S. Morey" written above the one which had been crossed out.

If this statement was true, it would certainly be a most remarkable story, but it is false, and was made by Hadley to shield himself from the consequences of the discovery of his having tampered with the affidavit. Let us see what Mrs. Morey and Justice Tarbox have to say respecting the matter. Mrs. Morey declares that Hadley—*alias* Wilson—called upon her and inquired if she had a son by the name of Henry L. Morey, to which she replied in the negative. Hadley insisted that she had a son by that name, and urged her to make for him an affidavit to that effect. This she absolutely declined to do, stating that her husband's name was Samuel C. Morey; that she had never had but two sons—the oldest was named George E. Morey, who died in infancy, and the second was George E. C. Morey, who was living, but whom she had not seen for some months. She added that she never had heard of any individual of the name of Henry L. Morey. Upon Hadley's persisting in her making an affidavit that her son was named "Henry L.," Mrs. Morey grew indignant and ordered him from her premises. This brought about a change of tone on Hadley's part, and an explanation that his insisting upon the matter was owing to his belief that her son's name was Henry L., and that she was denying the fact for the purpose of misleading him. Mr. Hadley then requested her to make an affidavit, to the effect that her name was Morey and that she had resided many years in Lynn, as it would show the existence of a family of that name in that city. Mrs. Morey responded to this suggestion, that, in view of his previous conduct, she would sign nothing that was not first approved by Mr. George O. Tarbox, a neighbor of hers and a Justice of the Peace.

Mr. Hadley then left and went to Mr. Tarbox's store. What transpired there is stat d by Justice Tarbox—who is an ardent Democrat, and was, at the time, a candidate of his party for election to the lower house of the State Legislature—to have been as follows: Hadley introduced himself as Mr. Wilson, of New York, and then proceeded, in the presence of Mrs. Tarbox, to relate to the Justice his efforts to obtain an affidavit from Mrs. Morey that she had a son by the name of Henry L. Morey, her refusal, his subsequent request for an affidavit to the effect that her name was Morey and that she had resided for many years in Lynn, and her reference of him to Mr. Tarbox. Mr. Tarbox replied that he knew the fact to be that Mrs. Morey had no son named Henry L., but he saw no objection to her making an affidavit as to her name and length of residence in Lynn. At Hadley's request Mr. Tarbox then furnished him with a sheet of note paper, and upon that sheet, at Tarbox's desk, Hadley drew up the following affidavit in the manner shown below:

I. the undersigned, Clara T. Morey, of the City of Lynn, County of Essex, and Comonwealth (sic) of Massachusetts, on oath do depose and say that I have lived in Lynn aforesaid for ten to fourteen years last past, and that my son, Mr.   Morey, has visited me frequently from time to time until within the past eleven months, and that since I know nothing of his whereabouts.

WITNESS my hand and seal this 26th day of October, A. D. 1880.

This being done, the paper was shown to Tarbox, and the blank space, which in the original, now in my possession, was left partly at the end of one line and partly at the beginning of the next, was explained by Hadley as being left for the purpose of inserting, when they got to the house, the full name of Mrs. Morey's son. Mr. Tarbox then accompanied Hadley to Mrs. Morey's, where she signed the paper and gave the name of her son as George E. C. Morey, when Hadley remarked that as her son was not named Henry L. it was a matter of no consequence and they would leave it as it was without mentioning the name of her son. Mr. Tarbox then swore Mrs. Morey to the truth of the statement signed by her, and he and Hadley— *alias* Wilson—left, the latter handing Mrs. Morey five dollars for her trouble. Upon returning to the store of Tarbox, Hadley wrote, on the back of the note sheet bearing Mrs. Morey's statement, a certificate to the administering of the oath, and Tarbox signed the same, receiving one dollar for his services. The certificate of the Clerk of the Court to the fact that Tarbox was lawfully empowered to administer oaths, was then obtained, and the paper was complete. Subsequent to the time of Mrs. Morey's subscribing and swearing to the paper, the blank space on the right of the word "Mr." was filled in by the insertion of the letters "H. L." These letters *were inserted by H. H. Hadley*, and they now appear in the original affidavit, which is in my possession, in his handwriting. After making this addition to the affidavit, Hadley telegraphed the Democratic National Committee on the same day—October 26th—"there is positive proof in my hand of H. L. Morey having lived here and in other Massachusetts towns. *One from his mother.*"

It is evident that Mr. Hadley's villainy is of a dull and stupid type, for he entirely lost sight of—forgot probably—this dispatch of his, *sent at the time of the perpetration of the alteration of the affidavit*, when writing his explanation of the appearance of H. L. Morey's name in that document. If he had remembered this telegram to the Committee, he would never have written *such* an explanation, for he would have known, if his statement was true, that the affidavit in his possession contained the name of "Geo. S. Morey," and not "H. L.," at the very moment when he was telegraphing that he had proof from H. L. Morey's mother of his—Henry's—residence in Lynn.

There appears in the original affidavit, to the left and over the word "Morey," following the letters "H. L.," which were inserted by Hadley in the blank space above shown, the words, in pencil, "Geo. S. Morey" in Hadley's writing, almost obliterated by rubbing. It is clear that the attempt to erase the letters "H. L.," and the writing in, in pencil, of the words "Geo. S. Morey," were done by Hadley after the National Committee caused the affidavit to be published on Saturday October 30th, as being made by the mother of Henry L. Morey. As published it contained the name of "H. L. Morey," but purported to be signed not by Clara T. Morey, but by Clara S. Morey. Another circumstance which shows that the insertion in pencil of the name of "Geo. S. Morey" was not made at the time stated by Hadley, is the fact that both Mrs. Morey and Justice Tarbox agree that the former gave Hadley the name of her son as George *E. C.* Morey. Hadley had forgotten the middle letters of George Morey's name when he subsequently doctored the affidavit so as to make it conform to his statement, and inserted it "Geo. S. Morey."

The Democratic National Committee cannot escape being considered participants in this false and fraudulent affidavit. After Hadley, *alias* Wilson, had forwarded that body his telegram announcing that he had evidence, from the mother of H. L. Morey, of his residence in Lynn, the *Boston Globe* sent a representative to Lynn to interview Mrs. Clara T. Morey, who had previously been seen on behalf of that journal, and she repeated what she had before said to its reporter, that she had no son H. L. Morey, never had known or heard of such a person, and had made no affidavit which contained his name. The same representative also saw Justice Tarbox, who said to him that the affidavit had been taken by him and that it did not contain the name of "H. L. Morey."

At a late hour at night on October 29th, the telegraph brought the *Globe*, for publication, the affidavit of Mrs. Morey, with the name of H. L. Morey therein. On the following day they again interviewed both Mrs. Morey and Justice Tarbox, each of whom declared, as they had previously done, that the name of H. L. Morey was not in the affidavit when signed and sworn to, and Justice Tarbox declared that if it was there on the day of its publication, as printed, the affidavit had been "tampered with."

Satisfied that this was the case, the *Globe* people communicated the facts above stated, in relation to the affidavit, to the Democratic National Committee, who waited until the morning of election day, *three days after receiving the information*, and then telegraphed Mayor Prince, of Boston —the Secretary of the Committee—that the affidavit had not been tampered with, and insinuated that Tarbox must have been bought. Nor was this all the warning or notice that the Committee had of the false character of that affidavit.

Upon its appearance in the daily journals of October 30th, it was brought to the attention of Mrs. Clara T. Morey, whereupon she made the following affidavit respecting her family:

COMMONWEALTH OF MASSACHUSETTS, Essex County, Lynn, October 30th, ss.:

Personally came before me Clara T. Morey, of Lynn, County of Essex and State of Massachusetts, who, being duly sworn, deposes and says: She married Samuel C. Morey in the City of Lowell, Mass., that she has had three children by the said Samuel C. Morey; that the first was a girl named Martha A. Morey; that the second was a son named George E. Morey, who died when he was a year old; that the third was a son named George E. C. Morey, who lives in the town of Medford, and that the above are all the children she has ever had; that her husband had three sons by a former wife—Samuel S. Morey, Francis A. Morey and Julian A. Morey—and these are all the sons he has had. CLARA T. MOREY.

Sworn to this thirtieth day of October, 1880, before me. BENJAMIN E. PORTER,
Justice of the Peace.

Justice George O. Tarbox, who took the affidavit of Mrs. Morey, for Hadley, *alias* Wilson, was very indignant upon being shown the affidavit sworn to before him, printed with the name of H. L. Morey inserted therein, and at once caused the following certificate and statement to be published:

LYNN, ESSEX COUNTY, MASS., October 30th, 1880

TO WHOM IT MAY CONCERN:

I, George O. Tarbox, of Lynn, Mass., Justice of the Peace, and who attested the signature of Clara T. Morey to a certain political document on October 26th, 1880, hereby testify that an affidavit (telegram), dated "New York, Oct. 29th, 1880," published in the daily papers, and having my name attached as Justice of the Peace, is not an exact copy of what Clara T. Morey signed and which I attested, *there being a very material alteration*. The published statement makes Clara T. Morey say, "My son, Mr. H. L. Morey, has visited me frequently from time to time until within the past eleven months." The document *did not say* "Mr. *H. L. Morey*," but simply "Mr. Morey," *without the "H. L."* I know that Clara T. Morey never had a son named "H. L." The document above referred to was read once by me to O. M. Wilson [Hadley], Chairman Barnum's agent, before it was signed, and twice after signing. Mr. Wilson stated that he only wanted the document to show there was a Mrs. Morey in Lynn. With this understanding I placed my official signature to the paper, not thinking that this evidence would be abused. GEORGE O. TARBOX,
Justice of the Peace.

Thus ended the second effort of the Democratic National Committee to support the original forgery. The affidavit of Mower Brothers & Phelan has been shown to have been untrue, and now we find Mrs. Clara T. Morey's affidavit is first tampered with, *after its execution*, by the agent of the Committee, then published in its altered condition, and then adhered to and defended, after public notice and denial of its being the paper sworn to, and after direct and personal notice to the Committee of the changes made in it.

Mr. Hadley's next move was to visit the Kirtland House, where he saw Mr. Andrew O. Carter, of the firm of Miles & Carter, proprietors of the hotel. He requested of Mr. Carter permission to look at the registers of the house for the year 1879. Two large books were handed him, the leaves of which he hastily turned and then requested permission to take one of the books away with him. This Mr. Carter refused to allow him to do, without further knowledge of him. Hadley thereupon left the hotel, but shortly returned, bringing with him Mr. Alfred A. Mower, who was known to Mr. Carter, and who assured that gentleman that it would be entirely safe to permit Hadley, *alias* Wilson, to take the register. It was further represented to Mr. Carter that the book was desired for use in a law suit, to be tried in Boston on the following day, and would be promptly returned.

Mr. Carter states that the entire time occupied by Hadley in inquiring for the registers, receiving and examining them, requesting permission to take one with him, being refused, going out and bringing in Mr. Mower, and finally obtaining the book he desired, was not over fifteen minutes, of which time "three or four minutes" only were devoted to the examination of the two registers. While one might, by chance, run across a given name in a hotel register, which he had never before seen, and with no date to guide him, within the period of "three or four minutes," it is extremely improbable—even if it be assumed that the name of "H. L. Morey" was, at that time, upon one of those books, and that Hadley discovered the name—it becomes almost a certainty, when the fact is known that to none of those about him, did Hadley either share the discovery or claim to have made any.

Mr. Carter—the then proprietor of the Kirtland House, of whom Hadley was seeking to obtain the register—says that Hadley neither exhibited the name of "H. L. Morey" to him, nor claimed to have found it in the book.

Mr. Roberts—the gentleman to whom Mr. Thompson had recommended Hadley, and who was the proprietor of the Kirtland at the time covered by the register Hadley was desirous of obtaining—says, that hearing that Hadley was possessed of the book, he requested permission to look at it for a moment, but was refused, Hadley declaring that he had sent it to New York by express, which statement was untrue.

Mr. Mower—who was acting as Hadley's friend and ally, and without whose aid Hadley could not have obtained the register—says that Hadley neither showed him the name of "H. L. Morey" therein, nor informed him that he had found it there.

These statements must convince every reasonable and fair-minded person, that the book was carried away by Hadley for an ulterior purpose, and when considered in connection with those below presented, they cannot fail to satisfactorily establish the fact, that at the time the register of the Kirtland House, covering a portion of the year 1879, passed into the possession of H. H. Hadley, *alias* O. M. Wilson—it did not contain the name of "H. L. Morey."

In this connection, attention is directed to the following truths:

First.—That no such person as H. L. Morey has ever been seen or heard of in Lynn by any human being.

Second.—That until after Hadley secured the custody of the Kirtland House register no person ever saw the name "H. L. Morey" therein.

Third.—That Mr. Carter, the then proprietor of the Kirtland House, in whose custody the book had been for some time previous to its removal by Hadley, had never seen Morey's name therein, or heard of the man, and has so sworn in an affidavit possessed by the author.

Fourth.—That Mr. Roberts has sworn, that during his proprietorship of the Kirtland House, covering about all the time covered by the register in question, he never heard of "H. L. Morey," never saw him, never knew his name to be upon that book, and does not believe it was there, prior to the time when Hadley carried it away.

Fifth.—That at the writer's request, Mr. Roberts made an examination of his cash books, covering the time of his proprietorship of the Kirtland, and that those books showed no one by the name of "H. L. Morey" to have been at his house during that time.

Sixth.—That during the period covered by the register it was the practice of the hotel management, late at night of each day, to prepare the book for the next day's business. This was done by leaving from one to three blank lines after the last name entered, and then writing, as a heading, the following day of the week and month, under which heading those arriving the next day would register their names. If perchance a guest or two should arrive after the book had been thus prepared, and before midnight, such of the lines as had been left blank, and were needed, would be utilized for his or their registration.

Seventh.—That the name "H. L. Morey," in each of the two places, where, after the book had passed into the possession of Mr. H. H. Hadley, it was subsequently found to appear, was written upon one of the lines so left blank, and was the last name entered under each of the days aforementioned.

Eighth.—That an analysis of the ink used in writing the various names in the register, as they appear under the dates containing the name "H. L. Morey," has shown that under the date of February 25th, 1879, the first four names registered were written "*with nut-gall ink*," while the fifth and last name there entered—that of "Henry L. Morey"—was written with "*an aniline ink*," which is entirely different from the other; that under date of Friday, October 17th, 1879, the two first names registered thereunder were written with "*logwood ink*," and the third and last name—that of "H. L. Morey, Lynn"—was written with "*an aniline ink*," while the entries of October 18th, 1879, immediately following the last mentioned entry of the name of "H. L. Morey, Lynn," were written with "*logwood ink*." It will be observed that while the ordinary entries in the register are written in different inks, under different days, that all *such* entries, under each date, are in the same kind of ink, and that neither are "an aniline ink ;" and that such ink was used solely in the Morey entries, each of which was written in *the same kind of ink*, although eight months intervened between the dates.

Thus are all doubts removed as to *when* the name of "H. L. Morey" was written upon the register in question. It was twice placed therein, after the book passed into the custody—upon a false pretense—of H. H. Hadley, the trusted and confidential agent of the Democratic National Committee.

Let us now see who had possession of the register, after it was turned over to Mr. Hadley, and prior to the time when it was produced in court by the defense in the Philp case. Hadley obtained possession of it on October 26th. He did not arrive in New York until late at night on the 27th, when he subsequently turned over the book, and such papers, affidavits, etc., as he had obtained in Massachusetts, to the Democratic National Committee; that body almost immediately delivered it to *Truth*, in whose custody it remained until produced in court. When the Committee forwarded the register to *Truth*, it informed the managers of that journal that it contained "an entry of the name of Henry L. Morey in two places." This relieves *Truth* from all suspicion of any complicity in the forging of Morey's name, while the fact is beyond dispute that at the time the book passed from Hadley's possession to that of the Committee it contained the two entries of the name of "H. L. Morey."

From all the facts and circumstances above recited, there is no escape from the conclusion that H. H. Hadley, *alias* O. M. Wilson, the agent and confidant of the Democratic National Committee, wrote the name of "H. L. Morey" in the Kirtland House register of the year 1879. Nor can there be any reasonable doubt from an examination of the entries themselves, that they were written by the same hand which penned the original Morey letter, and the erased and altered envelope, bearing the address of "H. L. Morey, Lynn, Mass.," which was enclosed to *Truth* as being the envelope in which Morey had received the Chinese letter from General Garfield.

It is eminently worthy of mention in this connection, that Mr. Hadley, in a statement made to me of various sums of money received by him from the Democratic National Committee, has admitted having received from Mr. William L. Scott, one of the Committee, five hundred dollars ($500) for obtaining the Kirtland House register.

The result, of the two preceding efforts of the National Committee, to sustain the original forgery upon General Garfield, have been shown to have not only failed, but to have involved very serious offenses, and the third attempt to support the same forged letter is now seen to have culminated in *the perpetration of two additional forgeries*, each of which appears to have been the work of its own agent and tool.

A single other incident of Mr. Hadley's trip to Massachusetts, where he endeavored to *create* an "H. L. Morey, of Lynn," remains to be told. If the reader will take the trouble to look back but a few pages, he will find in the telegram to Mr. Barnum, from the *Manchester* (N. H.) *Daily Union*, a recital of the story told John B. Mills, a reporter of the *Daily Union*, by one Edgar E. Mann, of Lawrence, respecting Henry L. Morey, whom Mann pretended to have known in many places, to have seen in Garfield's company, and to have been aware of the fact that he possessed many letters from General Garfield. As appears from that telegram, Mills had not been able, at that time, to obtain from Mann an affidavit as to the facts stated by him, although the National Committee had previously telegraphed for such a document.

While Hadley was in Boston he had such communication with Mills, as resulted in the latter's making another effort to obtain something from Mann in the way of a sworn statement, and in the making, by Mann, of the following affidavit, a copy of which, verified by the oath of John B. Mills, is in my possession.

"I, Edgar E. Mann, of Lawrence, Mass., do on oath, depose, and say that some time in the month of March, 1878, I was at Salem, Mass., on matters then pending in Court, and while there, near the Court House, I was approached by a man who called me by name and asked me if I did not want a job. He said he understood I was an expert workman. I asked him in what occupation. He replied shoemaking. I told him I was not connected with that trade. I told him I thought he could get expert workmen enough in Haverhill, in case he would pay for them. He asked me if I would aid him in procuring men in the shoemaking line. I then asked him his address. He took a card out of his pocket and wrote H. L. Morey, Lynn, Mass., on it. He asked me to send all the mechanics I found to this address at Lynn. EDGAR E. MANN.

ESSEX, MASS., October 28, 1880.

There personally appeared the above named Edgar E. Mann, and made oath that the above statement by him subscribed is true.
[SEAL.] JOHN S. GILE, *Notary Public.*"

What a fall was this. On October 25th, Mann was a very demi-god. He knew both General Garfield and H. L. Morey; had seen the two together in Washington, and knew Morey to have several letters from Garfield. He also knew Morey in, at least, three Massachusetts cities or towns. Three days later—on the 28th—when the pressure, or importunities, of those about him became too great to be longer borne, or when the inducements presented him became sufficiently tempting, Mann consented to commit his knowledge to paper and swear to it. Then it was that he stood disclosed to the world in his true light, as a coward and a falsifier. Not a word of his previous statement was he willing to swear to. General Garfield had altogether disappeared from his view, and H. L. Morey had been lost in a total stranger who had once, he believed, addressed him.

Mann's affidavit, when made, was, of course, absolutely valueless, save that when weighed with his original statement to Mills, it showed him to be wanting both in honor and honesty, and a stranger to the truth.

Such, as concisely as it can be told and the facts be made to appear, is the record of the conduct and actions of H. H. Hadley, during his trip to Massachusetts as the representative of the Democratic party, introduced and commended by the Chairman of its National Committee. There remain some communications which passed between Hadley and the Committee while he was thus absent, which must be presented, to complete the history of the trip, and we will now glance at them.

Upon the return of Hadley to Boston, from Lynn, on the evening of October 26th—Tuesday—he found awaiting him a number of telegrams from the Democratic headquarters. The dispatches received by him were all sent by the American Union Telegraph Company and are now in my hands. They are presented in the order of their receipt.

The first was sent in reply to one from Hadley to the Committee, informing it that he had obtained the Mower Brothers and Phelan affidavit and that of Mrs. Clara T. Morey.

"NEW YORK, October 26, 1880.

O. M. WILSON, Parker's, Boston.

Despatch received. We think we can use affidavits to full as good advantage Thursday as to-morrow. Proofs will appear in same paper as published original, in to-morrow's edition. Said to be very strong. Will supplement Thursday morning by what you get. Information here that stamps are genuine beyond question. If you have occasion to send any documents to us send by special messenger. *Prince* (the Mayor of Boston and Secretary of the National Committee) *will designate who*. Have telegraphed one hundred dollars Western Union. Nothing from your house.   E. B. D."

[NOTE—"E. B. D." was Edward B. Dickinson, the official stenographer, confidential agent, and acting Secretary of the National Committee. His rooms were upon the second floor of the house No. 138 Fifth Avenue, adjoining the private rooms of Mr. Chairman Barnum and the Executive Committee.]

The second telegram to Hadley was as follows :

" NEW YORK, October 26th, 1880.

O. M. WILSON, Parker's, Boston.

On further consultation, have decided it best you telegraph all you have so far. *Country very restless.* Telegraph by American Union line. I find it is too late to send telegraphic transfer. Offices close at five. *Call on Prince* (Mayor of Boston, and Secretary of the National Committee), or my father, if funds are needed to-night. Have telegraphed father to pay, and have mailed check.   E. B. D."

Upon receipt of this message, Hadley sent a long reply. His answer was dated, "Boston, October 26th, 1880," and addressed :

"To E. B. DICKINSON, 138 Fifth Avenue, New York."

"The following original affidavit is in my possession, and will come with me : (Then followed the full text of the affidavit of Mower Brothers and Phelan, previously spoken of herein.) Also the following, sworn to by Mr. Edgar E. Mann. (Then followed a summary of the affidavit of Mann, the full text of which is printed on a preceding page.) There is positive proof in my hands of H. L. Morey having lived here and in other Massachusetts towns. *One from his mother.*"   O. M. WILSON.

This telegram is a fitting finale to the remarkable mission of the Committee's trusted embassador, H. H. Hadley. A reference to the Mann affidavit, printed in full on the preceding page, will show that on October 26th, the date Hadley sent the above telegram, containing a summary of that affidavit, as "*sworn to*" by Mann, there was no such affidavit in existence, Mann's statement not having been sworn to *until the 28th instant*, two days thereafter. From what will hereafter appear, it would seem that it was a common practice with this representative of the National Committee, to secure the publication of papers as being "sworn to" by parties, when they were not verified. At the same time, it does not appear, that the National Committee took any steps to ascertain whether its agent, was, in fact, possessed of the originals of the documents which it received from him.

The third message from the Committee to Hadley, was received in Boston at 11.53 P. M. on October 26th. It read:

"NEW YORK, October 26th, 1880.

O. M. WILSON, Parker's, Boston.

Cripple (Edgar E. Mann) telegraphs from Lawrence, Mass., as follows : " Have you seen by Agent, Mrs. C. T. Morey, of Lynn ? Do you wish me to ? If so, telegraph, and if you will pay expense." Shall answer to-morrow morning that he must act in concert with you. What do you advise ? Will you see her, or shall we tell him to ? We will, of course, pay all necessary expenses to get the facts. Answer by night message.   E. B. D."

On the following morning, Wednesday, October 27th, the following dispatch was received by Hadley.

'NEW YORK, Oct. 27th, 1880.

O. M. WILSON, Parker's, Boston.

Important that you be here with all you have in time for to-morrow's papers. You can take one o'clock or four o'clock train, as you may be able. Have you seen Mrs. M.? Can you ascertain whether M. (Morey) had a press copy-book? Father has one hundred for you.
D."

Later in the day Hadley received his fifth message. It was as follows:

"NEW YORK, Oct. 27th, 1880.

O. M. WILSON, Parker House, Boston.

Don't come unless you have got through. Telegraph or send what you have. Have answered your dispatch fully.   WM. H. BARNUM."

From what we have learned of Mr. Hadley's performances, it would seem as if there could have been no question that he was "through." *He*, evidently was of that opinion, for he left Boston, at four o'clock that afternoon, October 27th, and arrived at the Democratic headquarters, at a late hour that night. Subsequently, he handed over to the Committee, the affidavits and other papers obtained by him during his trip, and their contents were, from time to time, doled out to the press by that body.

On October 28th, 1880, Mr. Barnum distinguished himself by sending to far distant points, a dispatch containing more than a thousand words, relative to the Morey letter. To a very considerable extent, the statements made therein were false, and one, at least, of the journals to whom this telegram was sent declined to print it. The editor of the *Carson* (Nevada) *Appeal*, upon receiving this message telegraphed Mr. Barnum : "The letter is recognized as a forgery out here, and you had better admit it as such and have done with the business." This was more than Mr. Barnum could stand. Advice from a wild Western journalist! That would never do. The question of the authenticity of the Morey letter must be forever put at rest ; the following reply was therefore sent:

"You are entirely deceived. *It* (the Morey letter) *is absolutely genuine*, and will be admitted so by every one. Very important that all sent you on the subject should be used."

Reference has been made herein, to one of the auxiliary organizations, the Hancock Republican Association, started early in the campaign for the purpose of affording aid and comfort to the Democratic party.

There was another "tender" which also demands notice. It was first heard of as early as July 15th, 1880, on which day General William F. Smith, more widely known as "Baldy" Smith, and others, met at the Westminster Hotel, in the city of New York, for the purpose of forming a central organization for the various "Hancock Legions" which were springing up throughout the country.

General Smith, if not the projector of this association, was certainly its most active and prominent member. On the evening of the meeting just mentioned, he presided, as he did, at the adjourned meeting, held at the same place a few days later—July 21st—at which time an organization was effected, under the name of the "National Association of Hancock Veterans."

Research discloses the fact, that on the Executive Committee of this organization was General Smith; that on the Advisory Committee was General Smith, and that the Chairman of the Executive Committee was General Smith; while it is noteworthy, that General Smith, was, at the same time, a Police Commissioner of the City of New York. One could hardly be censured for expressing the opinion, that General Smith, apparently, constituted a very large portion of the "National Association of Hancock Veterans." He was an early and ardent Hancock man, having attended the Democratic National Convention at Cincinnati in the interest of that gentleman, where he secured recognition from the *New York Herald*, which mentioned him, under date of June 29th, 1880, as one of "the Hancock boomers."

It was, perhaps, not wholly General Smith's fault, that, even at that early period, there were found individuals uncharitable enough to intimate that the General had "great expectations," while his subsequent, apparent activity in absorbing place and power in the "National Association," etc., quite naturally led to the whisperings, which were frequently heard, that his eyes were fixed upon the Department of War. From late in June, down to the day of election, General Smith was busy, in his way, "booming" Hancock. He was a frequent visitor at Governor's Island—the official residence of General Hancock—as well as at the rooms of the Democratic National Committee, and, in instances, even ventured to publicly address audiences on behalf of his favorite.

On the evening of the 25th of October, two public meetings were held, simultaneously, under the auspices of Smith's "National Association of Hancock Veterans," one at Tammany Hall and the other at Irving Hall. It must have been with some regret that on this occasion General Smith found himself unable to serve as the presiding officer of both meetings; but, as it could not well be, he acted in that capacity at one of the halls while another gentleman presided at the other meeting.

On the 28th of October, during the progress of the examination into the charge of criminal libel, which had been preferred against Kenward Philp, Chief Justice Noah Davis, of the Supreme Court, before whom the hearing was proceeding, directed Mr. Joseph Hart, the publisher of *Truth*, to produce the letter, which he (Hart) had received and published, and which purported to have been written by General Garfield to Henry L. Morey. Mr. Hart declined to comply with the order, and was at once committed for contempt of court. He subsequently agreed to produce the letter, and left the court room in the custody of his counsel for the purpose of obtaining the letter. At once the greatest consternation prevailed in Democratic circles.

Then it was that General Smith—having doubtless learned what had occurred in court—entered *Truth* office and inquired for Mr. Hart. Not finding that gentleman there, the veteran wrote, and left for him, the following letter, the original of which I have, and a *fac-simile* of which, reduced in size, is here presented.

"TRUTH"
142 Nassau Street

NEW YORK, *Oct 28*

Dear Mr Hart

The Republicans will file the Country with affidavits as to the letter being forged. If they even get a peep at it. The fac simile is all the proof required if you swear that that is from the letter in your possession. I wanted to ask you for it yesterday — they would not have got it from me till after Election.

Wm F Smith

The author, who has known General Smith for twenty years, regards this letter as eminently characteristic of that gentleman. "Baldy" Smith is nothing, if not impetuous, indiscreet, and, to a great degree, insubordinate; but there are portions of the letter which call for severe criticism.

The letter was, practically, an admission, by General Hancock's friend, of a belief that the Morey letter was a forgery, and the assertion that no Republican, should, with his consent, be allowed even "a peep at it" until "*after the election,*" was tantamount to a declaration that Democratic success was desired, let the means by which it was obtained be what they might. I regret to say, that, at that time, this was undoubtedly the sentiment, not only of many of the active leaders, but of a considerable portion of the file of the Democratic party.

General Smith says that he intended to have attempted to secure possession of the Morey letter on the day preceding the date of his note to Mr. Hart, and that, if he had succeeded, no one "would have got it from me [him] until after the election." I am aware of the fact, that a plan was arranged by which the letter was to be gotten into the possession of an individual, whom I will not here name; that counsel was consulted respecting the matter, and that the parties to the plot were advised, that if they obtained the letter, and the fact became known, they could refuse to produce it in court, and by being committed for contempt keep the document from the eyes of the court and the public until after the election. It is due Mr. Hart, of *Truth*, that it should be added that he was no party to the scheme, nor could he be led into it. I venture the opinion, however, that if General Smith had possessed himself of the letter, been ordered by the court to produce it and then failed to obey the mandate, the little incident related of a certain bovine, who undertook to prevent the legitimate use of a railroad track by placing himself in front of an express train, would have been the only light reading, which would, for some time, have afforded "Baldy" anything of interest or excitement.

Later in the day, Mr. Hart produced the original letter received by him, but without the envelope. He was directed to bring the envelope into court on the following morning—October 29th. He agreed so to do and so did, when Judge Davis directed his discharge from the order committing him to jail for contempt of court in declining to produce such documents. This order of discharge, upon Hart's purging himself of the contempt, was instantly made the pretext, by the Democratic National Committee, for sending to the country the following telegraphic address:

TO THE PUBLIC : NEW YORK, October 29th, 1880.
The Garfield letter is not a forgery. Mr. Joseph Hart, publisher of *Truth*, was honorably discharged this morning by the Republican Chief Justice of the General Term of the Supreme Court of New York, Hon. Noah Davis.   WILLIAM H. BARNUM, *Chairman.*

This dispatch, was one of the most dishonorable of the many vicious productions which appeared during the canvass over the signature of the Chairman of the Democratic National Committee. It was published on the morning of October 30th, but three days before the election, one of which was a Sunday. This was at a date too late for an effective refutation. It was written, not only days after General Garfield's explicit denial of the authorship of the Morey letter, or any knowledge whatever of its pretended recipient, but after every attempt to show the existence of Henry L. Morey had been, in fact, broken down. Indeed, at the time of its issuance, not a shadow of doubt remained in the mind of any one familiar with the proved facts, that the Morey letter was a gross and wicked imposition.

What can be said of the leaders of a great party, who could endeavor to influence the sentiment, and secure the votes, of the American people, at such a time, by such a manifesto, upon such a state of facts?

It surely can occasion no surprise, to learn that on the same day that Barnum issued the above address, the National Committee was still busily employed in scattering through the country, plates of the Morey letter, from which *fac-similes* might be published and circulated, to the very hour of the closing of the polls. That such was the case is established by the following letter, the original of which I possess. It is written upon a letter sheet, bearing the official heading of the Democratic National Committee, is signed by Mr. William L. Scott, the Pennsylvania member of that Committee, and reads as follows:

NEW YORK, October 29th, 1880.
DEAR MR. HART: We have requested the bearer, Mr. Andrews, to call on you and to make the necessary arrangements to get the plates, etc., off on the evening trains.
You can rely on him.   Yours truly, W. L. SCOTT.

Postmaster D. B. Angier, of Washington, D.C., was also examined as a witness in the Philp case. He testified that no such cancelling stamp as appeared on the envelope of the Morey letter, was in use in the Washington Post Office, on the 23d of January, 1880, the date the letter was claimed to have been mailed; that an entire new set of cancelling stamps were placed in use in his office, about the 15th of February, and the stamp upon the Morey letter was from one of such new set, which was entirely unlike the one in use in the Office, on the 23d of January. Thus was demonstrated the fact that the envelope in which it was declared the Morey letter had been forwarded, could not have been mailed from Washington, until after the 15th of February—a period at least three weeks later than the date of the letter. It also established the previously entertained opinion, that the microscopic researches *Truth* claimed to have made, had not enabled it to ascertain the real date.

When the Morey envelope was handed the Court for inspection by it, and by the Counsel for the prosecution, the Judge cut the sides thereof, so that it might be opened and examined with the light passing through it. The following discoveries were then made:

First.—That the month in the Washington post-mark had been erased, apparently by rubbing, but a microscope of great power failed to disclose what the month was. Yet some one had inserted in the so-called *fac-simile*, published by *Truth*, on October 27th, the word "Jan," and the figures "23."

Second.—That the envelope bore the receiving stamp, and sub-station stamp, of the New York Post Office, showing that it had been mailed in Washington to some one in New York, and had been delivered to some one in that city, and not in Lynn, Massachusetts. The date of its receipt, upon the receiving stamp, had been tampered with, one of the figures having been erased, and an attempt made to supply its place, not by a stamp, but by a line drawn by hand, while the letter to indicate the sub-station at, which it was delivered had also been erased.

Third.—That under the words "House of Representatives" in the left upper corner of the envelope, there had been something written which had been erased.

Fourth.—That the words "H. L. Morey," of the address, had been written below the place where the name of the party to whom the letter was originally addressed, was written; that the words "Lynn, Mass.," had been written over the other portions of the original address, which was to some one in New York, and that all of such original address had been erased. An examination thereof by the microscope showed that the first address was, as nearly as could be made out, Edwin Fox or Cox, Esq.

Fifth.—That the word "Personal" in the lower left hand corner of the envelope was written over an erasure.

All of the erasures spoken of were plainly visible to the naked eye, while some of the letters which had formed the original address, were also discernible without the aid of a glass. These disclosures of the forged and fraudulent character of the envelope, which were apparent to the most casual inspection, utterly discredited the letter claimed to have been sent therein; and yet, for ten days, Mr. Hewitt had been assuring the American public, from the rostrum, that upon his careful and thorough personal examination, the Morey letter was genuine—thus giving the sanction of his name and the weight of his character and social position to a clumsy forgery—when under his hand there lay all the while the means of detection.

If, as *Truth* and the Democratic National Committee, both claimed, they had never observed these patent evidences of fraud, the most charitable comment which can be made, is, that in their desperate efforts to injure General Garfield, and the party whose candidate he was, they did not avail themselves of the means in their hands to test the genuineness of the letter, with that prudence, care, sense of responsibility, and love of justice, which intelligent and fair minded men should, and would, have exercised.

Leaving the erasures on the envelope out of the question, the fact that the Washington post-mark had been tampered with, had not failed to be noticed by some one on *Truth*. Instead, however, of referring to it as a suspicious circumstance, it published what it asserted was a *fac-simile* thereof, in which the letters "Jan." and the figures "23" were inserted. Again, the receiving stamp upon the back of the envelope bore, with great distinctness, the words "Rec'd, New York," which at once disposed of any pretense that it had ever gone to Lynn.

On the following page will be found a *fac-simile* of the Morey envelope as it appeared when received by *Truth*. The upper portion of the plate shows its face, and the lower portion shows the reverse side.

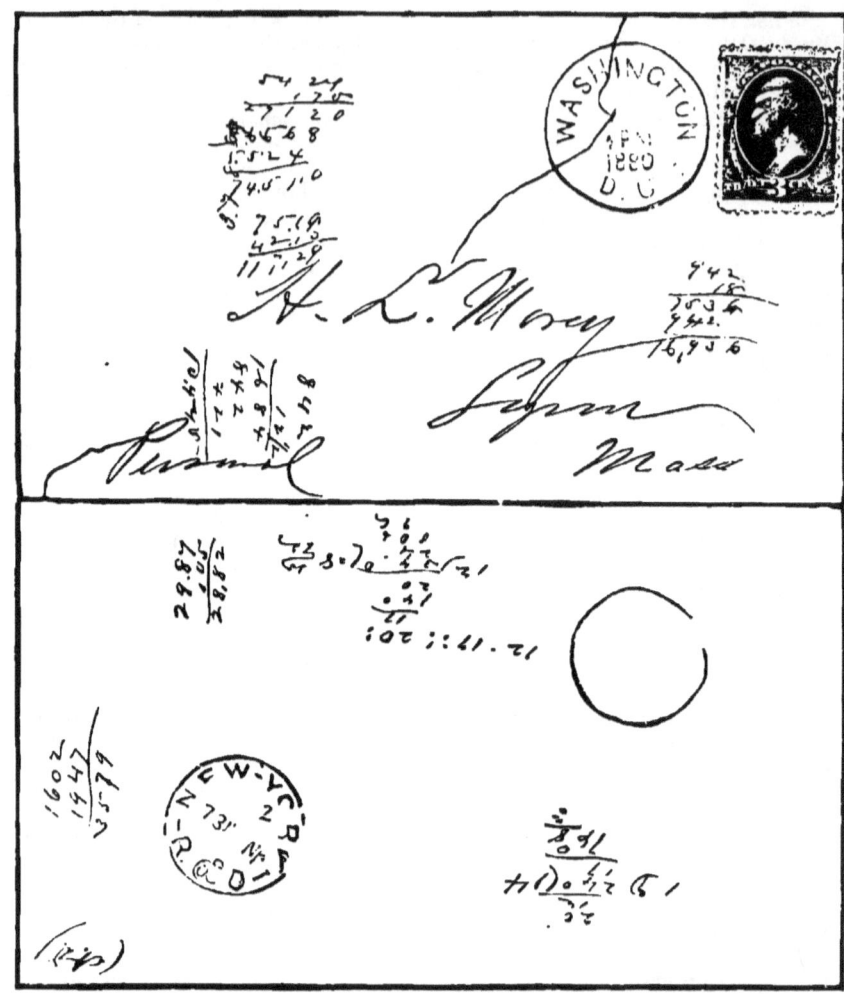

The No. 1 in the plate which follows is a *fac-simile* of the Post Office stamp in use in the Washington Post Office on January 23d. It is from a letter sent by a member of Congress to a gentleman in Brooklyn, N. Y. The No. 2 is a *fac-simile* of the Post Office stamp upon the Morey envelope. This stamp was never in use in the Washington office until February 15th, nearly a month after the date of the Morey letter. The difference in the two stamps will be at once observed. The No. 3 is a *fac-simile* of the Washington Post Office stamp as it appeared in *Truth*, of October 27th, 1880, after the letters and figures "Jan. 23" had been inserted in the office. A comparison of this stamp with No. 1 will make clear the blunder committed by the party or parties who caused the insertion in the *Truth fac-simile* of October 27th, of the letters and figures "Jan. 23." On the stamp actually in use in the Washington office on January 23d, the month and day were upon one and the same line; in the stamp on the altered *fac-simile* of the Morey-envelope they were shown as taking two lines.

On October 30th, 1880, *Truth* received the following letter, the original of which, now in my possession, is apparently in the handwriting of the penman of the Morey letter.

NEW YORK, Oct. 29th, '80.

EDITOR *Truth* :

I had no idea that the Morey letter would be brought to trial so soon.

I start immediately to Florida for Mr. Goodall, who will return with me by the 7th of November, if he is able to travel.

Garfield wrote the letter ; have no fear as to its proof, but we must have time to get ready.

Respectfully,

JOHN Q. A. SHEAKLEY.

On the morning of Monday, November 1st, *Truth* first published, in any form, a *fac-simile* of the letter purporting to be from one "John W. Goodall," of Lynn, Mass., who claimed to be the administrator of H. L. Morey's estate. This letter was the one received by *Truth* on October 18th, enclosing the Morey letter, and has been previously printed herein in full. Its publication at once brought forth the following card from Dr. J. W. Goodall, one of the most prominent and best known citizens of Lynn:

LYNN, Mass., Nov. 1st, 1880.

To THE EDITORS OF THE *Boston Journal* :

The statement published in the *Boston Globe* of this date and quoted from the *New York Star* and *Truth*, wherein John W. Goodall, of Lynn, Mass., is placed as administrator of the estate of one H. L. Morey. is an unmitigated falsehood, as it is an attempt to connect me with the Morey forgery case. One of the Democratic emissaries interviewed me in regard to the matter a few days since, when I told him that I never had any personal knowledge of any such man as H. L. Morey; also that no other J. W. Goodall, and no J. W. Goodall, lives in Lynn or its vicinity, and in the face of this the miserable sculpin has published this base falsehood and forgery, using what he took to be my name.

JONATHAN W. GOODELL, M.D.,

No. 4 Broad Street, Lynn, Mass.

An examination was made, on behalf of the prosecution in the Philp case, of the probate records of Essex County, and it was found that they contained no papers of administration on the estate of H. L. Morey by John W. Goodall or any other person.

On Monday, November 1st, Mr. William H. Barnum, Chairman of the Democratic National Committee, was interviewed at his home in Connecticut in relation to the Morey letter. This interview was made the subject of a special dispatch, by the Committee, to various party journals, especially those in States on the Pacific coast. As telegraphed, the interview began as follows :

"The Senator (Barnum) said: 'The genuineness of that (the Morey) letter *is now so fully established* that it should be clearly impressed upon the minds of all those who would be affected by the policy it declares.'"

Mr. Barnum then referred to the examination in the Philp case, and to a letter which Governor Jewell had, very foolishly, and without consultation with any one, been induced to write General Garfield, at the request of a gentleman claiming to represent Mr. Hart of *Truth*, who stated that Mr. Hart had become doubtful of the authenticity of the letter and would so declare in his paper, if he (Hart) could be satisfied that the previous course of *Truth* in respect thereto, would not be considered as reflecting upon, or working injuriously to the political aspirations of his said representative, who was a Republican whom he (Hart) was anxious to serve.

Mr. Barnum then discussed the question of Chinese labor and expressed himself as confident of success at the polls on the following day.

There were also sent to the press by the Democratic National Committee, simultaneously with the report of this interview, and for publication on the morning of election day, the three following telegrams, alleged to have been received by it. The contents of each one of the said telegrams was unqualifiedly false.

FIRST.

To Hon. W. H. Barnum,   NEWARK, Ohio, Oct. 31st, 1880, 11.12 P.M.
    Chairman, Democratic National Committee.

"The following dispatch was received here at 2 o'clock this morning and is authentic :

G. W. D., NEWARK, Ohio.   NEW PHILADELPHIA, Ohio, Oct 30th, 1880.

In haste I send you something far ahead of the Chinese letter. On last Thursday, Judge John H. Barnhill visited J. A. Garfield as a special committee of one from this city. On his return Friday evening, he was met at the depot by J. L. McIlvaine and others, who asked: "What is your report?" He replied by telling them to meet at his office at seven o'clock. Having heard his reply, and believing that something important could be gained, I secreted myself so as to hear all that would be said at the meeting. Precisely at seven o'clock some seven or eight persons met, and after a few moments of silence the still was broken by J. L. McIlvaine asking : "Well, Judge, what is your report?" The Judge arose, and said as follows : "I called on General Garfield at his residence, Mentor, Ohio, and was received very kindly.   After some conversation, I asked him if that Chinese letter was genuine, to which he replied, that having the utmost confidence in me as a sound Republican, he would say, as he did to Mr. Conkling, that he wrote the letter. But, Judge, you are an old lawyer and know that the best point in law is to deny well, and that it has been the policy of the leaders, with the exception of Blaine, of the Republican party, to fill this country up with a servile population from China, of about 50,000,000, and make voters of them, and as wealth and intelligence rules, the Republican party can then hold a perpetuation of power forever. This was the object of the Burlingame treaty, and the reason that Mr. Hayes vetoed the Chinese bill was that it would overthrow the Republican party." This idea satisfied all present, after which they dispersed.   Yours, etc.,   J. D. LONGHEAD.

Judge John H. Barnhill is a lawyer of New Philadelphia, Ohio, and is a prominent leader of the Republican party. J. D. Longhead is a lawyer and a man of prominence. I am personally acquainted with both gentlemen.   WALDO TAYLOR, Chairman, Democratic Congressional Executive Committee, of Licking County, Ohio.

I have inserted this document, at length, to again illustrate the statement that there was nothing so low, that the Democratic managers in 1880, did not, with alacrity stoop to its commission for partisan purposes.

The facts respecting this telegram were these. An insignificant sheet in Newark, Ohio, had published what purported to be Longhead's dispatch, on Monday, November 1st. Judge Barnhill was at once informed of its contents, and promptly, on the same day, telegraphed a denial of its statements.

In the face of this fact, the pretended dispatch was telegraphed by the Chairman of the Democratic Congressional Executive Committee of Licking County, Ohio, to Chairman Barnum, who hastened to send it broadcast over the country.

Judge Barnhill said of the dispatch:

I desire to say that every statement contained in the original dispatches, as published, is false and without any foundation in fact. I have not seen General Garfield, nor had any communication from him on any subject since his nomination for the Presidency. No such meeting or conversation as described in the article took place at any time. The story is a pure fiction and a wicked falsehood in every particular, and was doubtless invented and put in circulation by Democratic mud slingers as a desperate effort to aid a cause already cursed, among honest men, by fraud and forgery. The story upon its face, it is true, may be sufficient evidence to most men of its inherent falsehood, but yet it might deceive some one.

J. N. BARNHILL.

SECOND.

To W. H. BARNUM. NEWARK, Ohio, October 31st, 1880.

The *Morning News* to-morrow will publish the following extract furnished them by a well known gentleman of this city, from a letter written in the summer of 1861, by James A. Garfield to A. B. Way, a disciple preacher, then at Alliance, Stark County, Ohio: "The war has come and thank God for it. We now have the South just where we have been working for years to get it. I have made up my mind to enter the army, but will not remain there long, as it is a stepping-stone to political preferment, after which I intend devoting my attention to politics, as that pays better than religion, and office pays better than preaching the gospel. My object is now to make money honestly, if I can. And Members of Congress often have opportunities of making large sums outside of what their salary amounts to."

J. W. STEVENS, W. W. BURTON, Publishers *News*, Newark, Ohio.

THIRD.

The third dispatch sent out from Democratic headquarters on Monday, November 1st—the day before election—was received by the National Committee at 1.10 A. M. on that day. It was from William M. Price, Chairman of the Democratic Central Committee, of Alleghany County, Md.; was addressed to "Hon. W. H. Barnum, Chairman," and contained what purported to be the affidavit of one "Robert Lindsay."

As an attempt was subsequently made to support a paper, purporting to be this pretended affidavit, and as, if its contents had been true, the existence of Henry L. Morey would have been established, and the receipt, by Morey, of the published letter, purporting to be from General Garfield, would have been shown, it calls for much more than a passing notice. It is not, therefore, printed at this place, but will be found a few pages beyond, where it more appropriately belongs, as forming a portion of the history there given respecting the origin and support of the Lindsay affidavit.

It should here be noted how readily the local Democratic leaders throughout the country, and their followers, imitated not only the methods pursued by the Chairman of the National Committee, but the very forms of expression adopted by it.

On October 20th, when the Morey letter was first printed, Mr. Barnum sent it to the press with a telegram from himself, which began: "*The letter is authentic.*" THE LETTER WAS, IN FACT, A FORGERY, AND HENRY L. MOREY WAS A MYTH.

On October 31st, when Waldo Taylor forwarded the telegram purporting to be from J. D. Longhead, he began: "The following dispatch * * * *is authentic.*" THE CONTENTS OF THE DISPATCH WERE FALSE.

On the same day when William M. Price forwarded the telegram purporting to contain an affidavit of one "Robert Lindsay," he began: "The following affidavit of Robert Lindsay *is authentic.*" THE PRETENDED AFFIDAVIT WAS IN FACT A FALSE AND FRAUDULENT PAPER. There was no such affidavit as was then sent, signed or sworn to by *any* person, and "Robert Lindsay" was a myth.

What the Democratic National Committee accomplished in Massachusetts, in their efforts to find a Henry L. Morey, has been very fully made to appear. It remains now, to make clear the action of the same Committee in the attempts made in Maryland to find a "Robert Lindsay," and, by him, to establish the existence of an "Henry L. Morey," who should be shown to have been intimate with General Garfield, and the recipient of the "Morey letter."

On Tuesday, October 26th, 1880, one John W. Phelps, a Democrat, formerly of Springfield, Mass., but then, and for some time prior thereto, a resident of Cumberland, Md., where, as a contractor, he was engaged in the building of the George's Creek and Cumberland Railroad, prepared, caused to be written, and himself mailed, at the Post Office in Cumberland, the following letter addressed to the *Post* of Washington, D. C.

"CUMBERLAND, MD.

EDITOR *Post*.

DEAR SIR:---I see by the papers that Mr. Garfield denies writing what is now called the "Chinese letter." I wish to say through your valuable columns that I know he did write that letter, or at least my friend Morey, received the letter from Washington on the 25th of last January. I was then and am now a member of the "Employers' Union" of Lynn. Mr. Morey consulted with me and other members as to obtaining Mr. Garfield's views upon the labor question, particularly Chinese labor. We concluded to write him, did so, and received his letter in reply. I happened to be with Mr. Morey the 25th of January, when he got the letter, opened it, and we read it, therefore I know, as I said, of my own knowledge, that Mr. Garfield did write it.

I am at present at work here in Cumberland, and if you wish can go before a magistrate and make oath to the above fact.   Yours respectfully,
ROBERT LINDSAY."

At the time of mailing this letter, Mr. Phelps met Mr. David Lynn, a coal merchant of Cumberland, Md., and his then intimate friend, and remarked to him, "I have just gotten up something which I think will create a hell of a sensation." To Mr. Lynn's inquiries as to what it was, Phelps replied: "It is a letter purporting to be from one 'Robert Lindsay,' which has reference to the Morey letter, and I have mailed it to the *Washington Post*." He then requested Lynn to go to the telegraph office in Cumberland, in a day or two, and obtain for him any telegrams which might come addressed to Robert Lindsay. This Lynn did not do, not desiring to become mixed up in the Morey matter, and therefore a telegram which was subsequently sent to Cumberland by the *Washington Post*, addressed to "Robert Lindsay," remained in the office there, the operator not being able to learn of any such person in that city. The *Washington Post* was also notified, by the telegraph company, that the dispatch could not be delivered, as "Robert Lindsay" was unknown to its manager at Cumberland and could not be found. An affidavit by Mr. Lynn, showing the facts respecting Phelps' connection with the above letter, will be found in the Appendix.

Upon the receipt by the *Washington Post*, of the Lindsay letter, Mr. Walter S. Hutchins, the managing editor of that paper—his father, Mr. Stilson Hutchins, editor-in-chief, being out of the city—deeming the letter, if true, to be of importance, not only politically, but in a journalistic view as well, telegraphed "Robert Lindsay" to come at once to Washington. Receiving no reply, and learning that his telegram was undelivered, Mr. Hutchins sent Mr. Henry L. West, city editor of the *Post*, to Cumberland to find "Lindsay."

Mr. West left Washington, for Cumberland, on the morning of October 28th, and upon arriving there instituted and prosecuted the most thorough and systematic search for Lindsay.

The result of his trip was the ascertaining that the directory did not contain the name of "Robert Lindsay"; that the Post Office officials not only did not know but never had heard of him, while to their recollection, no letter had ever come to their office for him during their term of office; that the police authorities knew no such person; that the city officials had no knowledge of him; that he was not borne upon the subscription lists of the several newspapers published in Cumberland, nor upon the pay-rolls of the rolling mill, car shops, manufactories or other places employing men in and about the city; and that no one having charge of said subscription lists or the custody and care of the pay-rolls of the various establishments, where men were largely employed, had ever heard of any one in that locality by the name of "Robert Lindsay," save that, in one place, he was informed that some four or five miles out of Cumberland, on the line of one of the railroads, there was a colored man by the name of Lindsay, whose first name was thought to be Robert. Upon the receipt of this last mentioned expression of opinion, Mr. West telegraphed to the operator at the place where it was suggested the colored man lived, requesting said operator to ascertain if there was a "Robert Lindsay" residing there, but he received no reply to his message. Being fully satisfied that there was no "Robert Lindsay" in or about Cumberland, and that the letter was not genuine, Mr. West returned to Washington and reported to Mr. Walter S. Hutchins, the efforts made by him to find "Lindsay" and the result thereof.

Satisfied of the non-existence of "Robert Lindsay" in Cumberland, but thinking the letter from him might be interesting to *Truth* as a curiosity, Mr. Hutchins forwarded it to that journal enclosed in the following letter, the original of which I have.

    Largest circulation of any morning paper ever published in Washington.
     Office of the Washington *Post*,
      Stilson Hutchins, Editor,
       341 Pennsylvania Avenue.
          WASHINGTON, Oct. 29, 1880.

 DEAR SIR:—The enclosed letter was received at this office Wednesday. A dispatch was immediately sent to "Robert Lindsay," requesting him to come to Washington on the first train. It did not reach him. A reporter was sent to Cumberland and spent all day yesterday in searching for the man. He did not find him and my impression is that he is an humbug. Still I enclose his communication for your perusal and what other use you may desire to make of it.

           W. S. HUTCHINS,
Editor *Truth*.   Managing Editor.

Upon the receipt, by *Truth*, of Mr. Hutchins' letter, with the enclosure, that journal sent the "Lindsay letter" to the Democratic National Committee "with the request that it should endeavor to ascertain if the facts stated in the letter were true." The letter, so forwarded, reached the National Committee on Friday, October 30th. Mr. Barnum was not in the city at the time, and did not return until after the election. Mr. Abram S. Hewitt was in charge of the Democratic headquarters and the "Lindsay letter" was laid before him, together with the request of *Truth*. Mr. Hewitt has stated to the author that upon the matter being brought to his attention, he directed the sending of a telegram to the correspondent of the Committee at Cumberland, Md., requesting him to find "Robert Lindsay." In compliance with this direction a message of that character was sent to Mr. William M. Price, of Cumberland, the Chairman of the Democratic Central Committee of Alleghany County and an Elector on the Hancock and English ticket in the State of Maryland.

A few words as to Mr. Price, before further continuing the narrative of subsequent events, in which that gentleman will be found to have taken an active and prominent part. Mr. Price is an active and influential Democrat in his section of the State, and a friend and follower of United States Senator Gorman.

When Mr. Price was nominated, in 1880, as an Elector upon the National Democratic ticket, the *Cumberland* (Md.) *Leader*, a Democratic paper, published in his own city—the editor of which has been several times chosen by the Democracy to fill the important office of Clerk of the city of Cumberland—announced in its editorial columns of June 19th, 1880, that it should "scratch the name of William M. Price from our (its) electoral ticket." It specified six distinct reasons for such action on its part, summing up the grounds of its refusal to support Price in the strongest conceivable language, and declaring at the close of the article that "the Democratic party had no right to ask us to support a thing so contemptible" as William M. Price. Such was the opinion entertained and expressed concerning Mr. Price, by the organ of his party, at his own home, at a time when he was the candidate of the party for a seat in the Electoral College.

Mr. Price received the telegram sent by direction of Mr. Abram S. Hewitt, making inquiries respecting "Robert Lindsay," on the 30th day of October, and at once caused to be inserted in the *Sunday Civilian* of the following day this advertisement.

NOTICE.— If Robert Lindsay will call on the undersigned at once he will hear of something to his benefit. A liberal reward will be given for any information of the whereabouts of Robert Lindsay. WM. M. PRICE,
Oct. 31, 1t. Cumberland.

The advertisement neither brought Mr. Price the man "Robert Lindsay," nor any information as to any such person, wherefore, at about four o'clock in the afternoon of the 31st—Sunday—Price started from home to see what he could do in the matter, of and by himself. On the corner of Baltimore and Centre Streets, Cumberland, he saw James A. Birmingham, a special police officer in that city, in the employ of the Baltimore and Ohio Railroad Company, engaged in conversation with one, Richard Ryan, and one, "Buck" O'Neil. Price called Birmingham across the street, and inquired if he knew any "Robert Lindsay." Birmingham replied that he did not. Price then directed Birmingham to see if he could learn anything of any such person in or about Cumberland, and to get Ryan and O'Neil to aid him, and he (Price) would give them each five dollars for their services. Birmingham thereupon rejoined Ryan and O'Neil, and told them of what Price had said, whereupon the three started on a search for information as to "Robert Lindsay." They made numerous inquiries in all directions, but met with no success, and so reported to Mr. Price, whom they found between nine and ten o'clock that evening, on the corner of Harrison and South George's Streets, engaged in conversation with a gentleman who was unknown to them and who evidently was a stranger in their city. Upon reporting to Price, they were paid each five dollars for their services.

To ascertain who was the stranger seen with Price necessitates our leaving Cumberland, and taking a glance at affairs in New York.

After the Democratic National Committee sent its telegram to Price, it was, for some reason, deemed advisable by it not to rely solely upon the message forwarded, but to send to Cumberland its own representative. The individual selected was the ubiquitous H. H. Hadley, who was furnished with a letter of introduction and commendation to Mr. Price. A copy of this letter, certified to by Mr. Price as a correct copy, is in my possession. It is in his handwriting, and has never before been published. On the following page is a *fac-simile* thereof.

Hadley left New York for Cumberland, with the above letter, on Saturday, October 30th, and arrived at his destination on Sunday afternoon, October 31st, 1880. He went directly to the St. Nicholas Hotel, where he registered. I have the original leaf of the hotel register, containing his registry in his own handwriting. The following is a *fac-simile*, reduced in size, of his registration :

H H Hadley   New York city 37

Fac-simile of the letter to Mr. Price, referred to on the preceding page:

> New York, Oct 30, 1886.
>
> Wm M Price, Esq
>
> Dear Sir
>
> This will introduce Mr H H Hadley one of our staunch and trustworthy friends. He goes to your place on the matter spoken of in our telegram of today. He has our entire Confidence and we are bound by his acts. Please afford him all the assistance possible. He may ask of you to have check cashed which you will please do.
>
> Yours truly
>
> W H Barnum
> Chairman

> Dr Sir Above Send you Copy of the letter you gave me. I prefer to keep original at this time.
>
> yrs,
> W M Price

Soon after Mr. Hadley reached the St. Nicholas Hotel, he requested Captain C. C. Hedges, its proprietor, to find Mr. Price, whom he declared "he must see." Mr. Hedges sent twice during the evening to Price's house, but found that gentleman was not at home, but at church. About half-past nine Mr. Price came to the St. Nicholas, and there met Mr. Hadley. Upon being given the Committee's letter, introducing and commending Hadley, Mr. Price promptly began to disclose his true character by claiming to have found "Lindsay," and to have procured his affidavit. Mutual congratulations passed, and Hadley desired to see the important document, when a paper was handed him. Glancing it over, Mr. Hadley discovered that while it was drawn up to be sworn to, it was not yet an affidavit, *lacking both signature and jurat*. Calling Mr. Price's attention to that fact, Price replied that he understood all that, but the day was Sunday, and he could not put it in legal shape on that day. He added that it was all right, however, and would be properly completed on the morrow, at the same time urging that it be immediately telegraphed to New York, so that it could be sent to the country that night by the National Committee. To this proposition Mr. Hadley claims to have at first demurred, but upon Price's insisting that but one day intervened between the party and the day of election; that no one would know whether it was signed or sworn to, and that it would be made all right on the morrow, Hadley says he agreed to forward it, if Price would give him authority in writing so to do. Mr. Price readily assented to this, and paper being obtained from the hotel office, he wrote on a note sheet thereof, bearing the heading of the house, and delivered to Hadley the following paper, the original of which is in my possession.

ST. NICHOLAS HOTEL,
C. C. HEDGES, PROPRIETOR,
CUMBERLAND, MD. 18 .

H. H. HADLEY:
Please forward in my name to W. H. Barnum, Chm., the accompanying affidavit of Robert Lindsay which will be forwarded to-morrow, as soon as proper authentication and seals of court can be attached. W. M. PRICE, Chm.
Oct. 31st.

The matter being thus arranged, Mr. Price stated that he had been to some expense in the matter and should want to be compensated therefor. Mr. Hadley assented, adding that the Democratic National Committee would require the attendance of "Lindsay" in New York as a witness at the Philp examination. Mr. Price reflected a moment over this suggestion and some conversation followed. It resulted in an agreement being reached, that Price should have the paper signed and sworn to, should send "Lindsay" to New York and should receive for his services and expenses the sum of $300. Mr. Hadley requested a voucher and Mr. Price then drew up, signed and delivered to him a receipt for the amount named, which sum Hadley paid him. The original receipt, in Price's handwriting, is in my possession, written upon the back of a note sheet bearing the heading of the St. Nicholas Hotel, Cumberland, and a *fac-simile* thereof is given on the opposite page.

These matters being disposed of, Price and Hadley left the St. Nicholas and started toward the Queen City Hotel, owned and managed by the Baltimore and Ohio Railroad, the depot forming a part thereof. It was while going in that direction that Mr. Price was met by Birmingham, Ryan and O'Neil. The stranger, whom they speak of seeing with Price, was Hadley, as they subsequently learned. Later in the evening the whole party again met at the Queen City Hotel, and Price and Hadley went into the Baltimore and Ohio telegraph office, there located, where one of them began to write and continued writing for some moments. When the writing was completed, Price inquired of Birmingham, who meanwhile had entered the telegraph office, as to the politics of the night operator at that office, and received the reply that he did not know. Mr. Price then asked as to the politics of the General Agent of the Baltimore and Ohio road at Cumberland, that official having formerly been a telegraph operator at Parkersburg, West Virginia. Birmingham answered by saying that he believed him to be a Democrat, when Price wished to know the politics and residence of the operator of the Western Union Telegraph Company. Birmingham responded that he did not know that gentleman's politics, but could give his residence, which he did, and then left and went home, leaving Price and Hadley talking with each other. This was at about eleven o'clock at night.

[Handwritten note:]

Rec of H. H. Wady the sum of three hundred dollars in full for expenses in securing knower and getting affidavit of Robert Lindsay at expense of M. H. Barnum, chm. and can affidavit + Lindsay on to be sent to New York tomorrow morning evening

[signature]

Nov 1, 1880.

Sunday 31 - oct

After Hadley and Price had, on the night of Sunday, October 31st, arranged matters as above detailed, the telegram given on the following page was sent to Wm. H. Barnum, embodying the, as then unsigned and unsworn to, paper, which had been prepared as an affidavit to be subscribed and acknowledged by some one under the name of "Robert Lindsay." This telegram was furnished to the press by the Democratic National Committee, on Monday, November 1st, 1880, and was printed in the daily journals on the subsequent morning which was the day of the election. As sent to the press it read:

NEW YORK, November 1st, 1880.

The following dispatch was received at the National Democratic Headquarters at 1.10 this morning.

CUMBERLAND, Md., October 31st, 1880.

To Hon. W. H. BARNUM, Chairman.

The following affidavit of Robert Lindsay is authentic:

Robert Lindsay, being duly sworn, says that he resides in Alleghany County, Maryland; that he is personally acquainted with Henry L. Morey, whom he first met in 1874, and since at Lowell and Lynn, in the State of Massachusetts; also in Boston and in Philadelphia; that said Morey has frequently spoken to deponent upon the subject of cheap labor, and that in Boston, on or about the 4th day of February, 1880, said Morey showed to deponent several letters from prominent individuals relating to the subject of cheap labor; that three of said letters were from Hon. J. A. Garfield; and that deponent further swears that one of the letters then and there shown him by said Henry L. Morey was the identical so-called Chinese letter, which is now a matter of public controversy—or at least the words were the same as expressed in said letter, and that he recognized the engraving and photograph of said letter as being the photograph of the letter shown him by said Morey on the said 4th day of February; that said Morey expressed a determination to go from Boston to New Orleans, and deponent says he has not seen him since.

WILLIAM M. PRICE,
Chairman Central Committee, Alleghany County.

After this telegram had been forwarded, Mr. Hadley took the night train for New York.

Mr. Chairman Price now had his hands full. A paper had been telegraphed to the Democratic National Committee, over his name, as an affidavit, which was neither signed nor sworn to, and yet purported to be subscribed and acknowledged by a myth. He had received three hundred dollars for his work; had agreed in writing to forward an affidavit subscribed to in the name of "Robert Lindsay," and to send some one to New York as "Lindsay" on the following day—Monday. The contract was such as would have appalled any one but William M. Price, while it will certainly be difficult to find, in the history of the civilized world, another instance of as deliberate, reckless, insidious and wicked an attempt to secure the control of the government of a great nation, as was involved in this conspiracy.

This is how Mr. Price went about the work which he had assumed, and for the accomplishment of which he had obtained three hundred dollars.

At about ten o'clock on the morning of Monday, November 1st, 1880, Mr. Price stood at the Post Office in Cumberland. On the opposite side of Baltimore Street, stood James A. Birmingham conversing with some men, among whom were two who worked in the coal mines a few miles out from Cumberland. One of these miners was named Michael Cronley, alias "Knock," and the other was Francis P. Brady, alias "The Brute." Seeing Birmingham, Price called him across the street and inquired the names of the miners in the party he had just left. Birmingham named them, when Price inquired if one of them could not be got to sign the name of "Robert Lindsay" to a paper which he (Price) had. Upon Birmingham responding that he did not know, Price directed him to ascertain, saying that it would only have to be signed "Robert Lindsay," but such signing must be done in the presence of James Humbird, a Notary Public; that the man who would so sign the paper should receive five dollars therefor. Birmingham then left, and shortly joined such of the party across the street as still remained there and to whose number had been added his friend Richard Ryan. Informing Ryan of what Price had said, the former took Michael Cronley aside and told him what Price desired done and Cronley agreed to sign the paper. Birmingham, being informed of Cronley's willingness, went immediately to the office of Price and obtained the paper prepared for the signature and oath of "Robert Lindsay," when he rejoined Ryan and Cronley and the paper was passed to the latter. All three then went to the neighborhood of Humbird's house, but Cronley alone entered it.

What took place between Humbird and Cronley I can only relate by summarizing a statement made by Cronley on the day of his visit to Humbird's house, Monday, November 1st, to Thomas F. McCardell and Thomas Brown, two well known citizens of Cumberland. These gentlemen subsequently wrote out an account of Cronley's statements to them, and that individual informed me, in the month of April, 1882, that such account of his story was correct. So far as my information goes, Mr. Humbird has never denied Cronley's story, although made acquainted therewith.

Cronley stated to McCardell and Brown that he was inquired of by Birmingham if he would like to make five dollars from the campaign fund, and responded in the affirmative. Birmingham then told him to take the paper which he [Birmingham] had obtained from Price and handed him, and go to James Humbird's house and there sign the name of "Robert Lindsay" to it; if inquired of as to whether that was his name he was to reply that it was, and that he was sent there by William M. Price; that he took the paper and did as bidden, but, after signing the name of "Robert Lindsay" thereto, Humbird attempted to swear him to the truth of its contents, when he declined to be so sworn and left the house.

Birmingham, as will be seen in his affidavit, to be found in the Appendix, swears that Cronley, after leaving Humbird's, joined him and told him that he [Cronley] would not swear to the paper; that Cronley then went to the office of William M. Price and handed that gentleman the document; that Price handed Cronley fifteen dollars, five being for himself and five each for Birmingham and Brady, and that Cronley gave both the latter individuals the amount intended for them. Subsequently Birmingham and Ryan parted with Cronley, and shortly thereafter, met Brady, whom they invited to have a drink, which invitation was accepted. Birmingham then asked Brady if he would like to make five dollars, and upon receiving an affirmative reply he was told to go with Ryan to Price's office and to say to Price that his name was "Robert Lindsay." In answer to a question from Brady as to "who this Lindsay was," and "what it was all about," Ryan replied that Lindsay was a lecturer who was wanted for "an informal matter," but not being at hand, if he, Brady, would represent him "*it would be of great service to the Democratic party and probably be the means of electing Hancock.*" Birmingham then left the party, to go to his dinner, and Brady started, with Ryan, for Price's office. On the way thither, Brady, who had evidently been turning over in his mind Ryan's story as to "Lindsay," mildly remarked that he did "not think five dollars was enough for that"—the electing of Hancock.

This suggestion appeared to impress Ryan as having some force, for, upon the pair reaching Price's office, Ryan, after introducing Brady as "Robert Lindsay," took Price aside and conversed with him as to how much he [Price] was willing to pay for what he wished done, whereupon Price agreed that he would give twenty-five dollars. Ryan speedily informed Brady of the rise in the value of Hancock stock, and the terms proposed being made satisfactory to all, Price produced a newly made copy of the paper which Cronley had signed as "Robert Lindsay," but refused to swear to. This latter paper was all in the handwriting of William M. Price, and Brady, at once, without reading it, and in the presence of both Price and Ryan, signed the same "Robert *Linsey.*" Mr. Price, himself, then took Brady to the office of a justice of the peace, but not finding that official in, the two returned to Price's office, where Brady was put in Ryan's charge to go before Justice James F. Harrison and swear to the document. On the way to Harrison's office

Ryan learned that the Justice was in the office of the *Cumberland Times*. He there found him and informed him that a man was outside who wanted to swear to a paper and that he [Harrison] should "charge him five dollars for it." Harrison responded that the legal fee of ten cents was all he could, or should, charge, and went directly to his office. Shortly, Brady, whom Harrison did not know, entered and presented to the Justice the paper signed "Robert Linsey," the body of which, as well as the acknowledgment prepared for the signature of the Justice, Harrison recognized as being all in the handwriting of Price.

There were present in Harrison's office at the time Brady entered it, two men beside the Justice. One of these was William H. Porter, formerly Constable-at-large in Cumberland. Harrison, having heard something of the inquiries which had been made in that city for "Robert Lindsay," of whom he had never heard—although a resident of long standing, in Cumberland—was disposed to be extremely cautious. He inquired of Brady—who claimed to be "Robert Linsey,"—if that was his name; if the signature to the paper presented by him was written by himself; if he knew the contents of the paper he was desirous of swearing to, and if its contents were true. To all of these questions Brady answered in the affirmative, and then Harrison, for his own protection, wrote upon the paper the word "Witness" and requested Constable Porter to affix his signature underneath the same, as a subscribing witness. This Porter did, but upon obtaining a good look at Brady he felt certain he had seen him before and doubted if he (Brady) was the person he had just represented himself to be. Mr. Porter, subsequently, took some pains to investigate the matter, upon hearing a report that the name of the man who had sworn to the paper in Harrison's office was Francis P. Brady, hunted Brady up and at once identified him as the individual who had personated "Robert Lindsay" before Justice Harrison.

After Brady had sworn to the paper under the name of "Robert Linsey," he left Harrison's office and joined Ryan, who was waiting for him on the street, and together they returned to Price's office. Upon handing Mr. Price the affidavit, in its completed condition, that individual counted out twenty-five dollars which he gave to Ryan, who retained ten dollars, handed Brady ten dollars and gave Brady's friend, Cronley, five dollars.

In a full confession made by Brady to me on the 11th day of May, 1882, which was written down, subscribed and sworn to by him, and which will be found in full in the Appendix, he detailed at length the various efforts subsequently made by Wm. M. Price, his agents, confederates or tools, to prevent him (Brady) from making a full statement of his action and of the way in which he was led to do what he did; also of subsequent payments and promises made to him by said Price, or on his behalf, to induce him (Brady) to keep his mouth closed as to the transaction.

In the Appendix, will also be found the sworn statements of both Birmingham and Ryan as to their knowledge of and part in the matter. Also the affidavits of Mr. William H. Porter and Justice Harrison.

From the facts presented, it will be seen that on the afternoon of Monday, November 1st, Mr. Price had succeeded in getting signed and sworn to, an affidavit purporting to be made by "Robert Lindsay" or "Linsey," but which was, in fact, signed and sworn to by Francis P. Brady, who knew not its contents. The total expense Price had been put to was about fifty-five dollars and the cost of his notice in the *Sunday Civilian*.

I have in my possession the original affidavit in the handwriting of William M. Price, which was signed and sworn to by Brady, under the name of "Robert Linsey," on the first day of November, 1880, *one day after what purported to be the "Lindsay" affidavit was telegraphed, by Price and Hadley, to the Democratic National Committee.* I insert a copy of it because it contains several verbal changes from the unsigned, and unsworn to, paper, they telegraphed on October 31st as the affidavit of "Robert Lindsay." The words in italics are words in the original Brady-"Linsey" affidavit, not in the paper telegraphed as the affidavit, and the words in brackets are words in the telegraphed paper which are not in the said original affidavit:

"*This statement made and executed by me*, Robert Lindsay, [being duly sworn, says that he resides in], *now of* Alleghany County, Maryland, *shows that this deponent*, [that he], is personally acquainted with Henry L. Morey, whom he first met in *the year* 1874, and since at Lowell and Lynn in the State of Mass., also *at* [in] Boston, and [in] Philadelphia ; that said Morey has frequently spoken to deponent upon the subject, cheap labor, and that in Boston, on or about the 4th day of February, 1880, said Morey showed to deponent several letters from prominent individuals relating to the subject of cheap labor ; that three of said letters were from Hon. *James* [J.] A. Garfield ; and deponent further swears that one of the letters then and there shown *to* him by said Henry L. Morey was the identical so-called Chinese letter, which is now a matter of public controversy—or at least the words were the same as expressed in said letter, and that he recognizes the engraving and photograph of *the* said letter as being the photograph of the letter shown him by said Morey on the said 4th day of February ; that said Morey expressed a determination to go from Boston to New Orleans and *this* deponent says he has not seen him since.

Witness my hand and seal this 1*st day of November*, 1880.
ROBERT LINSEY." [SEAL.]
"*Witness*, WILLIAM H. PORTER."
"STATE OF MARYLAND, ALLEGHANY COUNTY, ss.
I hereby certify that on this 1st day of November, 1880, before me, the subscriber, a Justice of the Peace of the State of Maryland, in and for Alleghany County, personally appeared, Robert Lindsay, and made oath, in due form of law, that the facts, matters and things set forth in the above and written statement, are true as therein stated.
JAMES FORSYTH HARRISON, J. P."

It will be observed, that Price in his letter to Hadley, authorizing the latter to forward, in his (Price's) name, the paper which was sent the Democratic National Committee on Sunday night, October 31st, as an affidavit, spoke of it as made by "Robert *Lindsay;*" that in the receipt given to Hadley, he also referred to the man, whose presence in New York he promised, as "Robert *Lindsay;*" that the affidavit sworn to on the following day before Justice Harrison, and which he drew, contained the name of "Robert *Lindsay*" as that of the man whose statement it purported to be and who was to swear to the paper; and that in the certificate, written by him, for the Justice before whom oath to the paper was to be made, he also gave the name of the affiant as "Robert *Lindsay*." Poor Brady, who was hired to represent "Robert Lindsay," never having heard of Price's man "Lindsay," and being doubtless more familiar with "linsey-woolsey," wrote, when told to sign the name of "Robert Lindsay," the name of "Robert *Linsey.*"

The affidavit, after being signed and sworn to by Brady as "Robert Linsey," was forwarded the Democratic National Committee. The *man* "Robert Lindsay," whom Price had agreed in writing to forward to New York on Monday—November 1st—did not, however, get started. The first three days of November passed and the election was over and yet no "Robert Lindsay" made his appearance.

Then it was that *Truth* first began to discover that it was "left." The Committee no longer manifested any interest either in "Robert Lindsay," Henry L. Morey, his letter, or *Truth*. Believing the "Lindsay" affidavit true, and desiring the presence of "Robert Lindsay" in the Philp case, Mr. Hart undertook to produce that individual. The person who was, accidentally and hastily, selected by it, as its agent, to go to Cumberland and bring Lindsay to New York, was Richard Henry Wilde, a native of Louisiana. Wilde had been an officer in the Confederate army during the rebellion and subsequently served under Maximilian, in Mexico, until the death of that unfortunate protégé of Napoleon III, when he returned to New Orleans and became a prominent officer of a White League Regiment. He was also for a time a member of the Louisiana Legislature, and was known as the active representative of the Louisiana

Lottery Company, jealously guarding its interests. Thereafter, he entered the employ of that company, and subsequently, in the year 1879, came to New York, where he died in the year 1882.

In starting Wilde to Maryland for "Robert Lindsay," he was re-christened as "Henry Walton," given one hundred dollars, a copy of the issue of *Truth* containing the paper telegraphed by Price and Hadley as the affidavit of "Robert Lindsay," and a letter of introduction to William M. Price, of Cumberland.

Wilde, *alias* Walton, arrived in Cumberland about two o'clock in the afternoon of Thursday, November 4th, 1880, and registered at the Queen City Hotel as follows :

[signature: Henry Walton New York &c. 21]

He found Mr. Price at the Court-house engaged in the trial of a cause. The trial being concluded about half after three o'clock, Price left the court room with Wilde and, together, they walked down the street. Wilde, having previously handed Price his letter of introduction and the copy of *Truth* he brought with him, then informed Price that he had come for "Lindsay." Price answered: "You will have to excuse me; but as I do not know you, and the letter you have handed me may be forged, I will have to have better credentials." Wilde responded: "Why can't you telegraph to Hart (the publisher of *Truth*) and find out?" Mr. Price assented to this suggestion, and telegraphed Mr. Hart, as Wilde also did. Wilde then left Price and went to his hotel to await Hart's answer.

The telegram of Price was as follows:

CUMBERLAND, Md., November 4th, 1880.

J. HART, Publisher of *Truth*, N. Y.
Is Henry L. Walton all right? Answer. W. M. PRICE.

Wilde's message read:

CUMBERLAND, Md., November 4th, 1880.

JOSEPH HART, 142 Nassau Street, New York.
Price pretends to believe I do not represent you. Telegraph him I do, and I can reach you to-morrow at noon. HENRY WALTON.

Mr. Hart replied to Price that Walton was "all right," and requested Price to assist him in procuring "Lindsay." At about half after nine o'clock that evening, after receiving Hart's answer, Mr. Price went to the Queen City Hotel, and calling upon Wilde, *alias* Walton, said to him, "I can't find 'Lindsay' to-night; the man who knows him is busy, but as soon as I can I will bring him to you." Price then left and Wilde went to the telegraph office and sent the following message :

CUMBERLAND, MD., Nov. 4th, 1880.

JOSEPH HART, 142 NASSAU STREET, NEW YORK :
Can't get him before to-morrow, and can only get him there early Saturday morning. Shall I wait for him? Answer immediately. HENRY WALTON.

After Price had received Hart's answer vouching for Wilde, and at about nine o'clock that evening, *and before he called upon Wilde*, he had an interview with James A. Birmingham, at the latter's house, at which he said to him: "I want you to go up to-morrow to the Eckhart mines with a gentleman and show him *Brady*." Birmingham replied that it would not be possible, as he had "to be about the hotel and depot during train time." Price, after promising to obtain permission for Birmingham to attend to this matter, left the house and made the call upon Wilde which has been spoken of.

At about eight o'clock in the morning, on Friday, November 5th, Mr. Price went to the depot and obtained, from the General Agent of the Baltimore and Ohio Railroad, leave of absence for Birmingham. He then introduced "Mr. Walton" to Birmingham, and, taking Birmingham aside, said to him: "You go up to the mines and show Walton this man Brady, *alias* 'Bob Lindsay.'"

Birmingham then rejoined Wilde, *alias* Walton, who hired a conveyance, which Birmingham drove up the country, toward the Eckhart mines, stopping occasionally at various places, at each of which he would get out and inquire for Cronley and Brady.

When these inquiries were made by Birmingham, Wilde was never within hearing, being left in the wagon to care for the horse; for it was no part of the plan, either of Birmingham or Price, that Brady should go to New York, even if he would have been willing to so do, which would not have been the case. After each inquiry, Birmingham would report to Wilde that "Lindsay" could not be found, and finally told him that "Lindsay" was "not working" and was away from home. At about three o'clock in the afternoon the pair arrived back in Cumberland, and went in search of Mr. Price, whom they found coming from the Court-house. Wilde and Price then had some conversation on the street, and also in Price's office, to which they walked. At the close of their interview Walton left, to go to his hotel, asking Birmingham to come to the depot "at train time." At about five o'clock, Birmingham went to the depot and learned that the train due at that hour from the West, was about an hour and a half late. While about the depot, Wilde sent for him to come to his room, whither he went, when Wilde, as Birmingham swears, said to him : "Get somebody. I have to have somebody and I will give any one a hundred dollars." Birmingham answered that he could not find "Lindsay," when Wilde replied, "I have got to have that party."

Birmingham then left to go to supper, but met a friend who requested him—Birmingham—to accompany him upon an errand. On their way they met one "Lowly" Harbaugh and a stranger. Harbaugh introduced the stranger as Mr. O'Brien, and Birmingham invited the party to go with him to the saloon of "Buck" O'Neil and have a drink, which they all did. "Mr. O'Brien," was one James O'Brien, of Georgetown, D. C., who had arrived in Cumberland early that morning looking for work, and who had been told that Birmingham could probably get him something to do.

While the party were at O'Neil's saloon, "Buck" said to O'Brien: "Well, you found Birmingham at last," and then turning to Birmingham said: "That is 'Bob Lindsay' whom you have been looking for." To this remark Birmingham responded: "There is a man up at the Queen City Hotel who has offered a hundred dollars for 'Bob Lindsay,'" when O'Brien said: "Is that so? Well, I'm his man." Almost immediately thereafter the party started for the hotel, walking up the railroad track. One by one, all save Birmingham and O'Brien, branched off. They kept on to the Hotel, where they found the train for the East just coming in, and Wilde, standing on the depot platform. The train was obliged to remain twenty minutes at Cumberland that its passengers might be fed. Birmingham stepped up to Wilde, with O'Brien, and said: "Here is a man who wants to see you." O'Brien then said to Wilde that he was "Bob Lindsay," and Wilde agreed to give him one hundred dollars and his expenses if he would accompany him (Wilde) to New York and testify that he was "Robert Lindsay." O'Brien turned aside to Birmingham and informed him of Wilde's proposition, and Birmingham suggested that he—O'Brien—might go a part of the way, get what he could from Wilde and then leave the train and refuse to go further. O'Brien thereupon said to Wilde, that he would start with him, when Wilde purchased two tickets to New York. One of the tickets he retained himself, and the other he gave to O'Brien with ten dollars, which sum was to guarantee O'Brien his return fare. Wilde also gave Birmingham ten dollars for his services.

Just after the purchase of the tickets Wilde remembered that he had given Price the copy of *Truth* containing the Price and Hadley telegram of the so-called affidavit. Without that O'Brien could not tell how to shape his story. With it he could study up on the way to New York. Birmingham was sent to Price's house, which was close by the depot, for the copy of *Truth*, and returning with it just as the train was starting gave it to Wilde, who departed, taking O'Brien with him. On the following day—Saturday, November 6th—Mr. Price met Birmingham and inquired: "Did he get off all right?" to which Birmingham responded, "Yes, they started."

It has been previously shown herein, how James O'Brien was placed upon the stand in the Philp examination under the name of "Robert Lindsay;" how he was broken down upon cross-examination, was arrested on the charge of perjury, and made a full confession of his participation in and connection with the matter.

On the 24th of November, 1880, O'Brien was indicted for perjury, and on the 3d of December, of the same year, Samuel S. Morey was also indicted for the same offense. It being evident that Morey, by reason of his epileptic fits, was a man of weak mind, his plea of "guilty" was accepted, his sentence suspended, and he allowed to return home. O'Brien pleaded "guilty" on his indictment, and on the fourteenth day of April, 1881, was sentenced to the State prison for eight years, where he still is.

In Birmingham's affidavit, to be found in the Appendix, there appear some interesting statements of conversations with and payments made to him, by Price.

Thus ended the last of a long series of efforts made by the Democratic National Committee, through its agents, representatives, employes and allies, to establish the existence of the myth "Henry L. Morey," by the myth "Robert Lindsay," the perjurers Samuel S. Morey and James O'Brien, and other equally fraudulent, disreputable and unreliable witnesses. One cannot fail to feel indignant, when he learns that the tools alone were amenable to the law, while their far more guilty instigators and supporters could roam at will, only sorry that their wicked plots had proved unsuccessful.

In this connection, I recall a remark made by Mr. Hadley in one of his interviews with me. He said: "Upon one occasion I suggested to Mr. Barnum that I thought it would be well to go a little slow; that it seemed to me the pace was getting pretty rapid, and he was growing too careless and reckless; that if the press got hold of some of these matters they would give him the very devil. Barnum's reply to me was: 'Hadley, I don't care what they say about me. They may say I crucified Christ himself, if I only succeed in electing Hancock.'"

The writer has no means of knowing the truth of this statement. He gives it precisely as it was made to him, and he believes Hadley told the truth. Mr. Barnum's course was in perfect accord with such a policy as Hadley alleges he stated to him was governing his (Barnum's) actions. Nor was Mr. Barnum alone in holding such views. The *Sedalia* (Mo.) *Democrat*, a Democratic paper, in its issue of October 22d, 1880, said to its party in the city of New York:

"Go into the market and buy (votes). Where one Republican is colonized, colonize two Democrats; discount the repeaters; do as you please with the ballot boxes; *do anything to carry the state* (New York) *for Hancock*. Win, only win, and psalms will be sung for you in the churches, and fatted calves killed for you in State Houses and capitals. As for the right of such work, stuff! The civil war killed everything in politics but victory."

During the closing days of the Philp examination, and shortly after the election, the author obtained knowledge of one or two facts, which, being subsequently pursued, led, finally, to the entering of a *nolle prosequi* to the indictment against Philp for criminal libel. On the 12th day of November, 1880, the author determined, if possible, to obtain an interview with Mr. Hadley. He thereupon caused an officer serving under the District Attorney to be sent to Hadley's office with a subpœna. It was his intention, if Hadley had been found, to have met him and arranged for a future interview. The officer sent in search of Hadley shortly returned, with the information that that gentleman was not at his office. The writer subsequently learned, that Hadley left the city on the very day he was being looked for, having received word from a detective employed by him (Hadley) that an officer from the District Attorney had endeavored to find him at his place of business; that believing he was in danger of being arrested, he went to Jersey City, beyond the jurisdiction of the New York authorities, and from there sent the Democratic National Committee word of his supposed peril. In reply, he received, by the hand of a messenger, a letter, the original of which is now possessed by the author. It is here presented, in *fac simile*, and has never before been published:

HANCOCK AND ENGLISH.

Headquarters National Democratic Committee,

138 FIFTH AVENUE.

DUNCAN S. WALKER, 1st Assistant Secretary.
JOSEPH L. HANCE, 2d Assistant Secretary.
EDWARD B. DICKINSON, Official Stenographer.

Hon. WM. H. BARNUM, Chairman.
Hon. F. O. PRINCE, Secretary.
CHARLES J. CANDA, Treasurer,
52 William Street, New York.

New York, *Nov-12* 1880.

H H Hadley Esq
Dear Sir,
Get any friend of yours to go bail & Messrs Hewitt, Scott & Barnum will indemnify your friend — It is thought best that no member of the Committee appear in the matter.
Yours Truly,
Geo. B. McClellan

Mr. Hadley, being unable to furnish what bail he feared might be required of him, if arrested, and being wholly dissatisfied with the tone of the reply to his message, sent his brother to Democratic headquarters to see what could be done on his behalf. The matter being laid, by Mr. S. H. Hadley, before those in charge of the rooms of the Committee, the following letter, the original of which the writer is possessed of, was given that gentleman. It is written upon a letter sheet bearing the official heading of the Executive Committee of the National Committee, and reads:

NEW YORK, Nov. 13th, 1880.

MR. HEWITT:

MY DEAR SIR: This will be given you by Mr. S. H. Hadley, brother of H. H. Hadley. I knew of no course to pursue under the circumstances, except to send him to you. I hope you will be able to straighten matters out, as Mr. Hadley's conduct in the matter has been above reproach; he served us faithfully, and what he did will bear the most rigid scrutiny.

Hastily,
EDW. B. DICKINSON.

Hon. A. S. HEWITT,
9 Lexington Avenue.

Upon calling on Mr. Hewitt, that gentleman said to the bearer of the letter that it would be impossible for him, at that time, to go Mr. Hadley's bail; that his motives, if not his action, should he so do, would be misunderstood, and he must therefore decline to comply with the request made.

Believing himself deserted by those whom he looked to for assistance, Mr. Hadley left Jersey City, and went to Philadelphia, where he stopped for a time at the Bingham House, and subsequently at Guy's Hotel. He remained away for some weeks, during which time, Mr. William H. Barnum sent to John D. Townsend, Esq., a member of the New York bar and a prominent Democrat, a retainer of one thousand dollars, to protect Mr. Hadley and his interests, if he was arrested. Mr. Townsend thereupon communicated with the author respecting Mr. Hadley's being permitted to return home without being arrested, stating that a member of Mr. Hadley's family was seriously ill.

Of the money sent Mr. Townsend by Mr. Barnum, the first named gentleman only retained $500, giving Mr. Hadley $500. Of the sum so given Hadley, that individual retained $85, and the remainder thereof, $415, he gave to one N. MacGregor Steele, a lawyer in New York. Steele, upon receiving the amount stated, went at once to Lynn. He registered at the Sagamore House as follows:

[facsimile signature: Wm Gregor Steele New York]

Mr. Steele then called upon Justice George O. Tarbox and, presenting him with $100, endeavored to induce him to sign a prepared statement, which he (Steele) had brought with him, to the effect that when Mrs. Clara T. Morey signed and swore to the affidavit, drawn by Hadley, *alias* Wilson, before Justice Tarbox on October 26th, 1880, the name of "H. L. Morey" was written therein. This effort of Hadley's to entrap Justice Tarbox wholly failed, Mr. Steele being directed to take his money and get out. It was made for the purpose of placing it beyond the author's power to prove the falsity of the story Hadley had told him of his (Hadley's) originally writing "H. L. Morey" in Mrs. Morey's affidavit, of his subsequently running his pencil through the same and then writing above that name the words "Geo. S. Morey."

On the 4th of April, 1882, Mr. Hart, of *Truth*, received a second letter purporting to be from John W. Goodall. The original letter, so received, is in my possession and has never before been published. It is apparently in the handwriting of the penman of the Morey letter, and the following is a *fac-simile* thereof, reduced in size.

Truth:
No matter which way Dana turns on the Morey letter, he is a liar; he thought the letter genuine, is the reason he did not publish it, the signature was genuine. Heustis guess was correct, and Dana had to pretend it was a forgery as an excuse not to publish it — did he not have deducs $20-000, not to injure Garfield? When I showed him the letter he said — "astonishing — but it is just like him," if he had thought it a forgery, he would have said so to me, but he simply said "I've no use for it." as he handed it back to me.

That was a famous letter, and it made you famous, and made you known all over this country in a day; a decade in time otherwise would not have accomplished so much.

There is not a sentence in it that does not express some principle opposing of the Republican party. That is the only "infamous" part of it.

This is the last you will ever hear from
John W Goodall

Long after the election of 1880, letters were, from time to time, received by *Truth*, the *New York Star*, and other journals, referring to the Morey letter and matters connected therewith. These letters were signed "Esoteric," "Mrs. Elvius Carr," etc. Some of them contained elaborately constructed stories as to the early history of the Morey letter, and all were, evidently, prepared for the sole purpose of keeping alive an interest in the matter, on the part of the press, while adding to the mystery which, apparently, surrounded the authorship of the Morey letter. I have obtained possession of most of those letters and have fully satisfied myself that they came from, one and the same source—H. H. Hadley. I do not see that, at this time, they will add greatly to the history of the Morey letter, while it may be, that, at some future day, some of them will be of interest enough to demand their publication. If so, they will be made public, together with such other evidences and proofs of the facts herein stated as I have deemed it wise to reserve, for my own protection, should any one desire to raise an issue with me respecting the matters to which this work is devoted.

A SIDE SHOW IN WHICH MR. WILLIAM L. SCOTT PLAYED A PROMINENT PART.

As illustrating the eagerness with which the Democratic National Committee seized upon anything, which even the veriest confidence man threw into its net, in its desperate efforts to prove the existence of a man who never lived, the following is contributed.

On the 26th day of October, 1880, a telegram was sent from Chicago to the Democratic National Committee, informing that body that one H. Carter and friend had departed for New York, having in their possession certain letters from General Garfield, of a character similar to the Morey letter. This telegram was sent by H. Carter, *alias* Colonel H. G. Edwards, *alias* H. Carter Gray, etc., etc., a noted confidence man and swindler, but purported to be signed by the Hon. Lyman Trumbull, Perry Smith, Esq., and Mayor Carter Harrison of Chicago. After sending the dispatch, Carter and his friend took the east bound train. Reaching Pittsburgh, Penn., Carter telegraphed the Committee, that, for prudential reasons, they would not go to New York, but requested that some one should meet them at the Ebbitt House, in Washington, D. C. They arrived at the Ebbitt on the evening of Tuesday, October 26th, 1880, where they registered as "H. Carter, Chicago, Ill.," and "W. E. Andrews, Des Moines," and were assigned Parlor 418.

Upon the receipt of the second dispatch, Mr. Barnum telegraphed a prominent Democrat, then in Washington, requesting him to meet Carter and his friend at the Ebbitt. The gentleman so addressed, not knowing the nature of his mission, proceeded to seek Messrs. Carter and Andrews, whom he found occupying a parlor and two bed rooms, and both somewhat under the influence of liquor, yet able to converse after a manner. Carter inquired if his visitor understood what he was to meet them about, and received the reply that he did not, when Carter informed him that they had been recommended to the Committee as being possessed of letters from General Garfield of a nature similar to the Morey letter, and that they had come to Washington for the purpose of exhibiting such letters to him. To this the visitor made answer that he regretted he had not previously understood the matter; that he was not desirous of being mixed up with the Morey letter affair, and should decline to look at any papers relating thereto. Carter then inquired of his visitor what he proposed to do, to which that gentleman responded that he should at once telegraph Mr. Barnum that if he (Barnum) desired any one to attend to a matter of the character he understood this to be, it would be better to secure the services of some one else. He thereupon departed and at once telegraphed Mr. Barnum, declining to attend to the matter. His dispatch was delivered at about 12.30 in the morning, on Wednesday, October 27th. Mr. Carter was subsequently informed of what had been done, when he sent the gentleman who had called on him the following note—the original of which I have :

THE EBBITT. C. C. WILLARD.
MR. ―― [name withheld.] Washington, D. C., Oct. 27th, 1880, 2.15 A. M.
Am in the habit of having the messages or letters sent to me signed by the person who sends them. I drop the whole matter, as I see there is not ambition or principle enough in Barnum's district to promulgate matters. Shall return to the west in the afternoon to-day.
Yrs, &c., H. CARTER GRAY.

On the morning of October 27th, Mr. William L. Scott, of the Democratic National Committee, started for Washington, to confer with Carter and Andrews. While Scott was hastening to Washington, Carter and his friend were visiting at Fort Whipple, a Signal Service post between Washington and Arlington Heights, to which place they had driven out, and where they had introduced themselves to Captain Strong, the commandant of the post, in the following manner: Andrews first handed Captain Strong his business card, which the author has, and which reads:

```
                    Western
                Newspaper Union,
        Auxiliary  W. E. Andrews,  Publishers,
                     Manager,
                 Wholesale Paper
                     Dealers,
                 Des Moines, Iowa.
 Offices :
 Des Moines, Iowa,
 Kansas City, Mo.,
 Omaha, Neb.
```

Carter then borrowed the card from the Captain, wrote upon the back thereof, as his address, "Col. H. G. Edwards, Correspondent *New York Herald*," and returned it, stating that he had just arrived in Washington to assume charge of the Washington office of the *Herald*.

Introductions being over, Captain Strong extended the "distinguished" pair every courtesy; in return for his hospitality, when about to depart, Carter, *alias* "Col. H. G. Edwards," wrote, and delivered to Captain Strong, the following order, the original of which I have, upon the manager of "Rice's Surprise Party"—a theatrical troupe then in Washington—to pass members of the captain's family to his theatre.

H. H. MITCHELL, ESQ., Rice, Party: October 27th, 1880.
Please pass two to your entertainment, either at matinee or evening, and oblige,
H. G. EDWARDS, "*Herald*."

At about seven o'clock in the evening Carter and his friend returned to the Ebbitt, where they found a message, which informed Carter that Mr. William L. Scott had arrived, and was occupying parlor 12 at Willard's, where he would be pleased to see him. Carter went at once to Willard's, and upon reaching Mr. Scott's room, he was inquired of, by that gentleman, as to his desires: "What do you want?" said Scott, "money?" "No," responded Carter. "I don't want any money. I have enough," at the same time displaying some bills. "Well, what is it?" asked Scott, "is it place you want?" "No," replied Carter, "I don't want anything. What I am doing, I am doing solely for the benefit of the party."

Mr. Scott was delighted. He had found, in *Carter*, a patriot and a devotee of the Democratic party, who had letters from General Garfield, and had come from Chicago to exhibit them, to "benefit the party" and establish the authorship of a letter, which had been gotten up, almost under Scott's very nose, by a foster child of the National Committee. This satisfied the pure-minded representative of the Democracy of Pennsylvania, and, eagerly, he called for the letters. Carter made answer: that distrusting the gentleman who had called the previous evening he had left the letters, early that morning, with a friend in Georgetown, for safe keeping. "You can get them?" inquired Mr. Scott, to which Carter responded affirmatively. Mr. Scott thereupon ordered a carriage, and placed the same at Mr. Carter's disposal, the better to enable him to procure the letters and return with them as speedily as possible. Carter accepted the carriage, and drove to the Ebbitt House, where he informed the clerk that his friend Andrews was about to leave for the West, and that the bill for both was to be charged to him—Carter—who was not yet ready to depart. This being satisfactory, Mr. Andrews went to their rooms, procured the baggage of both and carried it to the depot. Carter re-entered the carriage, and directed the driver to take him to a variety theatre, the "Comique," situated on the corner of two streets just south of Pennsylvania Avenue, where he got out, directing the driver to await his return. Passing into the building at the front, Carter went immediately out of it on the side street, and walking to the depot joined his friend Andrews, when the two departed for the West, leaving their hotel bills unpaid.

The carriage remained in front of the theatre until midnight, when, hearing nothing from Carter, the driver returned to Willard's and reported where he had been. Mr. Scott paid a carriage bill of seven dollars on the following morning and returned to New York, a sadder, if not a wiser, man.

The whole affair, on Carter's part, was a huge joke of a confidence man, who was "on a lark." Mr. Andrews is, I learn, a man of fair standing, who, unfortunately, is addicted to too much conviviality, when absent from home. He fell in with Carter while in Chicago, and doubtless owes his appearance with him to over much indulgence in stimulants.

Not long after the time of this visit to Washington, Carter came to grief in Chicago, where he was living, like a prince, at one of the largest hotels, having passes on all the railroads and free tickets to all the places of amusement. These were obtained by him upon forged letters, in which he was introduced as Mr. Connery, the managing editor of the *New York Herald*, which gentleman he personated during his brief career in Chicago, after his interview with Mr. Scott of the Democratic National Committee.

Established Facts.

It has now been conclusively established:

I. That General Garfield had neither knowledge of or connection with the Morey letter.

II. That the Morey letter was prepared by persons in the employ of the Democratic National Committee, and the name of General Garfield forged thereto, in the interest of the Democratic party.

III. That the Morey letter and accompanying papers, envelope, etc., were so replete with apparent and intrinsic evidences of fraud and forgery, that no fair minded and honest man could, with the exercise of that care and prudence which the matter demanded, have failed to discover and declare it a forgery.

IV. That neither the handwriting of, nor the signature to, the Morey letter, bore any marked resemblance to the handwriting or signature of General Garfield.

V. That after the denial, by General Garfield, of any knowledge of Henry L. Morey, or of the letter purporting to be signed by him—Garfield—and addressed to said Morey, the Democratic National Committee not only persisted in asserting the letter to be genuine, but, by agents of known doubtful character, resorted to bribery, forgery, false swearing, false personation and perjury in its efforts to sustain the original forgery.

PART THIRD.

THE CONGRESSIONAL RECORDS OF JAMES A. GARFIELD AND ABRAM S. HEWITT, UPON THE SUBJECT OF CHINESE IMMIGRATION.

THE TREATY RELATIONS OF THE UNITED STATES AND CHINA EXPLAINED, AND THE HONORABLE, MANLY AND CONSISTENT COURSE OF GENERAL GARFIELD, IN DEALING WITH THE CHINESE PROBLEM, CLEARLY SET FORTH.

THE DECEPTIVE CHARACTER OF MR. HEWITT'S CHARGES AGAINST GENERAL GARFIELD SHOWN, HIS HYPOCRISY EXPOSED, AND HIS VERY QUESTIONABLE AND EVER CHANGING POSITION ON THE CHINESE QUESTION MADE PUBLIC.

THE TREATY RELATIONS OF THE UNITED STATES AND CHINA PRIOR TO 1868.

The first "treaty or general convention of peace, amity and commerce" between the United States and China was concluded July 3d, 1844, the second on June 18th, 1858, and the third in November of the same year. These treaties simply named the ports which should be open to American trade and be places of residence for American merchants, and prescribed rules for the regulation of our commercial relations with such open ports.

Such were the provisions of the treaties between the United States and China prior to 1868.

In November, 1862, General James A. Garfield was chosen to represent the Nineteenth Congressional District of the State of Ohio, in the Thirty-eighth Congress of the United States, and as such Representative took his seat in the National House of Representatives at the first session of that Congress in December, 1863. He was re-elected to a seat in that body at each election thereafter, down to and including the election in November, 1879, for members of the Forty-sixth Congress, and in January, 1880, while serving his ninth consecutive term as a Representative, was unanimously chosen a Senator of the United States from the State of Ohio, for the full term of six years, from March 4th, 1881.

In the year 1868 the Hon. Anson G. Burlingame visited the United States at the head of a Chinese embassy. The purpose of the visit was to extend and cement the friendly relations of China and the United States, and the entire country welcomed the visitors. Indeed, by none of the American people was a heartier reception extended to the embassy than by the residents of the Pacific coast, which, by reason of its closer proximity to China, had received, and almost wholly retained, such immigrants from China as had reached our shores.

On June 6th, 1868, on motion of the Hon. Fernando Wood (Democratic member from the city of New York), the National House of Representatives directed its Speaker, the Hon. Schuyler Colfax, "to extend to the embassy * * * a public reception in this Hall, at such time as may be convenient to the embassy and the public business." Such invitation was given and accepted for June 9th, at which time and place Mr. Burlingame and his associates were received and welcomed by the Speaker, Mr. Burlingame responding on behalf of the embassy.

The result of this visit of the representatives of China, of the interchange of courtesies which followed it, and of the welcome and hospitality extended the embassy, alike by the representatives of the American nation and by the people, led to the preparation and submission of a new treaty between China and the United States, the "additional articles" being signed July 28th, 1868, the ratifications being exchanged at Pekin, November 23d, 1869, and the treaty being officially promulgated in 1870.

Its provisions were such as then especially commended it to the favorable consideration of our government and its citizens, and its ratification was hailed throughout the United States, with manifestations of popular approval. No section of the country, no portion of the community, and no political or semi-political organization, made any objections thereto. On the contrary, its ratification was, universally, regarded as a brilliant achievement which would result in opening to us, as a nation, many avenues for the extension of our commercial relations, while affording our citizens, resident in China, much more freedom of movement and much greater protection than they had theretofore enjoyed.

THE CHARGES OF MR. ABRAM S. HEWITT AGAINST GENERAL GARFIELD OF FAVORING UNLIMITED CHINESE IMMIGRATION AND THE EMPLOYMENT OF CHINESE CHEAP LABOR.

When the tide of popular indignation—after the denial of General Garfield of all knowledge of the Morey letter and after the exposures made during the Philp examination—became so strong as to threaten to engulf the prominent members of the Democratic National Committee, Mr. Abram S. Hewitt stepped again to the front, and, with loud protestations of innocence of purpose, declared that he and his friends had been led into accepting and believing the letter genuine, because it *harmonized with the views of General Garfield upon the subject of Chinese immigration and labor, as shown by his speeches and votes in Congress.*

Mr. Hewitt was—so far as the public is possessed of any knowledge of the matter—the father of this statement, and he took great pains, and much apparent delight, in reiterating it upon every possible occasion. Indeed, he finally induced his fellow members of the National Committee to adopt it as a justification of their conduct in respect to the Morey letter, and to officially promulgate it as a charge against General Garfield.

The statements so made by Mr. Hewitt were untrue and deceptive, and could but have been known to him so to be when he started them, circulated them, and, by his incessant repetitions thereof, induced others to accept and believe them.

What follows will show with what pertinacity and affection Mr. Hewitt clung to this child of his imagination and partisanship.

I. In a speech delivered by Mr. Abram S. Hewitt at Chickering Hall, in the city of New York, on the evening of Wednesday, October 20th, 1880, the day the Morey letter first appeared in *Truth*, he said:

"It [the Morey letter] *expressed his* [Garfield's] *sentiments* on the Chinese Question *exactly.*"

II. In a speech delivered by Mr. Hewitt at Rochester, New York, on October 25th, 1880, he said:

"I thought I knew General Garfield's views on the Chinese question, but in the examination of that original [Morey] letter I found my knowledge confirmed."

III. In an interview had with Mr. Hewitt by a correspondent of the *New York Herald* on October 26th, 1880, that gentleman, in speaking of the Morey letter, gave as one of his reasons for asserting it to be a genuine letter of General Garfield's, the following:

"To say nothing of the corroboration to be found in General Garfield's record as to the sentiments of the letter."

IV. On Friday, October 29th, at a meeting held at Terrace Garden, in the city of New York, Mr. Hewitt was present, but, owing to a cold, could not speak, as had been his intention. His *prepared* speech was therefore read to those present, and was printed in the *World* of the following morning. In that prepared and studied address, Mr. Hewitt said:

"It cannot be denied that its [the Morey letter's] sentiments and declarations *are in full accordance* with the votes of General Garfield."

V. On November 12th, 1880—ten days after the election—the members of the Democratic National Committee held their final meeting. I am informed by a prominent officer of the Committee, who was present at the meeting referred to, that this most remarkable address was then and there written by Mr. Abram S. Hewitt, who presented it for adoption, whereupon it was accepted and directed to be signed and promulgated.

Among the many questionable statements of that address is the following:

"The [Morey] letter *seemed to be* in harmony with General Garfield's views upon the subject [of Chinese immigration and labor] covered by the letter, gathered from public records of undoubted genuineness."

VI. On the 13th of November, 1880, Mr. Hewitt, in a letter to Whitelaw Reid, Esq., wrote:

"There was nothing in its [the Morey letter's] declarations to arouse my suspicions. On the contrary, the sentiments expressed *appeared to be* in harmony with the views of General Garfield prior to his letter of acceptance, when the Morey letter purported to have been written."

VII. On November 24th, 1880—more than three weeks after the election and more than two weeks subsequent to the full exposure of the false character of the letter and the breaking down of the perjured witnesses, Samuel S. Morey, and James O'Brien, *alias* Robert Lindsay—Mr. Hewitt wrote *The Nation* as follows:

"So far as I have knowledge of his [Garfield's] opinions, and especially as tested by his votes, I *supposed* that the [Morey] letter expressed real sentiments."

VIII. Again, in the same letter, Mr. Hewitt said:

"The opinions expressed in the [Morey] letter, as I have already stated, were in entire harmony with the sentiments which I had always *supposed* General Garfield to hold prior to his letter of acceptance, when the Morey letter bore date."

IX. In the very lengthy dispatch of Mr. William H. Barnum, of date October 28th, 1880, which I have heretofore referred to as having been sent various journals, among which was the *Carson* (Nevada) *Appeal*, this accusation of Mr. Hewitt's against General Garfield was repeated in the charge that the Morey letter "expresses more tersely the sentiments of Garfield, as avowed by his speeches and votes in Congress."

X. On November 1st, 1880, Mr. Wm. H. Barnum was interviewed at his home in Connecticut, and a report thereof was telegraphed throughout the country. In that report Mr. Barnum was declared to have said that the "guilt of General Garfield as the author of the [Morey] letter" was "clearly established," and, reiterating Mr. Hewitt's assertions, to have asserted that "the sentiments" thereof were "very distinctly advocated by him in Congress."

GENERAL GARFIELD'S RECORD IN CONGRESS UPON THE QUESTIONS OF CHINESE IMMIGRATION AND CHINESE LABOR.

The only two matters referred to in the Morey letter were Chinese labor an the Burlingame treaty—the latter of which involved the question of Chinese immigration.

The objectionable portion of the Morey letter was its second sentence. viz.: "I take it that the question of employees is only a question of private and corporate economy (?) and individuals or companys (?) have the right to buy labor where they can get it cheapest. I am not prepared to say that it [the Burlingame treaty] should be abrogated until our great manufacturing and corporate interests are conserved in the matter of cheap labor." These expressions subjected their author to the charge of favoring the lowest of wages, and the importation of a species of "coolie" or slave labor, in the interest of capital—"our great manufacturing and corporate interests." These are the expressions which Mr. Hewitt has charged, over and over again, represented the sentiments of General Garfield as shown by his speeches and votes in Congress.

In the honest endeavor to ascertain what Mr. Hewitt had in mind when he so recklessly and vehemently asserted this charge, I have carefully examined more than seventy thousand pages of the records of Congress during the years of General Garfield's service in the House of Representatives. I have read and re-read all the debates in Congress from the date of the promulgation of the Burlingame treaty, down to the time of General Garfield's nomination for President in 1880, and I have found all that he said, and ascertained all that he did, upon the questions of Chinese immigration and Chinese labor.

Having thus examined the record of General Garfield upon these subjects, I assert, in the broadest manner, that nowhere does there appear anything which should have induced any honest or just man to make such an allegation as that which Mr. Hewitt sought to fasten upon General Garfield. His conduct toward, and treatment of, General Garfield, in the matter of the accusations, which he made with such freedom and persistency, may be the better judged when the facts appear.

The Congressional record of General James A. Garfield shows the following to have been his action upon the questions of Chinese immigration and Chinese labor, subsequent to the promulgation of the Burlingame treaty.

He permitted the introduction and reference of almost numberless bills and resolutions upon these subjects, at times when a single objection would have prevented such introduction and reference.

He voted for the appointment of the Joint Committee of Congress to investigate these subjects, and for the printing of the testimony taken and the report made by that committee.

He concurred, on June 17th, 1878, in the adoption of a resolution that the provisions of the Burlingame treaty might "wisely be modified so as to subserve the best interests of both governments, and the attention of the executive is respectfully invited to the subject."

He voted in April and May, 1880, for appropriations for the compensation and necessary expenses of certain commissioners who had just previously been appointed by the President and confirmed by the Senate, "to act with the Envoy Extraordinary and Minister Plenipotentiary of the United States to China, to negotiate and conclude, by treaty, a settlement of such matters of interest to the two governments," then pending between the same, as might "be confided to said Envoy and said Commissioners"—meaning thereby, among other questions at issue, the subject of Chinese immigration.

There certainly was no favor shown in these official acts toward Chinese interests or Chinese labor, while General Garfield's personal views upon the Chinese question, as expressed in private conversations, were equally as free from any suspicion of friendliness toward the unrestricted immigration of the Chinese.

I am possessed of a letter from a gentleman, well known throughout the country as an intimate friend of General Garfield, in which is given an account of a conversation had with the General upon the subjects here being considered, prior to his nomination at Chicago. The writer says:

"I may be pardoned for adding an item respecting General Garfield's sentiments on the Chinese question. I distinctly remember his using this illustration. He said the unlimited immigration of the Chinese was defended on the grounds of universal brotherhood and philanthropy—our duty to those people as brothers of our race. He said, we doubtless owed duties to them, but we also owed duties to ourselves. Then—and I give you almost his exact words—'I owe duties to my vicious neighbors, but if I know that by allowing their children to come into my door-yard and play with my children, there is danger that they will deprave my children and cause quarrels, in which all may be hurt and some killed, it is not one of my duties to those vicious children to allow them to come into my door-yard. My greater duty to my own forbids it. So, as a nation, it is not our duty to admit the Chinese if they will degrade our own people, or create serious strife among us, or between us and them.'

"I know from much conversation with him on the subject, that the above fairly represents General Garfield's feeling on this subject, and, therefore, that the Morey letter, in addition to being a forgery, was a gross misrepresentation of his sentiments."

That the writer of the above letter is correct in the statement that such were General Garfield's opinions, there can be no manner of doubt, and his account of his conversation with General Garfield finds unusual corroboration, if any was necessary, in a speech delivered by the General on June 4th, 1878, in the House of Representatives, upon the tariff—a subject which involved the entire question of protection to American labor. Mr. John R. Tucker, a Democratic member of Congress from Virginia, had on the eighth of the previous month, advocated the adoption, by the United States, of a free trade policy. In his remarks he had taken the precise position which General Garfield, in the conversation above reported, declared to be the standing ground of those who defended the unrestricted immigration of the Chinese, to wit, "the universal brotherhood of man."

Mr. Tucker had said :

"Commerce, Mr. Chairman, links all mankind in one common brotherhood of mutual dependence and interests, and thus creates that unity of our race which makes the resources of all the property of each and every member. We cannot, if we would, and should not, if we could, remain isolated and alone. Men, under the benign influence of Christianity, yearn for intercourse, for the interchange of thought and the products of thought, as a means of a common progress toward a nobler civilization.

"Mr. Chairman, I cannot believe this [the tariff system] is according to the Divine plan. Christianity bids us seek, in communion with our brethren of every race and clime, the blessings they can afford us, and to bestow, in return, upon them, those with which our new continent is destined to fill the world."

General Garfield, in reply, said:

"This, I admit, is a grand conception, a beautiful vision of the time when all the nations shall dwell in peace, when all will be, as it were, one nation, each furnishing to the others what they cannot profitably produce, and all working harmoniously together in the millennium of peace. If all the kingdoms of the world should become the kingdom of the Prince of Peace, then, I admit, that universal free trade ought to prevail. But that blessed era is yet too remote to be made the basis of the practical legislation of to-day. We are not yet members of 'The Parliament of Man, the Federation of the World.' For the present, the world is divided into separate nationalities, and that other Divine command still applies to our situation, 'He that provideth not for his own household has denied the faith, and is worse than an infidel,' and until that better era arrives, patriotism must supply the place of universal brotherhood.

"For the present, Gortchakoff can do more good to the world by taking care of Russia. The great Bismarck can accomplish more for his era by being, as he is, German to the core, and promoting the welfare of the German Empire. Let Beaconsfield take care of England, and McMahon of France, and let Americans devote themselves to the welfare of America. When each does his best for his own nation, to promote prosperity, justice and peace, all will have done more for the world, than if all had attempted to be cosmopolitans, rather than patriots." [Applause.]

We have now seen the affirmative record of General Garfield upon the Chinese question. To nothing therein contained did Mr. Hewitt's charges have reference or application. To what, then, did he allude? Let us see.

During all the bitter attacks made upon General Garfield in the campaign of 1880, but two of his acts or votes were mentioned as supporting Mr. Hewitt's assertions. They were:

First. His vote, in 1874, against an amendment proposed by Mr. Luttrell, of California, to an appropriation bill.

Second. His vote, in 1879, against the bill to restrict Chinese immigration.

The publication, during the campaign, of each of these acts or votes of General Garfield, emanated from the Democratic National Committee. That in respect to the first came about as follows :

The "Democratic Campaign Text Book," of 1880, published by the National Committee, devoted two hundred (200) pages to General Garfield. Every possible speech, action and vote, which, by any stretch of the imagination, could be tortured into an allegation or charge against him was there treated of, but nowhere—not even under the head of "Chinese Immigration"—was there a word with respect to this vote or any claim that it had the least bearing upon General Garfield's record on the Chinese question. In fact it had no such bearing, and it was not until some days after the publication both of the Morey letter and of Mr. Hewitt's repeated assertions of his claims respecting General Garfield's record, that the vote in question was anywhere referred to in the canvass. When it was thought necessary to support Mr. Hewitt's allegations, an editorial was prepared by the National Committee, and sent to, the party press, in which it was claimed that this vote of General Garfield's was evidence of his favoring Chinese as against American labor.

Let us now ascertain the facts respecting General Garfield's vote on the proposed Luttrell amendment.

In the year 1874, General Garfield was Chairman of the Committee on Appropriations, and had charge, in the House of Representatives, of the Sundry Civil, or as it is sometimes termed the Miscellaneous Appropriation bill. The rules prohibited the attaching to appropriation bills of new legislation, unless it was such as would reduce existing expenditures. This made it the *duty*, as well as the right, of the gentleman in charge of an appropriation bill, on its way through the House, to object to any amendment which might be offered thereto, whenever he believed such amendment would, if adopted, change existing laws. Such objection brought the matter directly before the Chairman of the Committee of the Whole, at the moment of the offering of the amendment, and the ruling of that gentleman, subject only to a vote in the Committee, if called for, or to a subsequent vote in the House, if the same was demanded, was final.

From the 11th to the 15th of June, 1874, the House passed most of its time in Committee of the Whole engaged in the consideration of the Sundry Civil Appropriation bill. During such time various amendments were offered. To most of them, General Garfield objected and made the point of order that the changes, thereby proposed, were in the nature of "new legislation." In each instance his point of order was sustained by the Chair and acquiesced in by the Committee and the House, or the amendment proposed was defeated by the House in Committee of the Whole.

On June 13th, the following item in the bill was reached :

"For the Navy Yard at Mare Island, California, for continuation of begun work, $250,000."

This sum it was necessary to appropriate, to provide for the payment of so much of certain work at Mare Island, then being done *under a contract* between the United States and one Murphy, as should be completed during the ensuing fiscal year. Mr. Murphy had been the lowest bidder for the work, the plans and specifications of which had been prepared and duly advertised, and proposals requested. After obtaining the contract, Murphy proceeded to employ Chinese laborers to do the work required thereunder. This excited the ire of two constituents of Mr. J. K. Luttrell, a Democratic member of the House from California, and they telegraphed him that white men could be had and that much feeling existed, and requested him to see the Department. The occasion presented Mr. Luttrell an opportunity to make for himself a spurious record upon the subject of Chinese labor, in a matter where no amendment could, by any possibility, effect a remedy. He therefore sought to amend the item, by a *proviso* under which the money appropriated would not be available to pay for the work done, if Chinese labor was employed.

It was simply an attempt to force a contractor with the Government, to do that which the Government had neither the right nor the power to compel him to do, and as to which it had no concern, under a threat of withholding from him that compensation for his work which it had solemnly agreed to pay him. It was a proposition which was inherently dishonest and dishonorable.

Aside from that, it was, as General Garfield believed, an amendment which could not, under the rules, be properly made to an appropriation bill, and for that reason, when it was offered, he objected to it and raised the point of order that it changed existing law.

Debate ensued, during which the facts respecting the letting of the contract were made clear and Mr. Luttrell was forced to read the telegram he had received. His amendment was then voted down, as it unquestionably should have been, and this without even a demand for the ayes and noes. No record, therefore, exists as to how any individual member voted, and nothing is known with respect thereto. It may, however, be assumed that General Garfield voted to sustain the point of order, which, both as a matter of right and duty, he raised. If this be the fact, neither his objection nor his vote furnishes the slightest indication as to his opinion upon the question of the employment of Chinese labor. The amendment was not offered in good faith, as the record shows, for, if adopted, it could neither have caused the discharge of a single Chinese laborer, nor the substitution in his place of a white man. The character and color of those employed upon the work were wholly matters for the contractor to pass upon. Congress had absolutely no power in the premises, and a vote for the amendment was simply a vote to hoodwink and deceive the white laborer.

Mr. Hewitt was not then a member of Congress, but it may well be doubted whether, if he had been, he would have voted in the affirmative upon that amendment, in the face of the facts disclosed in the debate, to wit: that the Government had let, to an individual, a contract for certain work at the Mare Island navy yard, and, neither legally nor morally, had any right to say who such contractor should employ, or what wages his employés should receive. But, be that as it may, the question that General Garfield was first bound to consider when the amendment was offered, was, whether, in his opinion, the same was new legislation. If he believed it so to be, it was his sworn duty to object to it and oppose it in every parliamentary manner. This he did, and his so acting can in no degree, however slight, be regarded as a criterion of his individual views upon the subject of the employment of Chinese labor.

If Mr. Hewitt does not consider this proposition as self-evident, he must face the reverse thereof, and declare that if a member of Congress, although required by law and the rules of the House to object to certain methods of legislation, makes such objection, that fact is evidence of his opposition to the subject matter of the proposed legislation. Let us see how that would operate in his own case.

Mr. Abram S. Hewitt was a member of the Forty-fifth Congress, and served upon the Committee on Appropriations. During the Second Session of that Congress, he had charge of the same appropriation bill—the Sundry Civil—as General Garfield had when Mr. Luttrell offered the amendment hereinbefore referred to.

When the bill was before the House, in Committee of the Whole, various members offered one or more amendments thereto, to each of which Mr. Hewitt raised the point of order that it was "new legislation" or "not germane to the purposes of the bill." Some of the amendments were of importance, as, for instance, that of General White, of Pennsylvania, who, under instructions from the Committee on Military Affairs, and at the instigation of the Chief of Ordnance, offered an amendment to the Revised Statutes, raising the annual appropriation for providing arms and equipments to the militia of the several States from $200,000 to $500,000. Mr. Hewitt objected to it as "new legislation," the appropriation made by the Revised Statutes being a "permanent appropriation," while the amendment would make it an "annual" one.

Did Mr. Hewitt's objecting to the amendment leave him open to the accusation, or even the suspicion, of being opposed to the appropriation of monies for the maintenance and equipment of the militia of the several States? Clearly not; and no one would more clearly recognize the absurdity, and more severely feel the injustice of such a charge, if made, than Mr. Hewitt himself.

Mr. Hewitt had therefore no right, morally or otherwise, to base any assertions, or entertain any "thoughts," "opinions," or "suppositions," as to General Garfield's "views," or "sentiments," respecting Chinese labor or Chinese immigration, upon his—Garfield's—action on the proposition contained in the Luttrell amendment. It formed no part of General Garfield's record upon the subject of the immigration of the Chinese to the United States, or their employment when here, for the reason that the proposed amendment, if adopted, could have affected neither the one question nor the other.

I come now to the consideration of matters connected with the action of General Garfield upon the Chinese bill. The claim that his course upon that measure showed his hostility to American as against Chinese labor *was* made in the "Campaign Text Book," and the bill itself, unquestionably, involved the subjects treated of in the Morey letter. Every other vote of General Garfield's has been conclusively shown to have involved no hostility to the restriction of Chinese Immigration, and no predilection for Chinese labor. The only remaining question, therefore, is, was the claim made in respect to the Chinese bill an honest one, based upon facts, and was Mr. Hewitt justified in grounding thereon his allegations and charges? This necessitates my showing not only what position was assumed and what action was taken by GENERAL JAMES A. GARFIELD with respect to the Chinese bill, but by MR. ABRAM S. HEWITT as well. The facts are as follows :

The Joint Committee which had been appointed to investigate the Chinese question, visited California, during the summer of 1876, and devoted weeks to a thorough investigation of the subject. The testimony taken by the Committee was very voluminous and covered almost every phase of the respective questions involved in the subjects referred to it.

Its report, submitted to the House by Mr. Piper, of California, on the 28th of February, 1877, was temperate in tone and fair in its recommendations, and was received and adopted without objection. It recognized the fact that the labor of the Chinese had been of great benefit to the people and interests of the Pacific coast, in the following statement:

"In the opinion of the Committee it may be said that the resources of California and the Pacific coast have been more rapidly developed with the cheap and docile labor of Chinese than they would have been without this element. So far as national prosperity is concerned, it cannot be doubted that the Pacific coast has been a great gainer."

The report then reviewed the evidence, showing the objections to the continued influx of the Chinese, which were, that by their manner of living they endangered the health of the city; by their vices they corrupted the morals of the youth; by their willingness to work for low wages they created a lack of employment for the whites and tended to degrade white laborers "to the abject condition of a servile class," while, by their increasing numbers, they retarded white immigration to the Pacific States; that they were alien in feelings and ideas to our form of government, and possessed neither knowledge of, nor appreciation for, it, and were therefore a "menace to republican institutions and Christian civilization." The conclusion of the Committee was as follows :

"This problem is too important to be treated with indifference. Congress should solve it, *having due regard to any rights already accrued under existing treaties and to humanity.*" Its recommendations were as follows: "The Committee recommend that measures be taken by the Executive, looking toward *a modification of the existing* treaty with China, confining it to strictly commercial purposes; and that Congress legislate to restrain the great influx of Asiatics to this country. It is not believed that either of these measures would be looked upon with disfavor by the Chinese government."

At the time of the presentation of the report to the House, Mr. Edwin R. Meade, a member of the Committee and a Democratic representative from the City of New York, obtained leave to print some remarks upon the subjects covered by the investigation. In that speech, Mr. Meade, speaking of Chinese immigration, said :

"The aspect of this subject which is most considered by the public is its relations to labor; and it is not improbable that something of the proverbial hostility between labor and capital has served here to magnify its importance." He then referred to the past usefulness of the Chinese and their labor to the Pacific Coast, but expressed the belief that "the equilibrium of demand and supply has been reached, and that, in the near future, the latter may exceed the former." With respect to the future policy of the country upon the subject, Mr. Meade said: "But while it is obvious that measures should be adopted restricting this growing coolie immigration, *a wise policy suggests due consideration and regard for existing treaty obligations with China.*"

On the 17th of June, 1878, the House of Representatives, by unanimous consent, and without debate, adopted the concurrent Resolution given herein on page 108.

It cannot fail to be observed, that in passing that concurrent Resolution, Congress in an eminently proper and orderly manner, alike compatible with the demands of a large portion of the inhabitants of the Pacific coast, and with the interests and honor of the Nation, was proceeding, with almost entire unanimity, to bring to a successful and equitable settlement the question of Chinese immigration.

On the 14th of January, 1878, Mr. Wren (Republican), of Nevada, introduced in the House of Representatives, a bill to restrict the immigration of Chinese. That body was then Democratic by a majority of nineteen, and Mr. Samuel J. Randall was its Speaker. The Committee on Education and Labor, to which it was referred, did nothing as to the bill during the session of that year. The Third Session of the Forty-fifth Congress began in December, 1878. Early in 1879 it seems to have occurred to the Democrats that, as a President was to be chosen in the following year, such action might be taken upon the Chinese bill as would accrue to their advantage as a party, and secure for them the electoral votes of the Pacific coast States in 1880. At once, the bill which had lain for a year in the committee, was reported back to the House with certain amendments.

Down to the time when this action was taken upon Mr. Wren's bill no partisan spirit had been manifested, in either branch of Congress, upon the subjects of Chinese immigration or Chinese labor. In both Houses, the resolutions for the appointment of the Joint Select Committee of Investigation had passed by a vote almost unanimous, and the same was true of the concurrent resolution calling the attention of the President to the subject of Chinese immigration and suggesting modifications in the provisions of the existing treaty.

The motives which operated upon the minds of the majority of the Committee on Education and Labor when reporting the bill back to the House on the 14th of January, 1879—one year to a day from the time the bill was referred to the Committee—were suspended, though the Democrats did not, for the moment, openly avow them. Their purposes soon, however, became clearly apparent when it was learned that a caucus of the Democratic members of the House had considered the bill and resolved upon forcing its passage, while the majority of the Committee reporting it had instructed its chairman not to permit the bill to be amended in the House.

The Republicans in Congress made no effort, either by caucus or otherwise, to oppose action upon the bill, although they believed it neither wise nor honorable to take such action as was proposed, pending the result of the correspondence then being carried on between our government and that of China.

In other words, the Republicans, as a party, stood by the report of the Joint Select Committee which had investigated the subject, declared that it should be solved by Congress, with a "*due regard to any rights accrued under existing treaties and to humanity,*" and recommended, as the thing to be first done, that "measures be taken by the Executive looking toward a modification of the existing treaty with China."

On January 28th, 1879, Mr. Willis, of Kentucky, called up the bill, and announced that, under instructions from his Committee, he should endeavor to pass the measure as it came from that body and without amendment.

Mr. Conger (Republican, of Michigan) stated that there were many Republicans who favored the passage of the bill if it could be somewhat amended, and they allowed to discuss it. Mr. Samuel S. Cox (Democrat, of New York) objected to debate, whereupon Mr. Page, of California—a Republican, and an earnest advocate of the bill—declared the course of the majority to be unfair and unexpected, and charged—without any denial thereof being made—that the Democrats had made the bill "the subject of a caucus," while the Republicans had been allowed "no opportunity to consider it at all."

Mr. Willis then demanded the previous question, which was seconded by a rising vote—Ayes, 116; Noes, 33; the yeas and nays not being called for.

Various efforts were then made to obtain unanimous consent to the following amendments. By Mr. Cannon (Republican, of Illinois) to have "travelers and diplomatic representatives coming to the United States, or passing through our territory, or students visiting the United States for the purposes of education," excepted from the provisions of the bill; by Mr. Conger (Republican, of Michigan) to permit "of the arrival on the coast of the United States of Chinese embassies or Chinese officers"; also to exempt from the provisions of the bill "ministers and their suites from China"; also to exempt from the prohibitions of the act any "shipwrecked Chinese" who, having been "cast away on the islands of the Pacific," should have been rescued, and to permit the vessel taking them on board, to bring them to and land them "at the first port" at which it should "arrive on our coast."

To each of these several amendments, Mr. Luttrell (Democrat, of California) objected, and thus prevented their consideration.

The subsequent proceedings are shown by the record to have been as follows:

"THE SPEAKER. The question is now on the engrossment and third reading of the bill as amended.

MR. GARFIELD. I ask unanimous consent, Mr. Speaker, to offer an amendment that this bill shall not take effect *until due notice has been given to China, according to the usages of international law,* of the termination of the treaty against which it is a palpable and flat violation.

THE SPEAKER. That is in the nature of debate.

MR. GARFIELD. My amendment will be received unless this bill is merely for party capital.

MR. COX, of New York. I object, unless I have a chance to answer the gentleman from Ohio."

The bill was then ordered to be engrossed and read a third time. It had its third reading, and the previous question on its passage was demanded, seconded and ordered, when Mr. Cox, of New York, and Mr. Conger, of Michigan, each called for the yeas and nays, which were ordered. The vote was then taken and the bill passed—Yeas, 155; Nays, 72; Absent or Not Voting, 61.

General Garfield was one of those who did not vote, although present. The bill as reported from the Committee, was far from satisfactory to him and to many others in the House, and the refusal of the majority of the House to allow any amendments thereto, even those of a humanitarian character, strengthened the feeling of dissent from the proposed measure. General Garfield was willing to vote for a bill which, while it contained restraining provisions against the unlimited immigration of Chinese, should recognize at least the moral right of China, as a party to treaties with this country, to be justly and fairly treated by the United States, and therefore it was, that, at the last moment, he asked unanimous consent to so amend the bill as that it should not take effect until China had received, "in accordance with the usages of international law," that "due notice" of the proposed abrogation of certain articles of the Burlingame treaty, to which, as a friendly nation, it was honorably entitled.

When this proposition was refused *even consideration*, General Garfield, still loth to say that no bill should be passed and yet desirous of not doing an unjust act, refrained from voting, believing the Senate would so amend the bill as that it might yet receive his approval.

Mr. Abram S. Hewitt voted for the bill, in the face of its gross imperfections and its unjust and dishonorable treatment of a friendly nation.

Eighteen Democratic members refrained from voting, while the following named Democrats voted "No" on the passage of the bill:

Messrs. Bragg and Bouck, of Wisconsin, Candler, of Georgia, Cutler and Hardenbergh, of New Jersey, Hart, of New York, Franklin, of Missouri, Robbins and Waddell, of North Carolina, Pridemore, of Virginia, Phelps and Warner, of Connecticut, Governor Swann, of Maryland, and James Williams, of Delaware. Benjamin A. Willis, of New York, was paired, but the announcement was made on the floor of the House that if present he would have voted "No."

The bill was received in the Senate on the day following its passage by the House, to wit: on January 29th, 1879, and was referred to the Committee on Foreign Affairs, from whence it was reported back, on February 7th, with a request that the Committee be discharged from its further consideration. One week later, February 13th, 1879, the bill was taken up by the Senate in Committee of the Whole. In the course of the debate which ensued, Senator Morgan (Democrat), of Alabama, stated that he should vote for the measure, but said:

"I admit, frankly, that I would much prefer a candid presentation of this question to China, through our State Department. We owe this much to China, as one of the treaty powers, in the way of courtesy, and we owe it to ourselves that we should not lightly, or in an abrupt manner, break a treaty by Act of Congress, or place upon it a narrow construction, at least until we have tried to amend it by agreement with China."

Senator Stanley Matthews (Republican), of Ohio, declared that he could not vote for the bill. He said:

"My respect for the sanctity of the plighted faith of the nation in a solemn treaty with a sovereign power," compels "me to seek some other method of securing these results than this arbitrary act of legislation."

On the following day, February 14th, 1879, the bill was further debated, and substantially all of the amendments which were refused consideration in the House—save the one offered by General Garfield—were adopted.

The measure was much improved by the Senate amendments, but was yet unsatisfactory to most of the great lawyers of that body, who, without regard to party ties, were united in the expression of their belief that the action proposed to be taken by the passage of the bill was impolitic, discourteous, unprecedented and unwarranted. As expressing their views, Senator Stanley Matthews (Republican), of Ohio, offered an amendment as a substitute for the pending bill, but Senator Conkling (Republican), of New York, having also prepared an amendment which he offered as a substitute for that of Senator Matthews, the latter accepted the Conkling amendment and withdrew his own in favor thereof.

In offering his amendment as a substitute for the pending measure, Senator Conkling referred to the bill under discussion as being "excessive, egregious, abrupt and unwarranted" in its character, but declared himself as willing

"to do that permitted by the Constitution; permitted by the comity of nations, and permitted by civilized usages between nationalities, to accomplish the whole purpose which the good of the people of the western coast demands."

The motion of Mr. Conkling, summarized, was to strike out all after enacting clause of the bill, and to insert a provision requesting the President "to immediately give notice to the Emperor of China, that so much of the existing treaty between" the two countries as permitted "the migration of subjects of the Chinese empire and their domicile in this country," was "unsatisfactory to the Government of the United States, and in its judgment pernicious, and to propose such modifications" in a new or supplemental treaty, to be submitted before January 1st, 1880, as would correct the evils complained of. In case China refused or omitted "to agree, by change of the existing treaty, to such modification, then the President of the United States was authorized to inform the Emperor of China that the United States" would, "by laws of its own, regulate or prevent the migration or importation to its shores of the subjects of China, and after the first of January, 1880," would "treat the obnoxious stipulations as at an end."

This substitute for the pending bill was wise, sound and honorable, and most tersely stated the views entertained, not only, by the great mass of Republican voters, but, by a majority of the conservative, thoughtful and fair-minded men of the country, without regard to party proclivities. It was what General Garfield *desired*, and what in the moment he took in the House, under objection, he *aimed to give expression to*. Several Senators spoke in favor of the proposed substitute. Senator Howe (Republican, of Wisconsin) said:

"Mr. President, if it be the pleasure of the Senate to abrogate a solemn international compact, both sides of which were negotiated by distinguished American citizens, without even asking the other party to that compact to consent to such modifications of it as will render it less obnoxious to us, I shall have but one word to say against doing that, and that word is 'No.'"

Senator Hamlin (Republican), of Maine, said:

"I am not willing to apply that remedy of might which subverts the remedy of right."

Senator David Davis (Independent), of Illinois, said:

"I would treat the Chinese Government as I would treat the British Government or the French Government, or any other civilized and Christian government in the world."

Senator Merrimon (Democrat), of North Carolina, said:

"I shall vote against this measure [the House bill] upon the ground that in my judgment, with all respect and toleration for those who think otherwise, it is an arbitrary invasion of the treaty rights of China, and a repudiation of the faith and honor of the country. * * * We ought to exhaust negotiation first."

Senator McMillan (Republican), of Minnesota, said :

"No nation has a right to do an act which violates a treaty which would not be justifiable in morals before the world."

Senator Wadleigh (Republican), of New Hampshire, said :

"I am opposed to this bill, in the first place, because it seems to me that it is a violation of the good faith of this nation and of this Government."

Senator Ingalls (Republican), of Kansas, said :

"Being compelled by the action of the Committee of the Whole to choose between a constitutional modification of an existing treaty and what I believe to be a flagrant act of national perfidy and dishonor, I prefer the former, and shall therefore vote for the amendment."

Senator Maxey (Democrat, of Texas), said :

"I am unwilling to set aside all the precedents known among the civilized nations of the earth so far back as the histories of treaties sheds light on the question,"

and declared that he should vote for the amendment of Senator Conkling.

Senator Edmunds (Republican), of Vermont, said:

"Before this bill passes, I wish to express my utter abhorrence of the principle that the bill is founded upon, which is, that, without negotiation, without notice, without any step that the fair and honest comity which should exist among nations, would require to be taken, we take a step of this kind, and undertake to abrogate, by legislation, a provision of a treaty with a friendly power."

Senator Eustis (Democrat), of Louisiana, said he should vote for the bill, but added:

"I believe the arguments which have been urged against its passage are overwhelming, except upon a single point, and that is the race question."

A vote being taken upon the proposed substitute of Senator Conkling, the same was lost : Yeas, 31 ; nays, 34 ; absent or not voting, 10.

Subsequently Mr. Conkling renewed the motion to substitute his amendment for the pending bill, Senator Henry G. Davis, of West Virginia, who was absent when the vote was previously taken, having entered the Senate Chamber. The motion was again lost, the majority against it being, however, but two.

The following twelve Democratic Senators voted for the substitution of Mr. Conkling's amendment for the House bill. The reader will see that they are the names of those of the strongest and ablest of the representatives of the Democratic party upon the floor of the Senate.

Senators Butler, of South Carolina; Cockrell, of Missouri; Henry G. Davis, of West Virginia; Garland, of Arkansas; Benj. H. Hill, of Georgia; Jones, of Florida; Kernan, of New York; McPherson, of New Jersey; Maxey, of Texas; Merrimon, of North Carolina; Randolph, of New Jersey; and Withers, of Virginia. Senator David Davis, of Illinois, who was classed as an "Independent," also voted for Mr. Conkling's substitute.

Senator Anthony (Republican), of Rhode Island, then moved an amendment, very similar to that of Mr. Conkling's, as a substitute for the pending bill, but the same was lost.

Senator Whyte (Democrat), of Maryland, then took the floor. He stated that he much desired to vote for the bill, but had theretofore refrained from voting on most of the amendments. He then offered an amendment, expressing his own views, and moved to insert the same in lieu of the then seventh section of the bill. Senator Whyte's amendment was very similar in character to that previously offered by Mr. Conkling, save that it was a substitute for a single section of the bill and not for the measure itself. A vote being had thereon, the amendment was rejected.

The bill was then read a third time, when Mr. Sargent and others called for the yeas and nays on its passage. They were ordered, and the bill was passed, yeas, 39 ; nays, 27. Absent or not voting, 9.

The following Democratic members of the Senate voted against the bill :

Butler, of South Carolina; Davis, of West Virginia; Hill, of Georgia; Jones, of Florida; Kernan, of New York; Merrimon, of North Carolina; Randolph, of New Jersey; and Withers, of Virginia. Senator David Davis (Independent), of Virginia, also voted against the measure.

Senators Barnum, of Connecticut, Harris, of Tennessee, and Johnston, of Virginia (all Democrats), seem to have been absent from the Senate when the vote was taken, and were not recorded. Senator Barnum, alone of the three, was paired on the bill, and, if present, would have voted for it.

Senators Saulsbury, of Delaware, Cockrell, of Missouri, and Whyte, of Maryland (all Democrats), were present, but refrained from voting. Of these three, Cockrell voted, in Committee of the Whole, for Conkling's amendment, which would have killed the House bill, and Whyte was, as we have just seen, opposed to the bill, unless it was further amended.

No member of the lower house of Congress was ever so thoroughly sustained and vindicated, in any position, upon a public measure, as was James A. Garfield, in the stand he took upon the Chinese bill, by the debate and votes had in the Senate. The entire discussion in that body turned upon the point which he so boldly and briefly enunciated, to wit: that the bill, as it stood, was "a palpable and flat violation" of the solemn obligations of a treaty, and was being enacted without that due notice to China which "the usages of international law" required. His position was not only upheld by the majority of his party associates in the Senate, but by nearly one-half of the entire Democratic membership of that body, who gave expression—either by direct statements or by their votes—to their preferences for such a course of procedure being adopted as General Garfield had outlined.

Who, then, would not rather have been James A. Garfield, when the Chinese bill was returned to the House, than Abram S. Hewitt? The *former*, had nothing to regret in his action and naught to explain, while the debates and votes in the Senate had, necessarily, greatly strengthened and fortified him. The *latter* was at a loss to know where he stood, what were his views, or what should be his future action.

The amended bill reached the House on February 22d, 1879, when Mr. Willis (Democrat, of Kentucky) moved to concur in the amendments of the Senate, and upon that motion called the previous question.

General Garfield then gave notice that he reserved " the right to call for separate votes on the amendments."

A motion having been made to adjourn, the same was voted down, ayes, 61; noes, 113. The previous question was then seconded, the main question was ordered, the vote by which the main question was ordered was reconsidered, and the motion to reconsider was laid upon the table. General Garfield then called " for a separate vote on each amendment of the Senate," when General Harry White moved to lay the bill and amendments on the table. The yeas and nays were called for and were eventually ordered.

The question upon the motion to lay the bill and Senate amendments upon the table was then taken, and there were: yeas, 95; nays, 140; absent or not voting, 55.

General Garfield voted in the affirmative upon this motion to lay the bill and Senate amendments upon the table. So also did the following Democratic members:

Messrs. Bridges and Mackey, of Pennsylvania, Bragg, Bouck and Lynde, of Wisconsin, Candler, Cook, Felton and Henry R. Harris, of Georgia, Franklin and Morgan, of Missouri,

Cutler and Hardenbergh, of New Jersey, John T. Harris and Pridemore, of Virginia, Hart, Fernando Wood and Benjamin A. Willis, of New York, Lander, Phelps and Warner, of Connecticut, Robbins and Waddell, of North Carolina, and James Williams, of Delaware

Mr. Abram S. Hewitt DODGED the vote. He was in the House that day. He voted, as appears by the "Record," *immediately before* the vote upon the Chinese bill, was taken and *immediately thereafter*, and was *not paired* upon that question.

Seventeen other Democratic members of the House, who were neither paired nor absent on leave, refrained from voting.

The amendments of the Senate were then concurred in, and a motion to reconsider the vote by which such concurrence was obtained and to lay that motion on the table, was agreed to.

The ayes and nays were not demanded on the motion to concur in the Senate amendments, the vote to lay the bill and amendments on the table being the vital vote which determined the fate of the measure. If that motion had prevailed, the bill would then and there have died, and that vote Mr. Abram S. Hewitt, as shown by the record, DODGED.

On March 1st, 1879, the President of the United States returned the Chinese bill to the House of Representatives with his objections thereto. His message was a well considered and temperate document, and in referring to the fact that the bill proposed to abruptly abrogate a portion of the last treaty with China, the President said:

"A denunciation of a part of a treaty, not made by the terms of the treaty itself separable from the rest, is a denunciation of the whole treaty. As the other high contracting party has entered into no treaty obligations except such as include the part denounced, the denunciation, by one party, of a part, necessarily liberates the other party from the whole treaty.

"I am convinced that whatever urgency might, in any quarter or by any interest, be supposed to require an instant suppression of further immigration from China, no reasons can require the immediate withdrawal of our treaty protection of the Chinese already in this country, and no circumstance can tolerate an exposure of our citizens in China—merchants or missionaries—to the consequences of so sudden an abrogation of their treaty protections."

The message of the President having been read, the question was: "Will the House, on reconsideration, pass this bill, notwithstanding the objection of the President?" The previous question was moved by Mr. Willis, the yeas and nays were demanded and ordered, and the vote was taken. It resulted, Ayes, 110; Noes, 96; two-thirds not having voted in the affirmative, under the provisions of the Constitution, the bill stood rejected.

General Garfield voted in the negative, and Mr. Abram S. Hewitt, having originally voted *for* the bill, and then having DODGED the vote, which would have laid it on the table, when it came back from the Senate, now squared the circle, and voted, with General Garfield, *against* the bill becoming a law.

The following named other Democratic members of the House voted to sustain the President's veto:

Messrs. Landers, Phelps and Warner, of Connecticut, James Williams, of Delaware, Henry R. Harris and Candler, of Georgia, Morse, of Massachusetts, Cutler and Hardenbergh, of New Jersey, Bliss and Willis, of New York, Waddell, of North Carolina, John T. Harris, and Pridemore, of Virginia, and Wilson, of West Virginia.

Thirty-eight other Democratic members of the House, neither absent on leave, nor paired, refrained from voting to pass the measure over the President's veto.

I have now presented a full summary of the entire public record of James A. Garfield upon all matters which related to, or were in anywise claimed to be connected with the subject of Chinese immigration, between 1870 and the time of his nomination at Chicago, in 1880, for President, save the numberless bills and resolutions which were from time to time offered by unanimous consent and referred to the proper Committees. Of the measures cited, which in fact related to Chinese immigration or Chinese labor, General Garfield voted in favor of all but one—the Chinese bill. As to that, the facts show, beyond a shadow of uncertainty, that he entertained no hostility to a proper regulation or limitation of Chinese immigration, and no predilection for Chinese labor.

His objection to the proposed Chinese bill was to the manner and the mode by which the evils complained of were sought to be remedied, and this objection he frankly avowed and sought to have overcome. His appeal to the House was that the bill might be so amended as that the national honor should not suffer, as it, inevitably, would had the pending bill become a law. He was met on the very threshold of his appeal by a single objection, which, under the rules of the House, prevented him from either continuing his remarks or having his amendment brought before that body. In the hope, and with the expectation, that the Senate would so amend the bill as to surmount his great objection thereto, to wit: that it proposed action on the part of the United States, which was in violation of treaty obligations, without that notice to a friendly nation which the usages of international law demanded, he refrained from voting on the bill. With eagerness and interest he watched the debate and votes in the Senate, and while he had the pleasure and the privilege of seeing his position sustained by the vast majority of the representative men of that body, of both political parties, he observed, with regret and mortification, the efforts there made to incorporate the provisions he deemed so important defeated by a majority of only two votes.

From that moment his course was clear. All his hopes of saving the bill were at an end, and but one thing remained to be attempted, to wit: to prevent, if possible, a concurrence by the House in the Senate amendments and thus to kill the measure. Therefore it was, that on the return of the bill to the House, General Garfield voted in favor of the motion to lay it upon the table, which, if it had prevailed, would have disposed of the measure in its then form. The motion was, however, defeated, and the bill was passed and sent to the President, who shortly returned it to the House with his disapproval, when General Garfield again voted to prevent its becoming a law, by sustaining the veto of the Executive.

From the outset to the close of the contest over this piece of legislation, the efforts and votes of General Garfield were not antagonistic to the purposes of the bill, but solely *to the manner in which it was attempted to accomplish those purposes.* His course was frank and dignified, was in the interests of justice and fair dealing, and was for the protection of the honor of the nation, and the advancement of honesty and amity in international affairs.

What are the facts as to Mr. Abram S. Hewitt? They may be stated thus:

I. With his eyes and ears both open, he endeavored to ruthlessly abrogate the provisions of a solemn international compact or "convention of peace, amity and commerce," by voting for the very crude House bill.

II. Upon the return of the bill to the House, with a few amendments made by the Senate, solely in the interests of humanity and a higher education, and which, as far as they went, greatly bettered the proposed statute, he DODGED the vote which threatened the life of the measure he had openly declared himself to favor.

III. When the bill, having finally passed both Houses of Congress, was returned to the House of Representatives, with the objections of the President thereto, he voted *against* the bill, which he had helped to pass, becoming a law.

General James A. Garfield never voted but one way upon the Chinese bill.

He was against it *in the form in which it was presented*. He so stated. He sought to amend it, and failing, he voted against its becoming a statute.

Mr. Abram S. Hewitt voted both ways and all ways upon the Chinese bill. He was for it, and voted *for it* once; he was then in doubt as to his position, and *dodged* the second vote; he was then opposed to the bill, and voted *against it* the third time it came up. There was no position which a legislator could possibly assume upon a pending measure, which Mr. Abram S. Hewitt did not appropriate to himself upon the Chinese bill, during its travels through the House.

On the eighth day of June, 1880, James A. Garfield was nominated, at Chicago, as the candidate of the Republican party for the office of President of the United States.

In his letter of acceptance, dated July 12th, 1880, General Garfield expressed, at some length, his views upon the subjects of Chinese immigration and labor. He said :

" It is too much like an importation to be welcomed without restriction; too much like an invasion, to be looked upon without solicitude. We cannot consent to allow any form of servile labor to be introduced among us under the guise of immigration. Recognizing the gravity of this subject, the present administration, supported by Congress, has sent to China a commission of distinguished citizens, for the purpose of securing such a modification of the existing treaty as will prevent the evils likely to arise from the present situation. It is confidently believed that these diplomatic negotiations will be successful, without the loss of commercial intercourse between the two powers, which promises a great increase of reciprocal trade, and the enlargement of our markets. Should these efforts fail, it will be the duty of Congress to mitigate the evils already felt, and prevent their increase by such restrictions as, without violence or injustice, will place upon a sure foundation the peace of our communities, and the freedom and dignity of labor."

Here we find the same candor and explicitness which was manifest in the few words General Garfield was able to utter in the House when expressing his desire to amend the Chinese bill. The position which he assumed at that time we find still adhered to in his later utterances. His nomination to the Presidency had worked no change in his views. He stood, in 1880, while a candidate for the highest office in the nation, as he stood, in 1879, on the floor of the House of Representatives, in favor of mitigating the evils incident to the unlimited immigration to this country of the subjects of China, but insisting—upon both occasions—that we were bound to observe our treaty obligations until all reasonable efforts to effect a change therein, by the ordinary and well understood methods of international law and usage, were first found to be of no avail.

It was in the face of these known facts that the Democratic National Committee, of which Mr. Abram S. Hewitt was one of its most prominent, active, influential and responsible members, published and circulated in its "Campaign Text Book," the charge that General Garfield was "Janus-faced" upon the subject of Chinese immigration. Mr. Hewitt charging Garfield with being "Janus-faced" upon the Chinese question, was Philip drunk accusing Philip sober, and General Garfield, when he learned of it, must have been reminded of the remark of Thucydides, when he said : "When I, in wrestling, have thrown Pericles and given him a fall, by persisting that he had no fall he gets the better of me, and makes the bystanders, in spite of their own eyes, believe him."

Nor was this the extent of Mr. Hewitt's offense. It was he, personally, who when the forged Morey letter appeared, went further and said and did more to make the country believe it was a genuine letter, than all other individuals collectively. Not content with merely asserting it genuine, without evidence, and in the face of intrinsic proof in the letter and its surroundings that it was a forgery, Mr. Abram S. Hewitt ran rampant over the State of New

York, shouting himself hoarse in asseverating that the sentiments of the Morey letter were those entertained by General Garfield, as his record would show. This allegation Mr. Hewitt continually repeated, not only long after General Garfield's explicit denial of any knowledge of, or connection with, the Morey letter, and after his declaration that he had never "*entertained*" such views as were therein enunciated, but even after the exposure of its false character. When, by reason of losing his voice, Mr. Hewitt could no longer make himself heard, his frenzy led him to writing the charge in a prepared speech, so that it might be printed; to being interviewed about it; to repeating it in private conversations; and, finally, to writing it in letters to individuals and to the press. Indeed.—after the election; after two perjured witnesses had been broken down upon the witness stand; after it had been conclusively established that the letter had never been sent to Lynn; after every attempt to prove the existence of any "H. L. Morey, of Lynn," had wholly failed, and after many of his party journals, and reputable people generally, without regard to their political proclivities, had become satisfied of its false and forged character—he alone, of those who had examined it at the Democratic headquarters and expressed the opinion that the signature to the letter was that of General Garfield, went upon the witness stand, and, *under oath*, undertook to sustain the letter and defend his course.

What Mr. Hewitt and his associates thought of an individual, who first voted *for* the Chinese bill and then DODGED the critical vote when the matter came before him the second time, I have not been able to ascertain. In respect to Mr. Hewitt's action, when the bill met him full in the face for the third time, I have been more fortunate, and have learned the views both of Mr. Hewitt and his associates as to his vote upon that occasion.

It is not often an individual is able to ascertain the real opinions of his *personal associates*, respecting any one act of his life. Still more rare are the instances in which an individual *unites* with his associates in giving expression, in public, to an opinion respecting one of his own acts. The country is therefore to be congratulated upon the fact, that as to Mr. Hewitt's last vote upon the Chinese bill—which vote was *against* the bill becoming a law—it is able to be put in possession, not only of what Mr. William H. Barnum, Mr. William L. Scott, Mr. Bradley B. Smalley, Mr. Orestes Cleveland, and other members of the Democratic National Committee, thought, in the summer of 1880, respecting it, but also of Mr. Hewitt's own views thereof.

I have the honor to present this morceau:

> "Upon the occasion referred to" (the effort to pass the Chinese bill over the President's veto), Mr. Abram S. Hewitt "voted NAY, thus illustrating his disrespect for the dignity and humanity of American labor, his contempt for the workingmen of his own race, and his willingness to force white American free laborers into competition for their daily bread with a race that knows no God, no morality and no obligations of social decency."

The reader may think this language somewhat strong. I beg him not to arrive at too hasty a judgment in respect thereto. It is the carefully considered and thoroughly matured expression of opinion of the gentlemen I have mentioned. The words within the quotation marks are theirs, not mine, and they were printed in the "Campaign Text Book" prepared, adopted, published and circulated by them. They applied the language to James A. Garfield. I have applied them to Abram S. Hewitt, who voted, "upon the occasion referred to," *in the same way as did General Garfield.*

If there be any who think too much consideration has been given to Mr. Hewitt's position and charges in respect to General Garfield and the Morey letter, they should remember that even the dead require adequate room for burial. In this instance, the subject to be interred was so odious and offensive as to demand particular attention and require more than the usual allotment of space.

PART FOURTH.

A SHORT RÉSUMÉ.

In bringing this narrative to an end, it is not my purpose to review, at any length, the history herein recited.

It seems to me appropriate, however, that I should recall the accountability of those whom the facts show to be responsible for this stupid, brutal and wicked forgery upon General Garfield.

It is a well settled rule of law that individuals, corporations, associations, committees and parties, political or otherwise, are responsible for the acts, either of commission or omission, of their duly selected and properly authorized agents, officers or other representatives, when acting within the scope of their authority. As I view the matter, I am compelled to state the responsibility of the several parties as follows :

I. THE DEMOCRATIC PARTY.

I arraign the Democratic party of the country, which, through its regularly designated channels, named for service upon its National Committee such men as William H. Barnum, William L. Scott and Abram S. Hewitt, Orestes Cleveland and Bradley B. Smalley, who united at least in giving the forgery endorsement, momentary character and wide circulation.

II. THE DEMOCRATIC NATIONAL COMMITTEE.

I arraign the Democratic National Committee :

First.—For placing the control of its affairs in the hands of an Executive and an Advisory Committee, so-called, upon each of which Messrs. Barnum, Scott, Hewitt, Cleveland and Smalley were the most prominent and active members.

Second.—For choosing as its Chairman Mr. William H. Barnum, whose political habits and methods were well known, and were generally recognized as not being of a character such as could command public respect and confidence.

III. MR. ABRAM S. HEWITT.

I arraign Abram S. Hewitt :

First.—For the evident personal gratification that he manifested whenever Mr. Barnum exhibited to him anything, which, if true, was calculated to injuriously affect the personal integrity or character of a political opponent, whatever might be the previous high standing of the gentlemen attacked.

Second.—For his continued and reiterated endorsement of the genuineness of the Morey letter, from the day when it was first shown him—and I fully acquit Mr. Hewitt of any knowledge of the letter previous to being shown it by Mr. Hart—down to the time of his leaving the witness stand, in the face of the non-existence of a single corroborative fact, with a full knowledge, during most of that time, of General Garfield's denial of its authorship ; with the most complete evidence before him, in the letter itself, and in the envelope in which it was claimed to have been mailed, of its fraudulent character; and with the exposure of the forgeries and perjuries by which its genuineness was attempted to be sustained by his own political friends and allies—the Chairman and agents of the Committee of which he was himself a prominent and active member.

Third.—For the grossly unjust and deceitful effort, upon his part, to fix in the public mind, the charge, first publicly made by him, that the sentiments of the Morey letter were in accord with General Garfield's views; and in persisting in the same after General Garfield's denial that he had ever "entertained" such opinions.

If Mr. Hewitt possessed any knowledge, whatever, upon the subject of General Garfield's opinions respecting Chinese immigration or Chinese labor, he knew his sentiments were the reverse of those contained in the Morey letter.

IV. MR. WILLIAM H. BARNUM.

I arraign William H. Barnum:

First.—For his apparent bad faith toward his personal and political friends and associates, in the matter of the presentation of the Morey letter to them, and in allowing them to declare it genuine.

Second.—For the efforts he made to sustain that letter, when, even if it be assumed that he did not *know* it to be a forgery, he could readily have ascertained the fact, and for the ways and means he adopted in his endeavors to "bolster" it up.

Third.—For his generally undignified, unmanly and disreputable management of the Democratic canvass, the level of which, as conducted by him, was upon so low a plane as to attract those who were quite willing to receive the funds he disbursed and perform any work therefor, without the slightest regard to law, order, decency, justice or right.

V. MR. SAMUEL J. RANDALL.

I ARRAIGN SAMUEL J. RANDALL:

For his hasty endorsement of the Morey letter as genuine, by which he added the weight, not only of his name, but of his high official position as the Speaker of the House of Representatives, to sustain this readily discoverable forgery.

Publicly, Mr. Randall refrained from further mention of the subject after the time when the letter was first exhibited to him at the rooms of the Democratic National Committee.

VI. "TRUTH."

Last and least, for it was not until the Democratic party, through its National Committee, its party journals, its representative men—Mr. Barnum, Mr. Hewitt, Mr. Randall, Mr. Cleveland, Mr. Cooper and others—gave the Morey letter endorsement, position and wide circulation, that it even attracted the notice of a single New York morning daily, and then only after it had been printed, *for three days*, in *Truth.*

With respect to *Truth* and its course, the facts seem to be as follows:

The paper was started, late in 1879, by Mr. Joseph Hart, upon a capital of $2,500 in cash. Mr. Hart had no experience as a journalist, and did not assume to act in such capacity, but held himself out, only and solely, as the publisher of the paper. The editor-in-chief, at the starting of the paper and for some time thereafter, was Charles A. Byrne, but one Louis F. Post—a bright and intelligent young lawyer, who was afflicted with constitutional laziness, was lacking in steadiness of purpose, and was running over with all manner of idiosyncrasies upon the subject of labor, land, greenbacks, religion and politics—was in the latter part of 1880 practically in control of its editorial columns. He had been Mr. Hart's counsel, adviser and friend, and possessed that gentleman's entire confidence and trust. He had, some time previous to the starting of *Truth*, been recognized as a Republican, but subsequently suffered from a chronic attack of bitterness toward the party and the gentleman who, in 1880, became its candidate for Vice-President. He has since been a Hancock man, a labor candidate for office and a Greenbacker.

I am fully satisfied, from all the information I have obtained, that much of the course of *Truth* after the middle of October, 1880, the coarseness and brutality exhibited in its editorial columns, and its generally unfair mode of treating the Morey letter and those who asserted it to be a forgery, were primarily and mainly due to Louis F. Post. It should be added, that while it is not believed he had any knowledge of the letter prior to its receipt by *Truth*, there is evidence, in his own handwriting, which establishes beyond all question that in his subsequent course in relation to the letter he did, or allowed to be done, acts which no lawyer should have done who cared aught for his reputation, and which tended to place his friend, his client and his patron—Mr. Hart—in a false and damaging position before the community.

I feel it due Mr. Hart, after learning the facts that I have respecting various matters which seemed to leave him in, at least, a very compromising position, to say that there can be no doubt that, relying upon the endorsement and support of the Morey letter given him by the Democratic National Committee, he thoroughly believed, for a long time, that it was a genuine letter. He himself admits that such belief, his zeal, his reliance upon Mr. Post's faithfulness to him and upon Post's legal abilities, led him not to give certain matters that care and attention which he should, and otherwise would have done, and which, if he had, would have early led him to a different conclusion and his journal to a radical change in its course.

After Mr. Hart and Mr. Post ceased having any business or other relations, Mr. Hart placed at my disposal everything which he had which bore in any manner upon the Morey letter, and rendered me such assistance as he could in my investigations after the truth. Such papers as have been furnished me by Mr. Hart, and have been used herein, will show upon their face to whom I am indebted therefor; and, while they supplied me with no new facts touching the authorship of the letter, they have been of great service in making the true inwardness of the letter and its endorsers the more apparent: they have welded the closer the links in the chain which the previously obtained facts had forged. Mr. Hart's papers and information were given me without a condition being asked or promised, and I have no hesitation in saying that they have been of material service. Common justice requires of me these statements which Mr. Hart will see, and know of, only by reading them herein.

I have felt constrained, in treating of the Morey letter, to criticise and condemn the action of the Democratic party. In so doing I have not intended to include the large number of patriotic, honest and right-minded men who are sincere in their opposition to the Republican party and who would scorn to do a dishonorable act for party success.

In speaking of the Democratic party, reference is made to it as it has been represented for a quarter of a century past by its active leaders—the men who have controlled its conventions, declared its policy and managed its campaigns. Those leaders and their followers, have, for twenty-five years, made the history of the party a continuous record of political blunders and crimes, the latter of which were perpetrated for the purpose of achieving that party success which their blunders had endangered.

The holding of men and women in bondage, the attempt to withdraw from the Union, the opening of fire upon the national flag as the emblem of national unity, the four long weary years of desolation and war, the riots of 1863 and their threatened renewal in 1864, the naturalization and other election frauds of 1868, the political murders at the South from 1872 to 1876, the use of tissue ballots, the bludgeon and the shotgun as Inspectors and Canvassers of elections, the cipher dispatches and the attempt to bribe members of an Electoral College in 1876, the disgraceful campaign of 1880—with the forgery of a letter upon General Garfield, and the endorsement, circulation and sustainment of the forgery—were each and all the act and deed of the leaders of the Democratic party, their allies and confederates, done with the sole object to aid and abet the party in its strife for power.

Such is the record, regret it as we may.

PART FIFTH.

The forgery of General Garfield's signature not a forgery in law. No punishment therefor possible. A remedy suggested for the future, to which the attention of the Legislatures of the several States is especially requested.

The question has been asked, times without number, as to what punishment could be inflicted upon those guilty of participation in the forgery of the Morey letter.

To these inquiries the only answer which could be given was that the forgery of the letter and signature addressed to "H. L. Morey," of Lynn, was not a forgery in law, and therefore could not be punished as such. If President Garfield had lived, an attempt to hold those concerned in the forgery, upon a charge of criminal libel, might, possibly, have been sustained by the courts, but of this even there is some question.

To my mind, the fact that no adequate punishment for the offense committed could be administered, rendered the exposure of the matter all the more necessary to the cause of good government. My opinion was that such exposure would not only have a tendency to prevent the perpetration of a similar offense in the near future—by demonstrating that not even "time," itself, could prevent the facts from being finally ascertained and laid bare to public notice and attention—but that it would inevitably result in the enactment of such measures as would, hereafter, affix a penalty to the commission of similar offenses.

As tending toward the accomplishment of the latter purpose, I have prepared a short bill, to which I invite the attention of the public generally, and of the members of the Legislatures of the several States particularly. I am by no means wedded to the text of the bill in question, and am aware that in many of the States some change in phraseology will be necessary to make it conform the more closely to the plan or arrangement of existing criminal codes or statutes. It is believed, however, that it fully meets the present requirements, and would, if enacted, tend to prevent the future repetition of offenses similar to those committed in respect to the Morey letter.

The bill has been approved by many prominent members of the New York Bar, to whom I have submitted it, among whom may be mentioned Francis N. Bangs, Esq., late President of the Association of the Bar in this city; Elihu Root, Esq., U. S. District Attorney; the Hon. Daniel G. Rollins, late District Attorney, and present Surrogate of the County of New York; Col. George Bliss, late U. S. District Attorney; Henry C. Gardiner, Esq., and George W. Lyon, Esq., late Assistant District Attorney of the County of New York.

An Act declaring certain Acts to be Forgeries, and providing for their Punishment.

Section 1. Every person who, with intent to injure or defraud, shall falsely make, alter, forge or counterfeit, or shall cause, aid, abet, assist or otherwise connive at, or be a party to, the making, altering, forging or counterfeiting of any letter, telegram, report or other written communication, paper or instrument, by which making, altering, forging or counterfeiting, any other person shall be in any manner injured in his good name, standing, position or general reputation, shall be adjudged guilty of forgery, and upon conviction shall be punished by a fine of not less than five hundred dollars, or imprisonment for not more than three years, or both.

Sec. 2. Every person who shall utter, or shall cause, aid, abet or otherwise connive at, or be a party to, the uttering of any letter, telegram, report or other written communication, paper or instrument, purporting to have been written or signed by another person, or any paper purporting to be a copy of any such paper or writing where no original existed, which said letter, telegram, report or other written communication, paper or instrument, or paper purporting to be a copy thereof, as aforesaid, the person uttering the same shall know to be false, forged or counterfeited, and by the uttering of which the sentiments, opinions, conduct, character, prospects, interests or rights of such other person shall be misrepresented or otherwise injuriously affected, shall be adjudged guilty of forgery, and upon conviction shall be punished by a fine of not less than five hundred dollars, or imprisonment for not more than three years.

Sec. 3. This act shall take effect immediately.

The New York Legislature, at its recent session, passed the bill as it appears above, and it is now a part of the statute law of that State. I am indebted to Senator Albert Daggett and Assemblymen Husted, Roosevelt and Howe for their earnest work in its behalf.

CONCLUSION.

In closing, I desire to tender my thanks to the many kind friends, by whose assistance—in meeting the necessary expenses incident to the long investigation—I have been greatly aided in reaching a successful termination in "hunting the rascals down." I have no intention to here recall them all by name, nor could I so do and regard their wishes. There are, however, a few to whom I feel under such special obligations, that I cannot refrain from mentioning them, and I am confident that in so doing I shall not be considered as in anywise making invidious distinctions.

I. To Chester A. Arthur, President of the United States, I desire to express my gratitude for his kind offices and interest in the investigation. It is entirely without his knowledge that any reference to himself is made herein, but I feel that the public are entitled to know the fact that in November, 1880, being then Vice-President, he learned of my determination to pursue the search for the facts respecting the origin, publication and support of the Morey letter, and sent me a message of encouragement, accompanied by a pledge that he would be personally responsible for the raising of two thousand dollars toward the necessary expenses of the investigation.

II. To the Hon. William E. Chandler, now Secretary of the Navy, to the late Marshall Jewell, Chairman of the Republican National Committee, and to the Hon. Richard C. McCormick, I am under many obligations for assistance, encouragement and advice.

III. To the editor of the *New York Tribune*, and his staff, both in New York and Washington; the editors of the *Philadelphia Press*, the *New York Mail and Express*, and the *Washington Post*, and the managing editors of the *New York Star* and *The Boston Globe*—the three latter of which journals are Democratic—I am indebted for much aid. My acknowledgments are also due Mr. Horace White, one of the editors of the *New York Evening Post*.

IV. To Colonel Henry J. Johnson and Captain W. E. Griffith, of Cumberland, Maryland, and to Captain J. G. B. Adams, of Lynn, Massachusetts, I desire to express my appreciation of the great value of their services, and their untiring devotion to the work of aiding in the ascertainment and exposure of the facts relating to the attempts made in their respective localities, to sustain the original forgery.

I ask, in conclusion, that every reader will, during the next meeting of the Legislature of his State, use his best endeavors to procure the passage of the suggested measure providing for the future prevention and punishment of offenses similar to that of which this work treats. If he will so act, he will have the consciousness of having done something toward rendering future elections more pure, free and honest, and thereby have prolonged the life of the nation, and perpetuated Republican ideas and institutions.

APPENDIX.

EXHIBIT I.

First.—In the course of my investigations I ascertained from Mr. J. Stanley Brown, General Garfield's Secretary, that during the session of Congress, which began in *December*, 1879, General Garfield was not in the habit of using paper of letter size, bearing the stamp of the "House of Representatives." He, almost invariably, used paper bearing his monogram, or paper bearing the heading of the "Committee of Ways and Means."

Second.—I also ascertained that all the paper prepared for the use of Members of Congress and bearing the heading "House of Representatives" was printed at the Government printing office, upon the order of the Clerk of the House of Representatives, and furnished to members, *only upon written orders signed by them;* and that there was no order from General Garfield for any paper similar to that upon which the Morey letter was written.

Third.—I further found that the heading "House of Representatives," borne upon the sheet of paper on which the Morey letter was written, was printed on *tablets* of letter size, and on one occasion only, and that was for the session above mentioned, and the quantity then printed was very small. The *stamp* used for that printing was used then, *and then only*, the style of lettering not meeting with favor among members.

Fourth.—I still further found that from November 8th, 1879, down to the first day of May, 1880, General Garfield never purchased a sheet of paper of letter size, either cut into tablets, or otherwise, bearing the heading "House of Representatives." This corroborated the "first" fact above stated.

Below will be found General Garfield's account with the Stationery Room of the House of Representatives, for the thirteen months from March 21st, 1879, to May 1st, 1880.

HON. J. A. GARFIELD,
  To *Stationery Room, House of Representatives.*

1879.			Dn.	1879.			Dn.
March 21.	2 blank books............	60	60				
"	4 tablets*............@ 30	1.20					
"	4 " ".............@ 20	80	2.00	Dec. 23.	1 box leads	05	
"	30.	1 blotter.	10	10	"	1 hand bag.............	2.63	
April	10.	1,000 envelope............	1.99	1.99	"	1 cork holder............	10	9.90
"	12.	1 box bands...............	11	11	28.	1 pint of mucilage.......	29	29
"	24.	By exchange in			29.	1 blank book............	13	
		McKinnon pen.......	50	50	"	1 bottle ink..............	19	
"	1 box pens	38	38	"	1 pen holder............	04	36
May	15.	1 blank book............	88		1880.			
"	½ ream note.......@1.10	28	1.10	Jan'y 12.	1 box note...............	50	50
July	5.	5 canvas books .....@12	60	60	Feb'y 2.	1 card note	22	22
Nov.	8.	1 bottle ink...............	10	10	"	1 " "	22	22
"	28.	1 journal	1.23		March 27.	2 automatic pencils.@15	30	
"	1 blank book............	35	1.58	"	2 pen holders...........	05	
Dec.	11.	1 pair shears.............	67	67	"	1 bottle ink..............	29	64
"	23.	1 pocket book............	2.35		29.	6 automatic pencils.@15	90	
"	1 box leads...............	15		"	2 boxes leads ......@ 05	10	1.00
"	1 ream note..............	1.00		30	1 basket.................	63	63
"	1 Japanese box	50		April 16.	1 box leads..............	05	05
"	1 box note	1.50		30.	1 " "	05	05
"	1 gold pencil	1.62				$23.65	$23.65

* These are the only "tablets" General Garfield purchased during the above designated thirteen months. They were obtained in March, 1879. The tablets of which the sheet containing the Morey letter was one were not then in existence. They were subsequently prepared for the next session of Congress.

I hereby certify that the above is a correct copy of the account of the Hon. James A. Garfield, for stationery, between March 21st, 1879, and April 30th, 1880, both inclusive, as the same appears upon the books and records of the Stationery Room of the House of Representatives.   LOUIS REINBURG,
    June 16th, 1882.   *Stationery Clerk.*

I certify that Louis Reinburg, whose signature is above, is the Stationery Clerk of the House of Representatives, and in immediate charge of the accounts of Members, of present and preceding Congresses, for stationery.   EDW'D McPHERSON,
    June 16th, 1882.   *Clerk of House of Representatives.*

EXHIBIT II.

The confession of perjury of Samuel S. Morey, who plead guilty to perjury in the Court of General Sessions in the city of New York. He went upon the stand before Justice Noah Davis in the Philp examination, and swore that "Henry L. Morey" was his uncle, and identified the forged entries in the Lynn hotel register as being in his uncle's handwriting.

My name is Samuel S. Morey; I am forty-nine years of age; was born in Lowell, Mass., and live in Lawrence, same State; am by occupation a laborer, and say, relative to the charge preferred against me, that for the last three years I have been in pretty straitened circumstances. I have been trying to get my pension restored to me. It was taken from me here while I was in South America, because not being here for a direct examination before the surgeon who examines them every two years. Last winter I suffered severely. I had no overcoat to my back, and hardly shoes to my feet, and had nothing in the house to eat, you might say. I worked but little of the time. I was having epileptic fits, and liable to fall at any time. People would not hire me, because they knew I was subject to those fits and I only got a day's work now and then. Last winter A. G. Clark helped me considerable.

Q. Who is A. G. Clark? A. The man who was on with me yesterday.
Q. What is his business?
A. He keeps a pool-room in Lawrence. When this case came up they came to me and wanted to know if I knew of anybody by the name of H. L. Morey. I told them 'I thought I did. Said I, "I think he is an uncle of mine, born in Andover, New Hampshire, and he afterward went from Andover and kept a grocery store in Fisherville." They ran on and kept bothering me, and finally they received a telegraphic dispatch from New York and wanted me to go on. Mr. Clark came to the wood yard where I was splitting wood. Said he, "Will you come on to New York?" I said "No, there is no use of my going on, I ain't going to get myself into any scrape." Said he, "You had better go." I said "No, I will not go." Said he, "Will you go up to Mr. Sanborn's law office?" Said I, "Yes, I will." I hesitated at first; finally I agreed to go. I got up there to Mr. Sanborn's. Mr. Clark went on foot and another man took me in a wagon. The other man's name I do not know. He is a resident of Lawrence. We went to Mr. Sanborn's office, and Mr. Sanborn, Mr. Clark. Mr. Murphy, and this man that went with me, and another man that I don't know—he had a crutch. They all urged me to go to New York. Said I, "I don't want to go." Said he, "Why?" Said I, "I don't want to get into any scrape." Said they, "*This thing will be all settled after election.*" *They all joined in saying this*—said it would only be a political case and so on. I said I had no money to go. They said, "Your expenses will be paid, and you will be well paid for going." I went to the door and said, "I won't go." They called me back again, and said something about going again and why I would not go; and I would not give any reason. Said I, "If I go on there we will be lodged in jail, the whole of us." They said, "You need not fear of being lodged in jail. We will stand by you, and we will see you well paid if you go." At that time Mr. Clark expressed fears that we would not be paid. Mr. Sanborn and the others assured us that we would be paid, and that they would be responsible for the payment of the money. They said, "Come back." I went back again. They said, "Will you go?" I said, "No." Mr. Clark spoke out and he says, "Sam, I never asked a favor of you before. This is the first favor I have asked of you. You know I have done considerable for you. Now, I want you to go to New York with me." Said I, "Mr. Clark, there is not another man in the City of Lawrence with whom I would go with but you, and now I don't want to go." Said he, "If you don't want to go, and won't go, don't you ever speak to me again, or look at me on the street, or ever ask another favor of me again." Said he, "You know I have done a good deal for you." I said, "I know you have. You gave me money out of your pocket, you gave me the coat that I have on my back, and the pants that I have on now." And says I, "I will go." Said I, "Mind, before we start, it will bring me into a scrape and you will get into a scrape yourself." By being in needy circumstances, not able to work a great deal, more than two or three or four days in the week, and sometimes going six or seven weeks without work, the inducement they held me out that this thing would be closed out after election; that I had no need to fear anything, I consented to come. I came on here. I gave correct testimony as you will see, and only in regard to H. L. Morey was my testimony false; and also when stated that I had been offered $100 by a Republican not to come on here and testify. My family record is true, except in relation to H. L. Morey, whom I don't know, and never have known, and knew at the time that it was a false statement.

Q. Have you ever been to the *Truth* office? A. Yes, sir; they sent for me the second time.
Q. How many times have you been to the *Truth* office?
A. I have been there a number of times.
Q. Did you ever have any interviews with a person by the name of "Josh" Hart? A. Yes, sir.
Q. With any one else besides him? A. There was another young man who wore spectacles.
Q. A man by the name of Post?
A. I do not know the name—a short man wearing spectacles and side whiskers. When I came here the first time we went to the Democratic headquarters in Fifth Avenue; I got here at eleven o'clock Saturday night. We went to the headquarters at eleven o'clock,

rapped there and couldn't find anybody. We went from there to the Continental hotel, registered our names and got a room.
Q. What did you register your name as? A. S. S. Morey.
Q. Clark came with you? A. Yes, sir.
Q. Any one else? A. No, sir; not at that time.
Q. Do you remember what day of the month it was?
A. It was the Saturday before election. Sunday morning we went down to the Democratic headquarters first, and found nobody there but some women cleaning up. We then, went and got some breakfast, came back, and they kept us there. I met a man by the name of Moore, first, and then a number of their headquarters men. I did not see Mr. Barnum. He had returned to Connecticut the evening previous. There was another short man there. I could tell his name if I heard it. Mr. Moore was Sergeant-at-arms of the Democratic Committee there, they said. I saw what I supposed was the Secretary, the man that wrote and gave me the check when we returned. He gave me a check for $150— $50 for expenses for Mr. Clark and $100 he was to give to me when he got the check cashed. The $100 was for coming on, I suppose. He didn't say what it was for. That Sunday he got a carriage and took us to the Central Park; from there we went down to Staten Island on the ferry-boat. We stopped down there until four o'clock in the afternoon, and went up to St. Vincent's Hotel, I think, up in the Park. We got supper there and returned to the Democratic headquarters and stopped there all night. They said in the morning that they couldn't let us out of their sight —they were afraid little Davenport would get hold of us. The next morning we got breakfast and went to the *Truth* office, and from there to the Court-house.
Q. Whom did you see at the *Truth* office? A. I saw a little short lawyer there.
Q. That fellow with a moustache and a red face?
A. It was not Howe; it was a little bald-headed man with Howe, I guess. I think his name was Hummell. We went from there to the Court-house. "Josh" Hart wanted to know about this Morey, and I told him the same as I testified to—as I have already testified to. After the Court adjourned until Thursday, then we went and got some supper and returned home on the nine o'clock train from the Grand Central Depot.
Q. How many times did you go to the *Truth* office?
A. I suppose I was in the *Truth* office half a dozen times.
Q. You said you had some interviews with "Josh" Hart?
A. Yes, sir. I had one with him at the Democratic headquarters on Sunday.
Q. What was that conversation, do you remember?
A. With regard to H. L. Morey, and one in reference to whether I had a brother an actor and slight-of-hand performer. I told him yes, and he asked me if I knew where he was then. I told him I supposed he was in South America; that was the last I had heard of him. He said, "Don't you suppose he is on here?" Said I, "Since I heard from him he has had time to come on here, and go back again." He said, "I think he is on here, and I think this letter was wrote by him." Said I, "I don't think it is, for I think if he had been on to the States he would come and see me." He took down what I said on paper, and said he would send a hack to Democratic headquarters at 8 o'clock, Monday morning. At 8 o'clock, or a few minutes past, on Monday morning, we left the headquarters and went to the *Truth* office, and from there we went to the Court-house. I had no further conversation with him. He showed me a letter, and asked me if knew the writing. I told him yes; that I should think it was my brother Frank's. The writing was very similar to my brother's. I had seen my brother write a good many times, and it was similar to his.
Q. Did Clark tell you who had asked him to get you to come to New York?
A. Yes, he said that Sanborn had told him to get me to come to New York.
Q. His lawyer? A. Yes, sir.
Q. Did he say anything more? A. He said nothing more, except that Sanborn, or somebody else, had received a telegram wanting me to come on.
Q. Did he say from whom he received that telegram?
A. He did not say anything to me about a fellow of the name of Wilson. Hart spoke about a letter which he had received from Mr. Goodall. He said this letter stated to have no fears that the Morey letter was genuine, and he (Goodall) was about to start to Florida to find Morey and bring him on here. That was all the conversation I had with him before I went to the Court-house. The first time I went to the *Truth* office, we started from the Democratic headquarters on Monday, I should think about twenty minutes past eight. That was the Monday before election. This was the first time I visited the *Truth* office. I met Mr. Hart and a gentleman with specs on—Mr. Post. Then there was a man there they called "Box." I think that was his nickname.
Q. What was said to you at that time that you remember? A. There is where he showed me the Goodall letter. Mr. Hart showed it to me, and said it was from Mr. Goodall.
Q. What did he say in regard to that Goodall letter?
A. He said that Morey had started to Florida for his health; that the Morey letter was genuine, and that he would start immediately for Florida and have Morey in time.
Q. When was the next time you went to the *Truth* office?
A. It was during the recess of the court on Monday.
Q. Did you have any conversation then? A. Nothing, except they said they guessed

that I was a clincher on them—referring to my testimony. Hart said this. We went from there and got dinner. "Box" went with me.

Q. What was the next time you went to the *Truth* office?

A. The next time I went to the office was after the court in the afternoon, when it was adjourned until Thursday. We had some conversation in regard to our being wanted again. Hart said he didn't know; he would take our names—Mr. Clark and mine—and if he wanted us again he would telegraph; and that was the last time I went to the *Truth* office before I returned home. We went direct from the *Truth* office to the Democratic headquarters. When we got to the Democratic headquarters we stopped there a few minutes. Mr. Moore was there, and this man that gave me the check, whose name, I think was Smalley, and one or two other gentlemen that I didn't know; and this man that gave me the check*—Smalley—I am sure, sat down and asked Mr. Clark what his expense had been. Mr. Clark said: "I counted my money, and put it down on a paper before I left home," and he counted it over to the man, and this man said, "never mind the cents;" said he, "Will $50 cover it?" Mr. Clark said "yes;" said he, "What shall we give Morey?" Clark said, "I don't know;" he asked me, and I said, "I will leave it all to you, sir." He then drew out a check for $150. He gave it to Mr. Clark, stating to Mr. Clark that $50 was for his expenses, and the $100 was for me. He wrote a receipt out, and I signed it, for $150, in my name.

Q. Did you get that $100?

A. We left New York at nine o'clock for Boston. We got into Boston, I think, about six, and took the half-past eight o'clock train from Boston for Lawrence. Upon our arrival in Lawrence, we went direct, I think, to the Pacific National Bank. Mr. Clark asked Mr. Taquit, the cashier, if he would cash a check for him of $150—a New York check—and Mr. Taquit said he would. Mr. Clark said, "You need not say anything about where you got it." He said he would not. I signed my name on the back of it. Mr. Clark passed it in and received the money. We went from there to Mr. Clark's pool room, corner of Essex and Jackson Streets. We went up there, took a drink, and Mr. Clark gave me $100. Thursday morning I went to work, but not feeling very well; I worked till noon time, when I went home feeling pretty bad. I retired to bed. I hadn't been to bed but an hour, I should judge, when somebody from New York came on—a person I didn't know at the time, but who I afterwards learned was Warner. I thought at the time when I first saw him that he had come to arrest me, and through the excitement I went into one of those epileptic fits. I had a number of them during the afternoon. They sent for the doctor, and when I came to, Warner told me he wanted me to go to New York with him that night. I told him I would not go; the doctor said I was utterly unable to go. During the night I continued to have these bad fits. On Friday he came again and still I was not able to go. Said he to my wife: "Is $200 any object for him to go on to-night?" My wife said: "No, it is not, he is not able to go."

Then on Saturday Mr. Clark came to see me. He wanted me to go. About half-past four he and Mr. Warner came to the house together in a carriage. We took the quarter to six train, I think, from Lawrence to Boston. Went to the United States Hotel, in Boston, and stopped there over night. Clark said he put his name down as A. Gillman. What my name was I do not know. It was not my right name. At eleven o'clock the next morning we left Boston for New York. We got in here about five minutes to six, and from the depot we went to the *Truth* office. I saw Mr. Hart there, and he said to Warner, "Take him to a hotel and have the bills charged to me." He took me to the Belmont Hotel. I think I registered my name as Asa Clements, and he registered his name as Gillman. We had another man in the party. Warner called him "Mack;" we went out and got some supper, and we stopped at the hotel all night, and yesterday morning walked to the *Truth* office. From the *Truth* office we went to the court room, and at noon time we went and got a lunch, and that was the last time I was to the *Truth* office. They brought me there last night. On the way from Boston to New York Warner said, "we must keep dark until we get into Court."

Q. Can you tell me on what bank the check for $150 was drawn?

A. On the Park National Bank.

Q. Whose name was signed to that check? A. I don't remember.

Q. What did they promise to give you this time? A. They said they would pay me well for coming on. Warner said this. No amount was specified.

Q. Was Clark present? A. I won't be certain; but he said in the presence of Clark, that all expenses would be paid for his time coming on. This was the last time.

Q. Had you ever seen Warner before? A. No, sir; not until I saw him in my house.

Q. Do you know where he lives? A. No, sir; but, by his talk and his language, I supposed he was connected with the *Truth* office. He had a *Truth* badge, under the lappel of his vest, so Mr. Clark told me—I did not see it.

Q. Who first spoke to you about coming on the first time? A. Mr. Clark.

Q. Was Warner on that time? A. No, sir; when we left here to go home the first time, Mr. Hart said if they wanted us again, they would telegraph us. After they gave me the check at Democratic headquarters, the man who gave me the check said if they wanted us again they would telegraph for us, and took Mr. Clark's name and my own.

---

* Mr. Morey was mistaken as to the name of the person who paid them. It was not Mr. Smalley, but Mr. Edward B. Dickinson.

Q. Who proposed to you first to have you say you had an uncle by the name of H. L. Morey? A. Clark.

Q. Who first showed you the register containing the entry H. L. Morey in two places? A. Hart.

Q. Where? A. Here, at *Truth* office.

Q. When was that register first shown you? A. The Monday morning prior to the election. That was the first time that I had been to *Truth* office.

Q. When that was shown to you, who suggested that you should swear that that was the signature of H. L. Morey? A. Hart asked me on a Sunday morning what kind of a handwriting H. L. Morey wrote. I said, "He writes a very coarse, bold hand." That was prior to my seeing the register, though when they showed me the register next day, I said I should think that that was his handwriting.

Q. As matter of fact that was not the handwriting of H. L. Morey, or of anybody else that you ever knew?

A. No, sir; I am reminded of another remark Clark made. When I met my uncle John yesterday, he shook hands with me, and Clark said, when we got out of our seats, "Who is that?" I said, "That is my uncle John." He said, "He will testify there is no H. L. Morey." I said, yes, he would. "They will all testify that there is no H. L. Morey." He said, "Well, I don't care. If you go to hell, I will go to hell with you."

(Signed) SAMUEL S. MOREY.

Taken before me, this 10th day of November, 1880.

B. T. MORGAN, *Police Justice.*

EXHIBIT III.

The affidavit of John C. Sanborn, as to Samuel S. Morey.

STATE OF MASSACHUSETTS, COUNTY OF ESSEX, CITY OF LAWRENCE, ss.

John C. Sanborn, being duly sworn, deposes and says: That he resides in the city of Lawrence, Mass., and has for some twenty years past.

That he is an attorney at law, at No. 239 Essex Street, in said city of Lawrence, and was such attorney at said place in the months of October and November, 1880; that about the middle of October, 1880, one Edgar F. Mann, of Lawrence, called upon deponent at his office and inquired for one Albion G. Clark, and as to whether deponent knew said Clark's whereabouts; that deponent replied that he knew that said Clark had at one time kept a saloon on Essex Street, but his belief was that he was out of business and that the best place to find said Clark would probably be at his house; that said Mann then left deponent's office, and after being gone for some time returned, saying that he had been unable to find said Clark; that while said Mann was in deponent's office, after his return as aforesaid, said Clark entered deponent's office to make an inquiry of deponent respecting some political matters of a local character; that deponent thereupon said to Mann, "Here is the man you want to see;" deponent seeing that neither of them knew each other; that then said Mann inquired of said Clark as to the whereabouts of one Samuel S. Morey; that said Clark stated that he did not know where said Morey then was, when said Mann produced a telegram to himself, purporting to come from the Democratic National Committee, and requesting him, the said Mann, to find the said Morey, and send him on to said Committee at New York; that thereupon one James O. Parker, who happened to be in deponent's office, and had a team at the door, took said Clark with him to go and find said Morey, and subsequently said Parker and said Clark returned with said Morey to deponent's office, where said Mann was remaining, waiting to learn if Morey had been found, and if he would go to New York; that a discussion followed, which, as deponent understood, resulted in Morey's declining to go to New York, and in said Morey's leaving deponent's office in company with Clark; that deponent subsequently heard from said Clark that Morey said he would go if his wife would consent.

And deponent further says that he understood that the reason of Morey's declining to go, was because he was subject to fits and liable at any moment to fall down in the street, with or in a fit, and wanted some one to go with him; and subsequently, deponent heard that said Morey had gone to New York, and that said Clark had accompanied him, and for said reason.

And deponent says, that, as he remembers the wording of the telegram, it was: "Send Sam Morey on at the Committee's expense," and signed "Wm. H. Barnum," and that during the conversation at deponent's office it was discussed as to who would pay the expense of the matter if the telegram should turn out to be a hoax, and it was finally informally agreed, that each of those present would pay a share of the car fares out and back.

And further deponent says he knows not. JOHN C. SANBORN.

Sworn to before me this 5th day of June, A. D. 1882.

[SEAL.] ARETAS R. SANBORN, *Notary Public.*

EXHIBIT IV.

The affidavit of David Lynn, as to the authorship of the Robert Lindsay letter mailed to the *Washington Post* from Cumberland, Md.

STATE OF MARYLAND, COUNTY OF WASHINGTON, HAGERSTOWN, ss.

David Lynn, being duly sworn, deposes and says, that he resides at Cumberland, Maryland; that he is a coal merchant in said city; that he has been well acquainted with John W. Phelps from about the spring of the year 1879; that said Phelps was for some time a contractor at Cumberland for the building of the George's Creek and Cumberland Railroad; that in the latter part of the month of October, 1880, this deponent met said John W. Phelps as he was going into the Post Office at Cumberland; that said Phelps upon seeing deponent said to him, "You are the very man I want to see; I will see you as soon as I mail these letters;" said Phelps then entered the Post Office and mailed some letters, deponent waiting for him; that said Phelps then joined deponent and took him down Liberty Street, which is a street not much frequented, and said to deponent, "I have just gotten up something which I think will create a hell of a sensation in the country;" that deponent inquired what it was, and said Phelps replied, "I have gotten up a letter purporting to be from one Robert Lindsay, which has reference to the Morey letter, and have mailed it to the *Washington Post;*" that he then requested deponent to go to the telegraph office in Cumberland and ascertain if there was any dispatch came there or any inquiry was made there for Robert Lindsay; that deponent thereupon left said Phelps, when said Phelps called deponent back and said, "Don't go there for a day or two. Give the letter time enough to get to Washington;" that deponent then left said Phelps, and although said Phelps and deponent were at the time on terms of great intimacy, deponent never made inquiry at the said telegraph office, as he did not desire to become mixed up with the Morey letter matter; that subsequently deponent heard that said Phelps had gone to New York, and also heard of him as being in that city; that shortly thereafter said Phelps returned to Cumberland; that deponent was standing on the portico of the Queen City Hotel, at the depot in Cumberland, when the train from the East arrived from which said Phelps alighted; that the moment said Phelps saw deponent he rushed toward him and requested deponent to come with him at once to his room, saying that he desired to see him upon business of importance; that deponent thereupon accompanied said Phelps to his room in the said Queen City Hotel; that upon arriving there, placing his hand upon deponent's shoulder, said Phelps said to deponent, "There is hell to pay about that letter. Now, Lynn, for God's sake don't give me away on that Lindsay letter business, particularly to Henry Loveridge,"—who was the President of the Maryland Coal Co., and Vice-President of the George's Creek and Cumberland Coal Co.—"because I have sworn to him that I had nothing to do with it, and I don't want him to have any knowledge of it."

That between the time when said Phelps informed deponent of his getting up the Lindsay letter, and the time of said Phelps' return to Cumberland as hereinbefore set forth, the fact of the receipt by the *Washington Post* of a letter purporting to be written by Robert Lindsay, and mailed from Cumberland, Md., had been widely published and the contents of said letter had created a sensation.
DAVID LYNN.

Subscribed and sworn to before me, this 18th day of March, A. D. 1882.
[SEAL] Jos. KEMSLER, *Notary Public.*

EXHIBIT V.

The sworn confession of James A. Birmingham, of Cumberland, Md., as to his employment by William M. Price, in connection with the search for a "Robert Lindsay," and the procuring of men to falsely personate a "Robert Lindsay."

STATE OF MARYLAND, CITY OF BALTIMORE, ss.

James A. Birmingham, being duly sworn, deposes and says, that he resides in the City of Cumberland, Alleghany County, Md., and has so resided there nearly thirty-four years; that at the present time he is a special policeman in the employ of the Baltimore and Ohio Railroad Company at Cumberland, and has held such position since May, 1880; that on Sunday, October 31st, 1880, immediately preceding the Presidential election of that year, at about four o'clock in the afternoon of said day, deponent was standing at the corner of Baltimore and Centre Streets, in front of a hardware store, when William M. Price came along and called deponent, and deponent thereupon joined said Price and walked a short distance along the street with him, away from the crowd with whom he was standing, when Price spoke to him; that said Price then said to deponent, "Jimmy, you are pretty well acquainted with the people in this county. Do you know any one by the name of Robert Lindsay?" that deponent replied, "I don't know any one by that name; the only person I know of by the name of Lindsay is a telegraph operator at Mt. Savage station"—which was about three miles from Cumberland—"but his name is William Lindsay;" that Price then said, "You go and find out if there is a Robert Lindsay in Cumberland, white or black;" and at the same time said to deponent that he would pay him the sum of five dollars; that Price add d, "You had better get some one else to look also; there are Dick

Ryan and Buck O'Neil standing on the corner; get them to go too, and I will give them five dollars;" that thereupon deponent joined said Ryan and O'Neil, and all three started out and made various inquiries for said Robert Lindsay, but nothing could be learned of any person by that name; that subsequently deponent went to his supper, and after supper deponent met said Ryan and said O'Neil, and all three went to the house of said Price and were informed that he was out; that later in the evening, between the hours of nine and ten o'clock, all three went back to said Price's residence, but did not find him at home; that we then started to go to the Queen City Hotel at the Depot, and on the corner of Harrison and South George's Streets we met said Price; that the three of us then informed said Price that we could not find or hear of any one by that name; that thereupon said Price gave deponent, the said Ryan, and the said O'Neil, the sum of five dollars each, and said to deponent, "Walk up to the hotel;" that at the time deponent and Ryan and O'Neil met said Price, on the corner of Harrison and South George's Street, as above mentioned, he had with him a stranger, a large man, whom deponent had never seen before, but whom later in the evening he learned to be one H. H. Hadley, of New York; that deponent has now been shown by Mr. John I. Davenport a photograph of a man, and deponent recognizes the said photograph as the picture of the man whom he saw at said time with said Price, and whom he later learned to be Hadley.

And deponent further says: that after Price requested him to "Walk up to the hotel," as related above, this deponent, and said Ryan and said O'Neil, started toward the Queen City Hotel, the said Price and said Hadley walking on ahead of deponent; that as deponent remembers, Price and Hadley left them to go to the residence of Asa Willison, the Collector of the Chesapeake and Ohio Canal. At all events, the said Price and Hadley, and said Willison, subsequently met deponent, and Ryan and O'Neil, at the said Queen City Hotel; that Price, Hadley and Willison then went into the telegraph office at the station, in the said Queen City Hotel; that both Price and Hadley went to the counter in said telegraph office where messages are written, and one of them then began to write, and continued writing for some moments; that Willison left and went out on the porch; that deponent is unable to say certainly whether it was Price or Hadley who did the writing, but his recollection is that it was Price; that when the writing was completed, said Price came to deponent and asked him, "What are the politics of Brendle, the night operator at the telegraph office?" that deponent replied that he did not know, when Price asked him, "What are the politics of Frank Legg?"—the General Agent of the Baltimore and Ohio Railroad at Cumberland, and who, previous to coming to Cumberland, had been a telegraph operator at Parkersburg; that deponent replied, "I think he is a Democrat;" that Price then rejoined Hadley, and after some talk with him returned to where deponent was standing, and asked deponent, "What are Snyder's politics?" deponent inquired, "What Snyder?" and Price replied, "Snyder, the telegraph operator of the Western Union Company;" deponent answered, "I do not know;" Price then asked deponent, "Where does Snyder live?" and deponent replied, "On Centre Street, fronting Hanover Street;" that Price then joined Hadley and Willison, and deponent left and went home, leaving them in conversation; that Ryan and O'Neil had gone previously, and were not present at the conversation between Price and deponent, relative to the telegraph operators; that the time of deponent's leaving was close to eleven o'clock on the night of said Sunday, October 31st, 1880; that on Monday, November 1st, 1880, shortly after ten o'clock in the morning, deponent, while walking along Baltimore Street, near Centre Street, met Michael Cronley, who is sometimes called "Knock," and one Frank Brady, who is nicknamed and spoken of as "The Brute," both of whom deponent had known for many years, and who were miners at the Eckhart Mines, and the three walked down to Liberty Street; that there we met some of the boys, miners and others, and stood engaged in conversation; that while so standing deponent saw Wm. M. Price standing at the post-office, which was on the opposite corner of Baltimore and Liberty Streets; that said Price called to deponent to come over, and deponent joined said Price, who requested him to "Walk along with me a few feet;" that said Price then said to deponent, "Are those fellows from the mines?" and deponent said, "Yes, sir;" Price then asked, "What are their names? who are they?" and deponent told him who they were, giving him their names as "Frank Brady, Mike Cronley, and Frank McMahon." Price then said, "They are none of them Bob Lindsay?" and deponent answered, "No." Price then said, "I have a paper and I wonder if one of them would not sign it as Robert Lindsay?" Deponent replied, "I do not know," and Price said, "Go and see and ask them;" that said Price left and went to his office, saying, "If one of them will do it, you come down to the office and get the paper. It will have to be taken to Jim Humbird," who was a Notary Public in Cumberland, "to sign it;" that deponent inquired if the paper would have to be sworn to. Price replied "No, and I will give the man five dollars;" that deponent thereupon went to join the party he had left, and on the corner of Baltimore and Mechanics Streets he found Dick Ryan and Michael Cronley, and he told said Ryan what Price had said, and Ryan had a conversation with Cronley, and returned to deponent and said, "Mick will sign it;" that thereupon deponent went to said Price's office, and told said Price. "Cronley will sign it, but he has not got to swear to this." Price replied, "No, but send him to Humbird's house to sign it." Deponent replied, "I guess he does not know where Humbird lives." Price said, "You show him;" that deponent then took said paper, offered him by Price, and went out, meeting Cronley on the corner where he had left him, and handed him the paper which Price had given him; that then deponent, Ryan and Cronley, went along Baltimore Street to Centre Street, and turned down Centre to where there was an old pump stood in front of Coolahan's grocery store, where Cronley stopped and inquired, "What is this paper?" Deponent replied, "I don't know. We will open and read it here." It was opened and Cronley went to read it, when Frank Brady stepped up and looked over Cronley's arm at the said paper; that deponent said to Cronley, "Don't let him see it;" that at the time deponent did not know what was in it, but thought it best not to let Brady see it; that Brady then turned and left us, and Cronley put the paper in his pocket, and we all, deponent, Ryan and Cronley, walked down to Union Street, and deponent pointed out Humbird's house; that Cronley went to the house and knocked for admission, and deponent saw him admitted; that after a few moments Cronley came out and joined deponent, and said, "Humbird wants me to swear to it," and deponent said, "Don't you do it;" that deponent thereupon left Cronley, and went to Price's office, and told said Price "Humbird wants Cronley to swear to it;" Price replied, "I'll see Humbird," and deponent left Price's office and went up to the corner of Baltimore and Mechanic Streets, and then waited some moments, when Cronley came up to deponent and said, "I have been to see Price and I got fifteen dollars from him, five for you and five for Ryan and five for myself," and then gave to both deponent and Ryan five dollars each, and stated that he had given the paper to Price, adding, "I am sorry I did not keep it;" that deponent left them to go to his dinner, said Ryan going along with deponent; that on their way they met the said Frank Brady, and Brady, Ryan and deponent went into Webster's saloon on North Centre Street and had a drink; that deponent does not remember that at that time he spoke to said Brady about going to Price's office with Ryan and representing Robert Lindsay, but he will not say that he did not; that then deponent went to his dinner, and he does not remember to have seen Brady or Cronley again that day; that deponent subsequently heard from Ryan that Brady had signed and sworn to another paper under the name of Robert Lindsay, before Squire Harrison.

And deponent further says, that the next interview he had with said Price came about in this manner: that on the evening of November the 4th, about nine o'clock, and after deponent had gone to bed, said Price came to deponent's house and inquired for deponent, who dressed himself and went down stairs, where he found Price seated in the parlor; that said Price said to deponent, "I want you to go up to-morrow to the Eckhart mines with a gentleman and show him Brady." Deponent replied, "I cannot get off." Price inquired "Why?" and deponent said, "I have to be about the hotel and depot during train time." Price responded, "I will get permission from Mr. Legg for you to go. You be up there in the morning and I will see you there;" that Price then left and on the morning of Friday, Nov. 5th, 1880, at about eight o'clock, Price came to the depot and went in and conversed with Mr. Legg, and then brought to deponent a man whom he introduced as "Mr. Walton," but whose right name deponent subsequently heard was Wilde; that after introducing Walton, Price called deponent aside and said: "You go up to the mines, and show Walton this man Brady, *alias* Bob Lindsay;" that thereupon deponent and Walton went to Hanse Willison's livery stables, where Walton procured a conveyance, and deponent and Walton drove to the Eckhart mines, stopping at the house of a Mrs. McMahon and inquiring for her son George McMahon; that after remaining there about five minutes, deponent and Walton drove to Frostburg and stopped at a saloon there, kept by one Sam May, where we had a drink, and deponent inquired of May to know if Brady or Cronley were in town; that May replied that he had not seen them; that after stopping there a few moments, deponent and Walton drove to the Hoffman mine, and there made inquiry of Frank Kelly, a blacksmith, if Brady and Cronley were working; that Kelly said: "they are," and deponent not wishing to go down in the mines, said to Walton: "We can't find them, they are not working," and thereupon we returned to Cumberland, reaching there in the neighborhood of three o'clock; that after leaving the horse at the stable, Walton requested deponent to walk with him down to Price's office, which deponent did. We found Price out, and were informed that he was at the Court-house, whither we started to go, when we met Price on the further end of the bridge. We joined him and turned and walked back with him—Walton and Price walking on ahead—to Price's office, where they went into the back room, deponent standing in the door-way. After Walton and Price finished their conversation Walton came out, Price saying to him, "I will meet you at the Queen City Hotel;" that deponent and Walton started up street, deponent leaving Walton at the corner of Baltimore and Mechanic streets and going into Tom Kane's place, leaving Walton going in the direction of the depot; that Walton turned back in a moment, and came to deponent saying: "I want to see you at the hotel at train time;" that shortly after, deponent went to the hotel and depot—it being about time for the arrival of the train leaving there for the East at about five o'clock. Upon arriving at the depot deponent made inquiry and learned that the train was about an hour and a half late; that Walton sent for deponent to come to his rooms, which he did, and found Walton undressed; that Walton then directed deponent to look for "that party," adding, "Get somebody—I have to have somebody and I will give any one $100." Deponent replied that he could not find "that party" anywhere, and Walton answered, "I will have to have him and reach New York, if I have to charter an engine to go on. I chartered an engine coming down from Baltimore to Washington, to catch the train for Cumberland at Washington, as it had left Baltimore when I arrived there, and I paid $100 for it. I have got to have that party:" that deponent left and went to go to supper, and on his way to Mechanics Street he met Howard Trievor, with whom he had some conversation, and whom he accompanied to Shantytown, at his request, to find one Brady Hummelschine.

whom Trievor wanted to warn that the police were looking for him; that on the way down with Trievor, deponent met "Lowly" Harbaugh and a stranger, and one other person whom deponent cannot recall positively at the moment, but whom he believes was Mat McGuiness; that Harbaugh stopped deponent and introduced the stranger with him to deponent as "Mr O'Brien;" that Trievor was in a hurry and called to deponent to come with him, when deponent said, "We are going down to Buck O'Neil's, won't you fellows"—meaning Harbaugh and his friends—"go with us?" that thereupon all the parties went to O'Neil's and had a drink; that while there, O'Neil said to O'Brien, "Well, you found Birmingham at last," and then said to deponent, "That is Bob Lindsay whom you are looking for;" that deponent replied, "There is a man up at the Queen City Hotel who has offered $100 for Bob Lindsay;" that O'Brien replied, "Is that so? well, I'm his man;" that then Buck O'Neil called O'Brien out to the porch and had a conversation with him; that thereafter the whole party—save perhaps McGuiness—started up the track toward the hotel; that Harbaugh and Trievor left at what is known as Williams' road, just before you get to the hotel and depot; that deponent and O'Brien went up to the depot and we found the train that was late just coming in, and as we got to the depot, Walton was standing there. Deponent said to Walton, "Here is a man who wants to see you;" that Walton then said to O'Brien, whom he had taken aside, "I will give you $100;" that there was other conversation, but that was the only portion of it deponent heard; that in a moment Walton left and went to the ticket office, and O'Brien turned to deponent and said, "This man wants me to go to New York, to swear I'm Robert Lindsay, and he has gone in to get a ticket," and deponent said, "Don't you go to New York with him; get what you can from him and jump off at Martinsburg. At all events don't you go beyond Washington with him;" that O'Brien said, "I can't go to Washington;" that then Walton came out from the ticket office and handed O'Brien a ticket and some money, and left, saying, "I have to go after a lunch;" that he turned about in a moment, and addressing deponent said, "Have you got the copy of *Truth?*" Deponent replied, "No," and Walton said, "Hurry up and go to Price and get from him that copy of *Truth* that he has;" that deponent went to Price's house, which is near the depot, and told said Price, "He has got a fellow—O'Brien—on the train with him;" that Price said, "That's all right." Deponent said, "He wants that *Truth*," and Price gave the paper to deponent, who got back with it to the depot just as the train was starting, and gave it to Walton, who left with O'Brien on said train.

And deponent further says, that just before sending deponent to Price for the *Truth*, said Walton gave deponent ten dollars.

And deponent further says, that the next time he saw said Price was on November 6th, 1880 (Saturday), when Price inquired of deponent, "Did he get off all right?" and deponent said, "Yes, they started."

And deponent further says, that after the said O'Brien had gone upon the witness stand in the Philp case in New York, under the name of Robert Lindsay, as appeared in the papers, and had been broken down and arrested upon a charge of perjury, said Price came to deponent and said, "That fellow O'Brien has given everything away. Don't you tell any one anything you know about it, and after everything is all hushed up I will pay you."

And deponent further says, that some time thereafter, and shortly before Christmas day, in the year 1880, deponent went to said Price and said, "I want some money." Price said, "I have not got any now. You come on Monday to my office;" that deponent went to Price's office on Monday and he was informed that Price was out of the city, and afterwards deponent, upon Price's return, met him at his office, and Price said, "The best way to fix this is in the way of a loan. You give me your note for what you want"—which deponent had informed Price was thirty dollars—"and at the end of thirty days I will pay it, taking up the note;" that thereupon Price drew up a note for deponent to sign, for the sum of $30, and deponent signed the same, and by Price's direction took it to Asa Willison to endorse; that Willison told deponent "to take it back and have 'Mr. Price endorse it;" that this was done and then deponent took it again to said Willison, who endorsed it after Mr. Price, and deponent took it to the Third National Bank in Cumberland and got it cashed, receiving the sum of $30, less the discount; that deponent supposes said Price took the note up, for he has never heard of it since having it discounted.

And deponent further says that said Price has from time to time had conversations with deponent respecting Brady and matters connected with the Lindsay matter, and upon one occasion, in speaking of the affidavit Brady had signed as Lindsay, deponent said, "That affidavit was sworn to before Squire Harrison. He will give you away;" that Price said, "No, he won't. He has got to do what we say, and so has Constable Porter, who witnessed it;" that at all the conversations said Price has had with deponent he has always cautioned deponent to "be sure and keep your mouth closed;" that the last conversation Price had with deponent was on Monday, May 22d, 1882 (yesterday), when he said to deponent: "I suppose the next man Davenport will be after will be you, but don't give him anything. Just keep your mouth shut and you will be all right."

And deponent further says that at the time said Wm. M. Price made the requests of deponent and employed him to find Robert Lindsay, and do the other matters herein detailed, in the year 1880, he—said Price—was the Chairman of the Alleghany County Democratic Committee, and an elector on the National Democratic ticket; that deponent was a supporter of General Hancock at the election of 1880.

And deponent further says that he never knew the contents of the Robert Lindsay affidavit until after the time of O'Brien's testimony in New York under the name of Robert Lindsay, when deponent, being at Price's office, he inquired of Price, "What was there in this affidavit?" Price replied, "There was not much. I will read it to you," and thereupon Price took from a drawer a paper which he said was a copy of the Lindsay affidavit, and ead it to deponent; that at the time when Price first spoke to deponent about getting some one to represent Lindsay in the signing of the affidavit, he said to deponent, "I want you to do this for me. It is worth something to me."

And deponent further says, that he makes this affidavit freely and of his own volition, and because of his desire to have the facts of his connection therewith, and the methods employed to lead deponent to do what he did in relation to the matter, made known.

And deponent further says, that this paper has been drawn up in his presence, and from his own statements, made line by line, and that the same has been read over to him in the presence of John M. McClintock, the U. S. Marshal at Baltimore, and that the same as it stands is correct.
JAMES A. BIRMINGHAM.

Subscribed in my presence this 23d day of May, A. D. 1882.   JOHN M. McCLINTOCK.
Sworn to before me, this 23d day of May, A. D. 1882.
[SEAL.]   THOS. KELL BRADFORD, *Notary Public*.

EXHIBIT VI.

The sworn confession of Richard Ryan, of Cumberland, Md., as to his employment by William M. Price, in connection with the search for a "Robert Lindsay" and the procuring of men to falsely personate a "Robert Lindsay."

STATE OF MARYLAND, CITY OF BALTIMORE, ss.

RICHARD RYAN, being duly sworn, deposes and says, that he resides at Cumberland, Md., and is employed there in the rolling mills of the Baltimore and Ohio Railroad Company, and has been for the past ten years; that on the afternoon of Sunday, October 31st, 1880, between the hours of three and four o'clock, deponent, with one James A. Birmingham and one "Buck" O'Neil, was standing near the corner of Baltimore and Centre Streets, when William M. Price passed along and called said Birmingham, who left deponent and O'Neil, and joined said Price; that after a short conversation with said Price, the said Birmingham returned to where O'Neil and deponent were still standing, and said: "Price wants us all to hunt for a man named Robert Lindsay, and says he will give us five dollars each to find him;" that at that time deponent had never heard of any one in that locality by the name of Robert Lindsay, but by reason of Price's offer we started off and went down to the rolling mill, where deponent was employed, and said Birmingham, being a special officer in the employ of the Baltimore and Ohio Railroad Company, got the keys to the office and we then went through the form of looking over the list of employees in said mill; that we also went to the round house of the said Baltimore and Ohio road, and made some inquiries there, and also inquired of people whom we met upon the street; that from some person, but who deponent does not remember, we heard the story that there was a colored man living near Cumberland by the name of Lindsay, whose first name was believed to be Robert, but we made no further pursuit of him; that subsequently in the evening of said Sunday, deponent, with said Birmingham and said O'Neil, went to said Price's house, but he was not at home; that subsequently we met Price on the street, and told him we could not find any one by the name of Robert Lindsay; that we then each received from said Price the sum of five dollars for our trouble, and then all of the party went up to the Queen City Hotel at the depot, where deponent and O'Neil only remained for a few moments, leaving Price and Birmingham there; that deponent does not remember who was with Price at the time, but has a recollection of having seen Asa Willison at the hotel or depot at that time; that at about nine or ten o'clock, on the morning of Monday, November 1st, 1880, deponent was on Baltimore Street, near the corner of Mechanic Street, talking with one Michael Cronley, a miner from Eckhart, when James Birmingham joined us, and taking deponent aside, said that Price had met him and wanted him to get some one to sign a paper in the name of Robert Lindsay; that Price had told him that the man need not swear to it; that deponent then spoke with said Cronley about it, and he (Cronley) said he would sign it; that Birmingham had stated that Price said it must be signed before Jim Humbird, a notary, and, therefore, deponent, Birmingham and Cronley, walked down within sight of Humbird's house, which Birmingham pointed out to Cronley, who went there and went into the house; that in a few moments Mr. Humbird came up the street, and entered the house, and Cronley very shortly came out and said that Humbird wanted him to swear to the paper; that he told Humbird that he could not write, but for him (Humbird) to write the name of Robert Lindsay to the paper, and he (Cronley) would swear to it; that Humbird said that he (Cronley) must sign it himself, and he finally did so; but upon it being insisted that he must swear to the paper, he refused to do so and left; that deponent said to Cronley, "I would not swear to it," and that Birmingham then left, saying he would go and see Price; that Cronley also shortly left, and that subsequently deponent met both Birmingham and Cronley, and the latter said that he had been to see Price and had given him the paper, and added, "I'm sorry I did not keep it;" that deponent does not remember receiving from Cronley any money at that time, but he does remember Cronley saying that Price had given him some money, but the amount he does not remember, and he will not say that Cronley did not give him a part of it.

And deponent further says, that shortly he, and Cronley and Birmingham started for Humbird's house, and while they were engaged in conversation on Centre Street, near Coolihan's grocery, Frank Brady, also a miner from Eckhart, joined the party, and, seeing the paper in Cronley's hand, which Birmingham had brought after going to Price's office, endeavored to see the said paper, and deponent's recollection is that said Brady looked at said paper, and as deponent supposed read it; that in a few moments Brady left and the remainder of the party then went down to point out Humbird's house to said Cronley; that after Cronley had come back from Price's office, at the time he said he had given Price the paper, but wished he "had not," said Cronley left deponent and Birmingham, and the latter two walked along the street; that after going a short distance they again met Frank Brady, and the three of us went into Webster's, on North Centre Street, and had a drink; that upon coming out, they stepped into the alley by the side of said saloon, and Birmingham then asked said Brady if he wanted to make a little money, to which Brady responded that he did, when Birmingham said: "Well, then go long with Ryan to Price's office, and tell him your name is Robert Lindsay;" that, thereupon, Birmingham left, and deponent and Brady went to Price's office, where deponent introduced Brady to Price as "Robert Lindsay;" that on the way to the office of Price some conversation took place between said Brady and deponent relative to what Brady was to receive, and upon reaching Price's office deponent had a conversation with Price as to how much he (Price) was willing to pay, the result of which was that Price agreed to give twenty-five dollars, and deponent so informed Brady; that then Price produced a paper, and told Brady to sign it, showing him where to write, and thereupon Brady signed the name of "Robert Linsey," and Price took Brady with him, to go, as he said, to Squire Brooks' office; that in a short time both Price and Brady returned, the former saying that Squire Brooks was not in, and directing deponent to take Brady and the paper over to some other squire; that deponent inquired if Squire Harrison would do, and Price replied that he would be satisfactory, when deponent and Brady started out for Harrison's office; that deponent, as he remembers, found Harrison at the office of the Cumberland *Times*, and Harrison came down to the street with deponent, who said to him that he had a man who wanted to swear to a paper, and he (Harrison) should "charge him five dollars for it;" that Harrison responded, "I can't do that; the law only gives me ten cents for taking an oath;" that Harrison then went to his office, and deponent told Brady that Harrison was in his office and for him to go up; that Brady went into Harrison's office and returned with the paper, and joined deponent, and they returned to Price's office, where Brady gave Price the paper; that Price then gave, either to deponent or to Brady, and deponent is not certain which, twenty-five dollars, of which Brady got ten dollars, deponent ten dollars and Cronley, who was on the street a short distance from Price's office, five dollars.

And deponent further says, that the understanding which he had of the contents of said paper was, that the man Lindsay had met H. L. Morey somewhere on the cars when traveling, and Morey had shown him the letter from Garfield, commonly spoken of as the Morey letter.

And deponent further says, that this statement is made by him voluntarily, and because he feels that the time has come when the way in which he came to be connected with the Lindsay affidavit should be made public,

And deponent further says that this statement has been taken down in his presence, and from his own story of the transaction herein related, and that the same has been read over to him in the presence of John M. McClintock, Esq., the U.S. Marshal for the District of Maryland.
RICHARD RYAN.

Subscribed in my presence, after the same has been read to the affiant } in my presence, and declared by him to be correct, May 25th, 1882. }

JOHN M. MCCLINTOCK.

Sworn to before me, this 25th day of May, A. D. 1882.

[SEAL.] THOMAS KELL BRADFORD, *Notary Public.*

EXHIBIT VII.

The sworn confession of Francis P. Brady, of Cumberland, Md., as to his personating a "Robert Lindsay," and signing and swearing to an affidavit under the name of "Robert Linsey." It details the connection which William M. Price and others had with the matter.

STATE OF MARYLAND, ALLEGHANY COUNTY, CITY OF CUMBERLAND, ss.

Francis P. Brady, being duly sworn, deposes and says, that he lives at Eckhart Mines and has so resided there, with the exception of some four or five years, ever since his birth, twenty-five years ago, the 18th day of December last. That on the morning of November the 1st, 1880, being Monday preceding the day of the Presidential election in that year, deponent and one Michael Cronley, also a resident at the Eckhart Mines, came into the City of Cumberland, over the Eckhart Mines railroad, arriving in Cumberland between eight and nine o'clock in the morning; that the object of deponent and said Cronley in coming to Cumberland that morning, was that being the day before the election there was to be a large Democratic parade, which he and Cronley desired to be present at; that after arriving deponent visited some of the drinking saloons, among which deponent remembers Minnaugh's, Weir's, Webster's and Albaugh's; that in said saloons, deponent with others, had various drinks; that in the neighborhood of ten o'clock, deponent saw the said Cronley, who had previously parted from deponent, standing on South Centre Street, just below Baltimore Street, in company with one James Birmingham, and one Richard Ryan; that deponent walked up to them, when he was told by them to "go away, you are not wanted;" that at said time the said Birmingham had in his hand a paper, which he and Ryan were showing to Cronley and endeavoring to explain something to him in regard thereto; that deponent wanted to see the said paper, but was refused a sight of it, and being told to leave he went away; that about half-past ten o'clock deponent was standing on North Centre Street, in front of Webster's saloon, when the said Birmingham and said Ryan came up to deponent, and all three went inside and had a drink; that upon leaving the saloon the party walked up to the little alley on the side of Webster's saloon, and turning down said alley some five or six feet, stopped, when the said Birmingham said to deponent—"Do you want to make five dollars?" that deponent replied "Yes, I would." That said Birmingham then said to deponent, "You go down with Ryan to Lawyer Price's office and tell him your name is Robert Lindsay;" that the Eckhart Mines, where deponent resides, is about ten or eleven miles from Cumberland by turnpike, and about twelve by railroad; that the said Birmingham and the said Ryan both knew this deponent well and intimately, and had for many years, and knew him to be Frank Brady and no other person; that after the remark of said Birmingham set forth herein just above, deponent accompanied said Ryan to Price's office, and there said Ryan introduced deponent to said Price as "Robert Lindsay." That at the said conversation with Birmingham and Ryan, deponent inquired who this Lindsay was, whom they wanted him to represent, and what it was all about; that said Ryan told deponent that Lindsay was a man "who traveled about the country delivering lectures," and that he was needed, but was not here, and if deponent would "represent him in an informal matter it would be of great service to the Democratic party," of which deponent was a follower, and would "probably be the means of electing Hancock." That deponent then said to said Ryan, while on the way to Price's office, that he did "not think five dollars was enough for that;" that thereupon, after arriving at Price's office and being introduced as aforementioned, the said Ryan called said Price into an adjoining room and they there had some moments' conversation; that when they returned to where deponent was sitting, Ryan stepped up to deponent and said, "It is all right, he will give twenty-five dollars;" that thereupon Price produced a paper, which deponent took into his hand and was about to read, when said Ryan said to deponent, "Don't you read it," whereupon deponent laid said paper down on Price's desk without reading it; that then said Price asked deponent to sign the said paper and showed him where to sign it; whereupon deponent took up a pen and wrote the name "Robert Linsey;" that then said Price told deponent to "come with him," and deponent and said Price went out, through a court or alleyway, to the office of a Justice of the Peace; that deponent does not remember the name of the justice, but the house, in which his office was, fronted on Mechanics Street, but could be reached by or through the court or alleyway aforementioned from the building in which Price's office was, which fronted on Baltimore Street; that they did not find the justice in, whereupon deponent and said Price returned to the office of the latter, where Ryan was waiting; that Price then said to deponent and Ryan, "Take it over to any Squire," and that Ryan asked, "How will Squire Harrison do?" That Price replied that Harrison would be satisfactory, whereupon deponent and Ryan started for Harrison's office; that as deponent remembers, Ryan met Harrison on the street near Harrison's office and stopped him, saying to deponent, "Here is Harrison, I will talk with him a moment and you walk along and go into Webster's," a saloon only a door or two away; that deponent so acted, and upon coming out in a moment thereafter, Ryan said to deponent, "Harrison has gone up into his office," and motioned to deponent to go up there; that deponent entered said Harrison's office and handed him the paper which he had signed in Price's office, as aforementioned, and which he had received from said Price; that said Harrison looked at the paper casually, and asked deponent one of the following questions, but which deponent does not now remember—"Did you sign this paper?" or "Is that your signature?" that to the question put, deponent responded in the affirmative. When said Justice Harrison swore deponent to the truth of the said paper subscribed by him, but which in truth and in fact deponent had neither read nor had read to him, and as to the contents of which deponent knew nothing; that deponent saw sitting in said Justice Harrison's office, at the time when he entered it, two men—one of whom he knows to be William H. Porter, and the other of whom he knows to be John W. Norris; that said Norris deponent did not know at said time, but deponent had seen Porter before; that before swearing deponent to said affidavit, Harrison asked said Porter to witness the execution of said paper, which said Porter did; that deponent has this day been shown by Mr. John I. Davenport the said affidavit which he received as herein described from said Price, and which he signed in the presence of said Price, and identifies the same as the said paper so received by him, signed by him and acknowledged by him before Justice Harrison.

And deponent further says, that after swearing to said affidavit, deponent left said Harrison's office, and met Ryan on the street, and said Ryan and deponent went together to Price's office, where deponent handed to said Price the said affidavit, and then Price handed to Ryan the sum of twenty-five dollars, which Ryan divided as follows: deponent received ten dollars, Ryan retained ten dollars and deponent's friend Michael Cronley was given five dollars, he being on the street just below Harrison's office; and then all three, Cronley, Ryan and deponent, went into Webster's saloon and had a drink, and deponent, and Cronley, and Ryan and Birmingham were together drinking a good portion of the evening thereafter, until about midnight, after the parade was over, when deponent returned home on the special train; that on the 14th of November, 1880, which was Sunday, deponent was again in the City of Cumberland, and while there met both Birmingham and Ryan, and on the same day had a conversation at the Washington House, Cumberland, with one Thomas F. McCardell and one Thomas Brown, both of whom are well known in Cumberland, and at that time deponent informed them of the facts in a general way. That subsequently, on the 19th of November, 1880, there appeared in the *Cumberland Daily News* a card from both said Brown and said McCardell, and subsequently in the said Daily *News*, on November 22d, 1880, there appeared a long card from said Brown. That in so far as said statements referred to the conversation had with deponent, and the statements made by deponent, they were substantially and fairly correct. That previous to the two publications herein above mentioned, there had been published in the *Baltimore American*, and also in the *Cumberland News*, an item regarding the said interview between deponent, and said McCardell, and said Brown; that upon the appearance of that item, deponent was visited, November 16th, 1880, at the mines, by one L. F. Harbaugh, commonly known as "Lowly" Harbaugh, whom deponent had met for the first time, to know him, when in Cumberland, on said Sunday, November 14th, 1880, and who, at the time of so introducing himself, said to deponent: "I am Mr. Price's agent in this matter, and I will come up to you at any time, if there is anything to communicate or anything to be done. I am all right, and I will see that you have no trouble about this affair, and that all your expenses are paid. There is money appropriated for that purpose, and I will see that you get it;" that at the time of said visit of said Harbaugh to deponent, he informed this deponent that he had come in consequence of the items which had appeared in the *Baltimore American* and the *Cumberland News*, and that it had been deemed advisable that deponent should publish a card denying the statements contained in said items; that deponent agreed to this, and thereupon, said Harbaugh and deponent, prepared such a card, which was published in the *Cumberland Daily Times*, on Monday, November 17th, 1880; that at said interview, said Harbaugh reiterated what he had previously said, about taking care of deponent, and seeing that he got into no trouble or expense by reason of his action.

And deponent further says, that most of the statements contained in his card in said *Cumberland Times* were untrue and false; that upon the publication of McCardell's and Brown's cards, contradicting deponent's statements, the said Harbaugh again visited deponent at the mines; that at that time, said Harbaugh showed deponent a memorandum of notes of conversations had by said Harbaugh with various people in Cumberland, principally saloon keepers, and told deponent of others which he had, but had not brought with him, and he also had a talk at the mine with Michael Cronley, and made a memorandum of that, and also saw one James Finn, a saloon keeper at Pompey Smash, and also one Frank Kelly, a blacksmith at Eckhart, and conversed with them as to their seeing deponent in Cumberland on November 1st, 1880; that said Harbaugh informed deponent that his purpose in having had all these conversations with the saloon keepers in Cumberland, and with Cronley, Finn and Kelly, was to get up a memorandum which would account for all deponent's time while in Cumberland, on said first day of November, 1880, and so show that it was impossible for deponent to have been in Justice Harrison's office and sworn to the Lindsay affidavit.

And deponent further says, that on Thursday, the 24th day of March, 1881, there appeared in the *Cumberland News*, an item purporting to set forth that deponent had been in Cumberland demanding a settlement from Price and his confederates; that it was at that time that deponent next saw said Harbaugh, of whom he demanded payment for the trouble, annoyance and expense to which he had been put by reason of his having represented Robert Lindsay in the matter afore detailed; that said Harbaugh thereupon took deponent to the house of said Wm. M. Price, and Harbaugh told Price that deponent wanted his money, the bill being $20; that Price replied that he had not been able to get to his office, having a sore wrist; that as soon as he could get out he would see that deponent was paid; that thereupon deponent remained in Cumberland until the following day, and then went to said Price's office; not finding Price there, deponent then went alone, to his, said Price's, house, and there had a long interview with him, and received from him the sum of five dollars on account of deponent's bill, and the promise that on the following day deponent should have the remainder; that at said interview said Price assured this deponent that there was no danger to be apprehended by deponent; that if Cronley had not talked so much nothing would have come out about it.

And deponent further says, that on the following day he called upon said Price at his office to obtain the balance of his bill, $15—and that said Price then wrote out a bank check and enclosed it in an envelope, which he addressed to said Harbaugh, directing deponent to take it to said Harbaugh, who would give deponent the money; that at said time said Price cautioned deponent again about the absolute necessity of his keeping his tongue quiet about the affair, saying to deponent, "that nine out of every ten cases tried in the Court-house in Cumberland are lost to one of the parties because they have talked too much;" that this caution was given deponent because of the publication aforementioned, on said day, in said *News*, of the statement that deponent was demanding his pay from his employers; that deponent received from said Harbaugh the $15, upon the presentation of the envelope received by deponent from said Price; that deponent has never had any further interviews with said Harbaugh upon the matter, nor has he had any further interview with Price respecting the affair, since the one last above mentioned herein, until Tuesday, April 25th, 1882; that on Thursday, April 20th, 1882, deponent, with Michael Cromley, had a long interview with Mr. John I. Davenport at Frostburg, which lasted until about half past one in the morning of Friday, the 21st; that on Tuesday, April 25th, following said conference with said Davenport, deponent came into Cumberland and was standing on Baltimore Street at the corner of Mechanic Street, in conversation with some friends, when said William M. Price came along and called deponent, asking him "if he was engaged," to which deponent replied, "not particularly." Price then said, "Will you take a walk with me up street?" Deponent assented and accompanied said Price to his residence, when Price informed deponent that he had heard that Mr. Davenport had been to Frostburg, and desired deponent to inform him, Price, as to what Davenport wanted and what he had to say, and then said to deponent, "My advice is that if Davenport comes again up there, you had better get together and knock thunder out of him, and any one who comes with him. There is no law in Alleghany county, and no court which will prosecute you if you will do this. You shall have all the counsel you require, and, at the worst, only a case of assault and battery could be made of it."

That during the said conversation deponent inquired of said Price, as to how Davenport could have obtained possession of the original affidavit which deponent had signed as "Robert Lindsay;" that Price inquired if it was the fact that Davenport had such paper, and deponent replied that it was, and he had been shown it by Davenport; that said Price replied that such possession could only have been obtained by the treachery or violation of confidence of the Democratic leaders in New York, and that if such was the case he, Price, had documents in his trunk which would crush them, and let every one in Alleghany County out; that said Price then told deponent that he had made nothing out of the affair, but was out of pocket two hundred dollars by reason of it, but that if deponent got into any trouble by reason of it, or was molested on account thereof, he should be furnished with the best counsel, and paid for his time and trouble.

And deponent further says, that he has had no further conversations with said Price respecting the matter; that the said William M. Price, at the time of deponent's being taken to his office, and signing the said affidavit as Robert Lindsay, was the Chairman of the Alleghany County Democratic Committee, and an elector on the National Democratic ticket; that in the repeated interviews, detailed herein, with said Price, said Price has always addressed deponent as "Brady," by which name said Price has known deponent.

And deponent further says, that he makes the above statement freely and voluntarily, and of his own desire to have the truth known in regard to his action and the circumstances under which he was induced to act as he did in signing said affidavit as "Robert Linsey," and swearing to it under said name.

And deponent further says, that he does not know any one in Cumberland, or in that neighborhood or vicinity, by the name of Robert Lindsay, nor has he ever heard of any one in that locality of that name, and deponent believes that in representing Robert Lindsay he was personating a myth, and that all persons connected with the said Lindsay affidavit knew such to be the fact at the time of the getting up and execution of said affidavit.

And deponent further says, that this affidavit has been drawn up in his presence and from his own statements, made line by line, and has been fully and carefully read over to him in the presence of Col. Johnson, Postmaster at Cumberland, and others, and that the same, as it now stands, is correct. FRANCIS P. BRADY.

Sworn to before me, this 11th day of May, A. D. 1882. J. WM. JONES, J. P.

EXHIBIT VIII.

The affidavit of Justice James F. Harrison, of Cumberland, Md.; before whom Francis P. Brady swore to the "Robert Lindsay" affidavit in the name of "Robert Linsey."

STATE OF MARYLAND, ALLEGHANY COUNTY, to wit.

On this sixth day of June, A. D. 1882, personally appeared before me, the subscriber, a Notary Public of the State of Maryland in and for Alleghany County, Jas. Forsyth Harrison, a citizen of Cumberland, Md., and by profession an attorney at law, who having been first duly sworn according to law, did depose and say for himself, that in the month of November, 1880, in addition to practicing law, he was duly appointed, qualified and commissioned as a Justice of the Peace of the State of Maryland, in and for Alleghany County. That the statement below, which was published by your affiant in the *Cumberland Daily News*, of the issue of Saturday, November 13th, 1880, is true and correct to the best of your affiant's knowledge and belief.

To the Editor of the *Daily News* :   CUMBERLAND, November 12th, 1880.

On November 1st, inst., a deposition and affidavit were made before me as a Justice of the Peace, by a man purporting to be Robert Lindsay. Mr. Wm. H. Porter, constable, and Mr. John W. Norris, night brakeman on the yard engine of the Baltimore and Ohio Railroad in this city, were present at the time in my office. Mr. Porter's name as a witness was attached to the deposition. The deposition and certificate, and date, too (Nov. 1st, 1880), were in the handwriting of Mr. Wm. M. Price. I was in the *Daily Times* office, when I was approached by Mr. Richard Ryan, who informed me that there was a man at my office who wanted to make an affidavit. Mr. Ryan said to me, "Charge him $5.00 for it." I replied I could not do it, as the law only allowed a fee of ten cents for an affidavit. The man purporting to be Robert Lindsay came into my office alone, and the only persons present were Mr. Robert Lindsay, Messrs. Wm. H. Porter and John W. Norris and myself. After the man was sworn, he asked me, "How much is it?" I replied, "Ten cents." He pulled out a quantity of silver and threw down onto my desk ten cents. I may add that I have no knowledge of the man who was in my office, nor did I certify that he was Robert Lindsay. No person other than Mr. Richard Ryan ever approached me prior to the taking of the deposition of the alleged Robert Lindsay, when the sum of $5.00 was suggested to me by Mr. Richard Ryan to charge for the affidavit. I was suspicious that there was something wrong about it, and in self-protection I called upon Mr. Wm. H. Porter to attest his name to the deposition as a witness. This is the sum and substance that I know of my own knowledge of the Robert Lindsay case in Cumberland.   JAS. FORSYTH HARRISON.

Sworn and subscribed to, before me, this sixth day of June, A. D. eighteen hundred and eighty-two.

[L. S.]   F. F. McCARDELL, *Notary Public.*

EXHIBIT IX.

The affidavit of Wm. H. Porter, the subscribing witness to the Robert Lindsay affidavit. It corroborates a portion of Brady's confession, and identifies Brady as the man who swore to the affidavit under the name of Robert Lindsay.

CITY OF CUMBERLAND, ALLEGHANY COUNTY, STATE OF MARYLAND, ss:

William H. Porter, being duly sworn, deposes and says: that he resides in the city of Cumberland and has for the past thirteen years; that in the fall of the year 1880, deponent was Constable-at-large in the city of Cumberland; that on the first day of November, in the year 1880, being Monday preceding the day of Election, this deponent was seated in the office of James F. Harrison, a Justice of the Peace, on North Centre Street, in said city of Cumberland, when a man came in and presented to said Justice Harrison a paper which was signed, and which the man said he desired to swear to; that upon seeing the signature to the paper, the said Justice Harrison said to said man, "Are you Robert Lindsay?" to which said man responded, "I am;" that said Harrison turned to deponent and said, "perhaps you had better witness this paper," whereupon, he (Harrison) wrote on the left-hand side of the paper the word "Witness," and deponent on the line below wrote his name; that deponent observed that said paper was in the handwriting of Mr. Wm. M. Price, then an elector on the National Democratic ticket and Chairman of the Alleghany County Democratic Committee; that after deponent had witnessed the signing of said paper as aforementioned, the said Justice Harrison administered to said man who had signed it the usual oath of acknowledgment and certified to the said fact; that at the time of the said execution of the said paper, deponent did not know what the contents of said paper were, nor did he become acquainted therewith until he subsequently saw the same in print; that the man who executed said paper wore his cap pulled down over his face and his coat collar turned up, and deponent, while he did not place him for the moment, thought his appearance was familiar, and subsequently deponent recalled his name and he then knew, and has since become confirmed in his knowledge, that the said man, who as herein described, executed and swore to said paper, was one Brady, a miner, from Frostburg; that deponent has been shown the said original paper witnessed by deponent and identified his signature thereto, and the handwriting of the said paper as that of said Price, and the signature of said Justice Harrison to the acknowledgment.

And deponent further says, that there was another person, John W. Norris, present, when said paper was executed.   WM. H. PORTER.

Subscribed and sworn to before me this 2d of October, 1882.

[SEAL.]   FRANCIS M. OFFUTT, *Notary Public.*

EXHIBIT X.

The confession of perjury of James O'Brien, alias "Robert Lindsay," who is now in the State Prison at Sing Sing, New York, serving out an eight years' sentence for perjury. He went upon the stand before Judge Noah Davis, in the Philp examination, and swore that he was "Robert Lindsay;" that he knew "H. L. Morey," and that Morey had shown him the so-called Morey letter, at about the time of its receipt from General Garfield.

My name is James O'Brien, *alias* Robert Lindsay; I am twenty-one years of age, and was born in Washington, D. C., and reside in Georgetown, D. C., and am by occupation a laborer. I was in Baltimore on the day of election. I went up there for the Republican party, to stop Democratic repeaters from going to Baltimore from Washington. I went home that night and received word at my house that a man had brought word there from another man from Cumberland, to come up to Cumberland; that he had a job of work for me. He had been down to Washington a week or two before that, and I asked him if he could get a job, to get it for me, and as soon as I received the information I started to go. The next night I left at half-past nine o'clock, I think that was the time the train started. I arrived there in the morning and went to the man's house, and he informed me that a policeman by the name of Birmingham had promised to get me a job. So I waited around that day. It was raining very hard. At night me and him together went up town to see if we could see this Birmingham, and we could not find him. I was to stop at his house. We came back home and went to bed. The next morning I got up and stayed around the house awhile and went up town and there met one Louis Harbaugh, and me and him walked around together. We went to the Water Works there, looking for this Birmingham; I could not find him. In the afternoon we went back to this friend's house again. He keeps a saloon, and we sat there playing a game of "seven up." We ate supper there about five o'clock and we started to go up town again to see if we could see Birmingham, and as we were going up the street we met Birmingham and another man coming down, and said he to Birmingham, "Come on and let us go back to 'Buck's' [he was my friend], and get a glass of beer." There was another man with him, and the four of us went back. I think Harbaugh walked with Birmingham. During the time Harbaugh had introduced me to Birmingham.

So we got to Buck's and Buck introduced me again. I said we had been made acquainted. We drank two or three glasses of beer, and went outside on the porch. After that Buck called me and I got out there. He said, "Jim, how would you like to make $100?" I said, "What doing?" He had told me before that they had been hunting for Robert Lindsay the Sunday before that, and the fellows all around there had a guy, "Who found Robert Lindsay?" I didn't know who Robert Lindsay was, and had never heard of him. And they told me that there was a man there hunting all around for Robert Lindsay, and he could not be found. And this man, whose name was Walton, told him to get anybody that would come and answer to the name of Robert Lindsay, and that they would give him $100. So I told this man, "I don't know nothing about this; I don't want to get into any scrape." He said, "You don't have to do anything, except to go to New York and show that there is such a person as Robert Lindsay." Said he, "They can't make you swear that you made out the affidavit." I didn't make out the affidavit, I said. "Well," he said, "if you don't want to go, you need not go. You can get the money in advance, and jump off the train if you want to." I said, "No, if I start I will go all the way."

So going to the train we met this man Walton at the depot, and Birmingham introduced him to me. He introduced me as Lindsay, but before we got up there we sat down to talk it all over. Before we got to the hotel at the depot where this man was stopping, said I, "Does this man (Walton) understand that my name is not Lindsay?" He said "Yes. He told me to get a man to answer to the name of Lindsay." So when we got up there he introduced me as Lindsay. Walton said, "Do you understand what you are going to get?" "This man says I am to receive $100." I said, "Yes, you are." He said. "All right." So when he came out with the ticket, he said, "Here is your ticket to New York and $10. I could not get a round trip ticket. But that is to pay your way back."

So then we started along, and he explained everything; even got me a *Truth* paper so I could see the letter. Birmingham got me that, so I could see it, and study it. Coming on I asked him if there is any trial about this affair. He said, "No, none at all." Then I said, "I can't be hurt much. I will go." When we arrived here we stopped at some office. We went in a cab, and went from there to the *Truth* office, and there I was introduced as Lindsay.

Q. Whom did you see there? A. Mr. Hart, Mr. Post and a man by the name of Byrne.
Q. Did you have any conversation with them?
A. Walton then walked out, and he and Hart had some private conversation. When Hart came in he said, "Walton has told me all about it. I understand it."

When we were leaving Cumberland, Birmingham held out his hand and said to me, "Good-by, Barry," and looked up into Walton's face, as much as to say, "I know all about it." Coming on the train I said to Walton, "Who is going to pay you this money?" He said, "The *Truth* will pay you through me." Soon after we arrived here they examined me.

Q. Who examined you?

A. First Post. This Birmingham told me to make up a story about the Workingman's Union. "That is what you represent and that is all you have got to do," he said, and when I got on the stand I told them about mines. After that I went to supper. Before I went to supper, Hart said, "Have you got any change?" I said, "No." He said, "Here, you had better take this," and he gave me ten dollars. He first offered me five dollars. The next day being Sunday, I said I wanted to get a clean shirt, and then he gave me ten dollars. We went to supper, and a man went with me; they call him "Box." His name is Ellin. We went with him to supper, and he never left me while I have been here. He slept with me, and never let me go out of his sight. When we came from supper, Hart said to Box, "You had better take him to Tony Pastor's Theatre." We came back after the performance, and then I was cross-questioned by Howe about the mines, and he said, "That would do; that is all you will have to swear to."

Q. How many times have you been at *Truth* office?

A. I have been there all the time, I might as well say, except to go to the theatre or to meals or to the hotel to go to bed.

Q. Did you go to the Democratic headquarters? A. No, sir.

Q. Did you say to Box at any time that your name was not Lindsay? A. No, I did not.

Q. Did you have any conversation with any one in regard to that for which you came on here? A. No one at all. Mr. Hart said to me, "I know your name is not Lindsay." He said, "Walton knows your name; he heard it there in Cumberland."

Q. This Walton said that you were going to get this money through the *Truth?*

A. Through the *Truth.*

Q. Then when you made a statement yesterday that your name was Lindsay, you knew at the time that it was untrue? A. Yes, sir.

Q. Is that all the statement that you want to make; have you told us all in regard to this transaction that you desire to state?

A. I desire to state it all. Mr. Hart told me that Walton told him all about this. He said, "I will pay you, and d——n it, I will pay you double to put him in a hole." They asked me if I knew where Main Street was in Lynn. I said no, I knew where the main street is; and Post and Hart said: "That is just the way for you to answer in Court." Post said to me, "If they ask you any questions, don't have any hesitation in answering them. About this secret organization, just tell them you are bound by oath not to divulge any secrets. If they ask you any questions, answer them right up, openly." Hart said, "Suppose they bring Garfield and put him on the stand?" and Howe said, "I wish they would." When I came I did not understand that I would have to do any swearing at all. If I had known that, I would not have come. I was out of work and didn't have any money. Hart asked me how I would like to have a job in New York. I told him I would like it very much, and he said: "Well, we won't say anything about that now, until this is over."

Q. You never lived in Cumberland, did you? A. No, sir.

Q. Do you know a person by the name of William H. Thompson? A. No, sir.

Q. You came to Cumberland through Birmingham?

A. No, through Buck O'Neil, who lives in Cumberland, and keeps a saloon there.

Q. Who is Birmingham? A. He is a police officer at Cumberland.

Q. What is his full name? A. I do not know. They call him some kind of a nick name.

Q. How did you know Buck O'Neil?

A. I was in Cumberland last summer, and then three weeks before I went up there, at the time of the Baltimore Centennial, and at the time of the National Fair, at Washington, Buck O'Neil and Joe Albaugh came down to Washington and saw the Fair and also the Baltimore Centennial, and while in Washington they came to see me, as I was acquainted with both of them.

Q. When was it that Buck O'Neil wrote you? A. He did not write. He sent a man, who came to my house on election day. I was boarding on Market Space, Georgetown.

Q. Then a man came from Cumberland, and asked you to go to Buck O'Neil's?

A. That was either election day, or the day before election. But I didn't hear it until election night. I went to Cumberland the next night, that was the Wednesday night.

Q. Whom did you see there? A. Buck O'Neil.

Q. In his saloon? A. Yes, sir.

Q. Whom else did you see?

A. There was some fellows standing around there. I met on the street as I was going to Buck O'Neil's house, Frank Quigly, and a man who they call "Poodle" Warner. They asked me to go back as far as Buck's, and get a glass of beer. We went back and stood there drinking. It was raining hard and I remained there all day. That was Thursday. Wednesday it took me almost all night to come from Washington, until 3 o'clock in the morning. Thursday I saw Buck O'Neil. He said, "stay around," that probably Birmingham would come down. He told me that Birmingham had a job for me. I stayed around there. The invitation was that I should stay at his house until I did get work.

Q. Up to that time had you ever known Birmingham? A. No, sir.

Q. Did he tell you who Birmingham was? A. He told me he was a policeman.

Q. When and where did you with Birmingham first meet Walton?

A. It was Friday evening, in front of the Queen City Hotel, which is the depot at Cumberland.

Q. What did Birmingham say to Walton, in your presence?

A. He said to Walton, "This is Mr. Lindsay." He said, "You understand." When Walton said to me, "Has the man told you what you are to receive?" and I said as I have stated.

Q. Do you know the first name of Walton? A. No, sir; I do not.

Q. What sort of a looking man is Walton?

A. He is a tall man, and talks very fast, and stoops over; he has darkish chestnut hair, with two little buds of side whiskers, and moustache, and I do not remember whether he has got a goatee or not. He has a kind of sallow complexion. He had a lightish overcoat, and a hunting coat resembling corduroy.

Q. Does he talk fast or slow? A. Neither fast or slow.

Q. Did he say where he came from? A. He said he came from the *Truth* office, and there is where he brought me. I stopped at French's.

Q. When you refused the other day to state the name of your employer, and asked for an opportunity to advise with counsel, that was granted you; and then you came back and said you had seen William H. Thompson. Did you know any such man as William H. Thompson? A. No, sir.

Q. How did you come to suggest the name of William H. Thompson?

A. That was the first name that came into my mind.

Q. Whereabouts did you go in the *Truth* office?

A. I sat in the rear room—the editor's room.

Q. Who paid you? A. I received a ticket and $10 from this Walton in Cumberland when we got on the train. After I arrived here, I received $10 more from Hart.

Q. Is that all you had? A. That is all I had.

Q. Who told you the story which you were to tell?

A. Walton told me to make up one of my own, and they got me a paper in Cumberland, to study this letter that was published, and told me to make it up; and Birmingham told me to say that I belonged to the Workingmen's Union.

Q. Who told you that it was necessary to say, among things, that you belonged to Lynn, Mass.? A. No one; only from the affidavit I saw printed in the paper. They told me to swear to this affidavit that was made out. I think it was this man, Walton, who told me that. The first time I saw that affidavit was after leaving Cumberland, in the cars.

Q. Did you have any conversation with any one here on your arrival, in regard to that affidavit, or did any one ask you if you had read an affidavit?

A. I think it was Howe who asked me if I had read that affidavit, and asked me if I had made it, and I said yes.

Q. You had not made it? A. No, sir.

Q. Do you know who was the man who made that affidavit? A. I do not.

Q. Were you ever in Lynn, Mass.? A. Never, in my life.

Q. Did you ever in your life-time see a person by the name of H. L. Morey? A. No, sir.

Q. Did you ever see the original Morey letter until it was shown you in court? A. No, sir.

Q. Did you ever hear of the Morey (Garfield) letter until you saw a printed copy of it, after you left Cumberland to come to New York? A. No, sir.

(Signed), JAMES O'BRIEN.

Taken before me. Nov. 10th, 1880.

B. T. MORGAN, *Police Justice*, New York City.

EXHIBIT XI.

The affidavit of Henry L. West, City Editor of the *Washington Post*, as to his search for Robert Lindsay.

UNITED STATES OF AMERICA, DISTRICT OF COLUMBIA, CITY OF WASHINGTON, ss.:

HENRY L. WEST, being duly sworn, deposes and says, that he resides in the City of Washington, D. C., and has for some years past; that he is the City Editor of the *Washington Post* in said City, and was such City Editor during the Fall of the year 1880.

That on the 27th day of October, A.D. 1880, and shortly before the Presidential election of that year, deponent was given by Mr. Walter S. Hutchins, the managing editor of said *Washington Post*, a copy of a letter mailed at Cumberland, Md., addressed to the *Washington Post*, and signed Robert Lindsay, and which related to the then recent publication of the so-called Morey letter, the existence of one H. L. Morey, the receipt by said Morey of the letter purporting to be from James A. Garfield upon the subject of Chinese labor; that deponent was directed by said Hutchins to proceed to Cumberland, Md., and endeavor to find Robert Lindsay; that he left the city upon such errand early on the morning of the 28th of October, 1880, and upon arriving in Cumberland about midday, went at once and examined the **directory for the year 1880 of the residents of Cumberland**, but could find no one by the name of Robert Lindsay mentioned therein; that deponent next visited the post-office in said city, and there saw and conversed with Col. H. J. Johnson, the then postmaster, relative to his knowledge of any person by the name of Robert Lindsay in that neighborhood and as to whether any letters had ever to his knowledge or that of any employee of his office, passed through the said post-office addressed to the Robert Lindsay! That after the most careful inquiries there and then made, said Johnson informed deponent that he not only never knew or heard of a Robert Lindsay in or about Cumberland, but that no letter had ever passed through that post-office, during his occupancy of the postmastership for any person of the name of Robert Lindsay.

And deponent further says, that subsequently he made similar inquiries of the Captain of Police, or a police official of the city, as to whether he knew or had ever heard of any person by the name of Robert Lindsay in that locality; that deponent received to all such inquiries so made of said officer answers in the negative.

And deponent further says, that subsequently he made similar inquiries of an official of the city, whose name and title have at this moment escaped his memory, but said official, deponent had been informed, would be more likely to know of any such person as Robert Lindsay, if such person there was in that vicinity, than almost any one else who could be thought of. That to all of his said inquiries so made of said official deponent received answers that no person by the name of Robert Lindsay was known to or had ever been heard of by said official.

And deponent further says, that he, at that time, then visited the respective offices of the several newspapers published in said City of Cumberland, and there made inquiries, if on their respective lists of subscribers, not alone in the City of Cumberland, but throughout the County of Alleghany, there was any one by the name of Robert Lindsay; and still deponent could find no Robert Lindsay, nor obtain any information of any person by that name.

And deponent further says, that subsequently he started out upon a thorough and systematic search through all the factories, mills, works and shops in and immediately about the City of Cumberland—that at each of said places he hunted up the foreman or person who had charge of the pay-rolls or lists of employees in his factory, mill or shop, and had made an examination of each of said rolls or lists, and also made personal inquiries of said foreman or other person, as to their knowledge at any time, of any person in that neighborhood by the name of Robert Lindsay. That the examination as above detailed of said payrolls or lists of employees, and his inquiries, resulted in his neither finding nor hearing of any person by the name of Robert Lindsay in the vicinity of Cumberland, save that in one shop deponent was told that they believed that some four or five miles out from the city, on or near the line of one of the railroads running out from Cumberland, there was a colored man of that name.

And deponent further says, that as he remembers, he then went to the Western Union Telegraph office and telegraphed the operator at the place where, or nearest to the place where he had been informed the aforesaid colored individual was—but the name of which place deponent does not now remember—inquiring of said operator, if he knew of any colored person, or could ascertain of any colored person in his neighborhood of the name of Robert Lindsay. That to such inquiry, deponent never received a reply, and after telegraphing Mr. Walter S. Hutchins of the result of his investigation deponent returned to Washington.

And deponent further says, that he has herein detailed all that he did while in Cumberland on his said mission, and all the persons whom he called upon, or had intercourse with, respecting a Robert Lindsay, and that his said search and investigation was made in the most careful and painstaking manner, and for the purpose of finding of the person who had sent the letter to the *Washington Post*, and signed himself Robert Lindsay.

HENRY L. WEST.

Subscribed and sworn to before me, this 29th day of May, 1882.
    [SEAL.]   GEORGE R. HERRICK, *Notary Public*,
                     In and for the District of Columbia.

It has not been the purpose of the author to here present all the evidence in his possession as to the matters and things stated in this work. His intention has been, simply, to furnish some of the more important and interesting exhibits, and this, he thinks, it will be found he has done.

THE END.

www.ingramcontent.com/pod-product-compliance
Lightning Source LLC
Chambersburg PA
CBHW030344170426
43202CB00010B/1242